D1594617

KISSINGER & CYPRUS

A Study in Lawlessness

KISSINGER & CYPRUS

A Study in Lawlessness

GENE ROSSIDES

BOOKS BY AHIF

U.S. Relations with Turkey and Its Impact on Greece and Cyprus

The First Victory: Greece in the Second World War by George C. Blytas
Published jointly with Cosmos Publishing

Cyprus 35 Years Later: What is Needed for a Solution?

The United States and Cyprus: Double Standards and the Rule of Law

Blood and Tears: Greece 1940-1949. A Story of War and Love
by George Papavizas

Greece's Pivotal Role in World War II and Its Importance to the U.S. Today

The Truman Doctrine of Aid to Greece: A Fifty-Year Retrospective
Published jointly with the Academy of Political Science

*Modern Greeks: Greece in World War II, The German Occupation and
National Resistance, the Civil War* by Costas Stassinopoulos

BOOKS BY AHI

Handbook on United States Relations with Greece and Cyprus

Doing Business in Greece

American Hellenic Who's Who (5th edition)

The Rule of Law and Conditions on Foreign Aid to Turkey

*United States Foreign Policy Regarding Greece, Turkey & Cyprus:
The Rule of Law and American Interests*

Cyprus: The Tragedy and the Challenge by Polyvios G. Polyviou

*Crisis on Cyprus, Report for Senate Judiciary Subcommittee
Regarding Refugees*

KISSINGER & CYPRUS

A Study in Lawlessness

GENE ROSSIDES

AMERICAN HELLENIC INSTITUTE FOUNDATION

WASHINGTON, D.C.

Published by
American Hellenic Institute Foundation
1220 16th Street, N.W.
Washington, D.C. 20036

Jacket design by George Lois

Library of Congress Cataloging-in-Publication Data

Rossides, Eugene T.
Kissinger and Cyprus : a study in lawlessness / Gene Rossides.
pages cm
Includes bibliographical references and index.
ISBN 1-889247-08-1 (978-1-889247-08-3 : alk. paper)
1. Cyprus--History--Turkish Invasion, 1974. 2. Kissinger, Henry, 1923- 3.
United States--Foreign relations--1974-1977. 4. United States--Foreign
relations--Cyprus. 5. Cyprus--Foreign relations--United States. 6. United
States--Foreign relations--Turkey. 7. Turkey--Foreign relations--United States.
8. Aggression (International law)--History--20th century. I. Title.
DS54.9.R64 2014
956.9304--dc23
2013036963

ISBN: 978-1-889247-08-3

Printed in the United States of America

Dedicated to
the memory of the victims of
Henry Kissinger's lawlessness
and to
Christopher Hitchens who led the way.

Contents

Map done August, 13, 1974 by the Bureau of Intelligence and Research projecting Turkish moves on Cyprus.

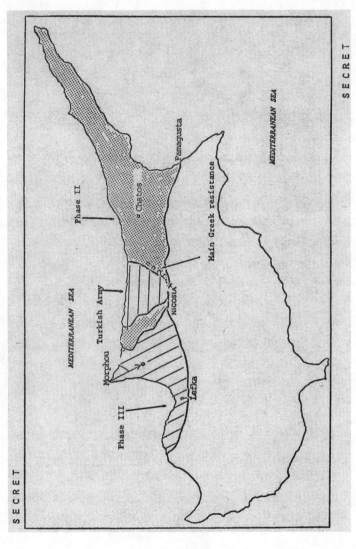

Map of Cyprus, dated August 13, 1974, by the Bureau of Intelligence and Research, U.S. Department of State. Reprinted from Kostas Venizelos and Michalis Ignatiou, *The Secret Archives of Kissinger* [in Greek] (Athens: Livani Publishing, 2002), 236.

List of Illustrations

List of Political Cartoons

by Pat Oliphant

Foreword

The United States moved into a leading position in international relations slowly and hesitantly. Although the nation's large population and thriving industrial economy seemed by the late nineteenth century to warrant a leading role in international affairs, the American people and many of their political leaders were not convinced that the United States should extend its reach beyond the country's already expansive frontiers. Involvement with foreign peoples and with foreign power relations in Europe, Asia, and Latin America raised serious moral and political questions for those who were not dedicated to a simplistic brand of *realpolitik*. Convinced as they were that the United States stood for something more complex and idealistic than national supremacy, they asked questions and raised doubts that are still with us today. Where, in the age of modern weapons and terrorism, should we draw the line between what might be useful in defending our national security abroad but is unacceptable in our legal system at home? How tolerant should we be when our forces or those of our allies cross the boundaries well established during the years since the end of World War II in international law? How ardent should our support for democracy and international law be when our friends trample on human rights and overthrow elected regimes?

These and other enduring questions about morality, law and politics provide the context for Gene Rossides's study of America's policies toward Cyprus and of Henry Kissinger's role in setting and implementing those policies. The author does

1

not do an academic fairy dance around the legal and moral dilemmas created when the United States condoned Turkey's brutal exercise of power in Cyprus. Rossides leaves no doubt in the reader's mind that Kissinger's policies traded America's legal and moral position for a short-term political gain. Even the gain, he notes, was questionable. Meanwhile, the policies violated American law and flaunted international law. The destruction of property was significant. Forced ethnic removal took place with America's tacit approval, as did the introduction of a foreign population to the island. American arms were involved in the entire process in a specific violation of American law.

There are many reasons to conclude that this was a sorry and ultimately expensive episode in America's policies in the Middle East. Most telling is the fact that the aggression involved a relatively large, well-armed nation attacking and subjugating a small, defenseless country. Preventing this sort of aggression was a major objective of the United States when it took a leading position in creating the United Nations. To those who remember or have studied the first stages of World War II, this is a particularly telling issue; then, German power was used against Czechoslovakia and Poland to achieve national aims that are similar to those that Turkey achieved in Cyprus—with America's support.

Telling as well is the fact that a democratically elected government was overturned in the process of conquering and dividing Cyprus. The Turkish minority and the Greek Cypriot majority had for the most part lived in peace and had attempted to create a constitutional government embracing political ideals that the United States had long considered one of its most important contributions to world history. Most Americans believe their government has and should continue to support those ideals. Many believe that the American model offers appropriate guidelines for people seeking to create more stable and equitable governments in their societies. The developments in Cyprus that Gene Rossides describes in detail bring into question America's moral leadership in the developing world.

Also brought into question is an American polity that could be influenced excessively by one advocate of a brand of *realpolitik* at odds with our nation's democratic values and democratic government. Henry Kissinger's contempt for democratic constraints on the nation's foreign policy was evident throughout the Cyprus affair. Particular circumstances allowed him to exercise more power than even the President of the United States can normally have in peacetime. Our society is based on the central concept that we are governed by law, not by individuals who consider themselves to be above the law. We can be grateful to Gene Rossides for making us rethink these issues and to reconsider America's policy toward Cyprus. These issues will not go away. They call for policies that balance our desire for national security with our dedication to American concepts of equity, democracy, and world peace.

Professor Louis Galambos
Johns Hopkins University

INTRODUCTION

On July 15, 1974 the military dictator of Greece, Brigadier General Dimitrios Ioannides, with the encouragement of the U.S. Secretary of State Henry Kissinger, overthrew the democratically elected President of Cyprus, Archbishop Makarios, and installed a puppet regime. Five days later, with the encouragement of Kissinger, Turkey invaded Cyprus with the declared goal of deposing the puppet regime and reestablishing the previous status quo. On July 23, the puppet regime fell and the legitimate government of Cyprus was restored. The same day, the Greek junta dictator Ioannides fell from power. Yet Turkey did not withdraw its invasion forces after achieving its declared objectives. Instead, on August 14, three weeks after the legitimate government of Cyprus had been restored, Turkey commenced the massive second phase of its invasion with Kissinger's abetment and approval. Over the following three days, Turkey occupied an additional 30 percent of Cyprus and expelled 180,000 Greek Cypriots from their homes and properties (and 20,000 more in ensuing years). It has occupied northern Cyprus ever since, planting more than 200,000 illegal Turkish settlers and demanding that the island be partitioned into separate Turkish Cypriot and Greek Cypriot entities.

The Cyprus tragedy of 1974 is directly linked to Kissinger, who, as both secretary of state and national security advisor, was fully in charge of U.S. foreign policy at the time. Kissinger's actions and deliberate inactions regarding Cyprus profoundly harmed U.S. interests.

It is not a pleasant task to document the unlawful conduct of a U.S. secretary of state. The story needs to be told, however, for its bearing on current U.S. policy toward Cyprus, Greece, and Turkey and on the importance of the rule of law in U.S. foreign policy worldwide. At issue are the democratic values set forth in the United States' documents of freedom—the Declaration of Independence, the Constitution, and the Bill of Rights—that is, democracy based on majority rule, the rule of law, and protection of minority rights. These values are crucially relevant to the foreign policy issues facing the United States today in Afghanistan, Iraq, Israel and the West Bank, Iran, Syria, North Korea, the Arab Spring nations, and elsewhere.

The Arab Spring, ongoing since 2011, is basically a movement demanding the rule of law and democratic values, including the right of assembly, the right to protest and petition, and freedom of speech and religion. The United States can show its support for these democratic aspirations of the Arab Spring by openly supporting for Cyprus a "constitutional democracy based on majority rule, the rule of law and protection of minority rights," as called for by Vice President George H. W. Bush, then the Republican presidential candidate, on July 7, 1988. Publicly calling on Turkey to end the occupation of Cyprus by removing its troops and settlers would be a dramatic signal to the Arab nations and the world community that the United States has retaken the moral high ground—a realistic way to counter anti-American hostility and Islamic fundamentalism.

The United States can also demonstrate its dedication to the rule of law by acknowledging and denouncing Kissinger's lawless conduct and flagrant violation of democratic values in his handling of the Cyprus problem from 1974 to the end of President Ford's administration on January 20, 1977. Kissinger worked hard to sell the idea that the Cyprus problem was an ethnic conflict between Greeks and Turks on Cyprus going back centuries, rather than an issue of Turkey's aggression against Cyprus beginning in the summer of 1974. Kissinger was, at a minimum, an accessory to Turkey's war crimes, and he, along with the Turkish military and political leaders and military commanders in Cyprus, should long ago have been indicted and tried before an international tribunal and now before the International Criminal Court. Although Kissinger is unlikely to be brought to justice at this late date, the United States should acknowledge his role and do what it can to rectify the wrongs that it has tolerated for forty years. Kissinger should be forced to account for his actions, if not in the International Criminal Court, then at least in the court of public opinion. It is in the interests of the United States to do so in support of the rule of law because it is the right thing to do and because it bears on current U.S. foreign policy issues around the world.

The State Department has continued to ignore and coverup the role played by Kissinger in Turkey's invasion of Cyprus in 1974, and the responsibility of the United States to rectify its wrong. Furthermore, the State Department has failed to acknowledge publicly that the Cyprus crisis would have been avoided had Kissinger followed the policy recommendations put forth by the career foreign service officials, Thomas Boyatt and his colleagues, in 1974.

The author hopes that this volume will generate renewed interest in the Cyprus problem, the importance of the rule of law in U.S. foreign policy, and the responsibility of the United States to redress the situation in Cyprus.

Overview

This book explores four themes. The first is Kissinger's illegal actions and responsibility for the Cyprus tragedy of 1974 and its aftermath. The second is Cyprus's importance as a strategic, economic, and political asset to Europe and the United States. This asset includes substantial natural gas reserves in the off-shore waters south of Cyprus in its Exclusive Economic Zone (EEZ). The third theme is Turkey's actions as a rogue state, its violations of U.S. and international laws, its history of unreliability as an ally of the United States, and its moves towards Islamic fundamentalism. The fourth theme is the vital importance to the United States of absolute allegiance to the rule of law. It is in the interests of the United States to rectify its wrong by pressuring Turkey to withdraw its troops and settlers from Cyprus.

Chapter 1 discusses Cyprus's strategic, economic, and political value to the West, the United States, and Israel. Chapter 2 gives a brief history of and background to the Cyprus problem. Chapter 3 examines Kissinger's encouragement of the Greek junta-initiated coup against the elected government of President Makarios of Cyprus, and chapter 4 details his encouragement of Turkey's two-phase aggression against Cyprus in the summer of 1974. Chapter 5 sets forth Kissinger's violation of U.S. laws and failure to uphold international law in these actions. Chapter 6 refutes the account of these events and his role in them that Kissinger gave in his memoirs.

Chapter 7 recounts the initiation in Congress of legislation to embargo arms shipments to Turkey and the battle with the Ford administration over the embargo led by Kissinger. Chapter 8 details Turkey's actions as a rogue state and its violation of U.S. and international laws and calls for actions against Turkey. Chapter 9 examines Kissinger's national security argument and his failure to acknowledge Turkey's unreliability as an ally. Chapter 10 compares President George H. W. Bush's actions regarding Iraq's invasion and occupation of Kuwait with Kissinger's actions regarding Turkey's invasion and occupation of Cyprus. It discusses President Dwight D. Eisenhower's response to the aggression against Egypt by Britain, France, and Israel in the 1956 Suez crisis, and stresses the relevance of the rule of law in the foreign policy issues facing the United States today.

The title of chapter 11, "Kissinger the war criminal," comes from Jussi M. Hanhimäki's review of *Nixon and Kissinger:*

Partners in Power (2007) by Robert Dallek. Hanhimäki wrote that "over time, Kissinger the war criminal came to replace the image of a globe-trotting super-diplomat." This chapter makes the case for Kissinger's role as an accomplice and accessory in the war crimes and crimes against humanity committed by the Turks in their aggression against Cyprus and the Greek junta's war crimes in their coup against President Makarios. The final chapter, "The Rule of Law in the National Interest," sets forth actions the United States should take to rectify its wrong in Cyprus.

Acknowledgments

I have used comments from several key persons, including the late Christopher Hitchens, a noted journalist and author and an expert on Cyprus; former undersecretary of state George Ball; former secretary of state Cyrus Vance; Robert Kaiser, a *Washington Post* assistant editor and foreign correspondent; Martin F. Nolan, the White House correspondent for the *Boston Globe;* and others. I have also used excerpts from an interview of Kissinger by Oriana Fallaci, and from memoirs by James Callaghan and Andrei Gromyko.

By good fortune, I visited a gallery that was selling the originals of cartoons by Pat Oliphant, one of the leading political cartoonists of the era who witnessed these events. I purchased six dealing with Turkey and Cyprus and reproduce them and a seventh in this volume with Oliphant's permission.

Many thanks to editors Madeleine Adams and James Ashton for their numerous helpful suggestions; to Yola Pakhchanian, director of publications for the American Hellenic Institute Foundation, for her research, manuscript preparation, production assistance and for overseeing every step of the publication of this manuscript; to Carol Thomas for manuscript preparation; to my brother Daniel W. Rossides, professor emeritus of sociology of Bowdoin College, and my son Michael Rossides for their many helpful suggestions and encouragement; to Nick Karambelas and his daughter Alexandra for their manuscript review. A very special thanks to George Lois for the jacket design and to Louis Galambos, Professor of History; Editor, The Papers of Dwight David Eisenhower; and Co-Director, The Institute for Applied Economics, Global Health, and the Study of Business Enterprise, Johns Hopkins University, for his Foreword and helpful suggestions.

Gene Rossides

1

Cyprus: Strategic, Economic and Political Value

Cyprus is a strategically located island in the Eastern Mediterranean, with an area of 3,572 square miles. Its population in 1974 was about 650,000, with Greek Cypriots accounting for 80 percent of the population, Turkish Cypriots 18 percent, and Armenians, Maronites, and others comprising the remaining 2 percent.[1] While its predominant cultural heritage can be traced to the first Greek colonization in the thirteenth century B.C., Cyprus has had a number of rulers, including Assyrians, Egyptians, Phoenicians, Persians, Romans, Byzantines, and Crusaders. In 1489 the island was taken over by the Venetians, who ruled it until 1571, when it was conquered by the Ottoman Turks. Cyprus's involvement in the strategic affairs of Western Europe began in 1878, when Great Britain acquired Cyprus in an agreement with Turkey. Today, Cyprus serves Western Europe and the United States as a stationary aircraft carrier in the Middle East. Its high mountains and its listening posts, which are superior to those in Turkey, are still in general use—they formerly enabled the West to monitor the Soviet Union's activities during the Cold War.

The discovery of natural gas deposits in the Eastern Mediterranean in Cyprus's territorial waters—the continental shelf and Exclusive Economic Zone (EEZ) south of Cyprus—has also made Cyprus an economic asset of significance to Europe's energy security. Cyprus, together with Egypt, Israel, and Lebanon, can help bring energy security to Europe, an issue of vital strategic importance not only to the European Union but also to the United States and NATO.

On February 17, 2003, Cyprus signed an agreement with Egypt for joint exploration of natural gas and oil in an area 125 miles wide between the two countries. A similar agreement with Lebanon is pending ratification by Lebanon's parliament. On December 17, 2010, Cyprus and Israel signed an agreement delimiting the maritime boundary between them in the Mediterranean Sea, an agreement which enables Israeli-Cypriot cooperative exploration of gas and oil resources in the Eastern Mediterranean south and east of Cyprus. This exploration began in September 2011.

In 2012, Cyprus's foreign minister Erato Kozakou-Marcoullis described the care Cyprus has taken in building relations with its neighbors while exploiting the hydrocarbon resources in its EEZ:

> The discovery of hydrocarbon deposits offshore is a major development for all countries in the Eastern Mediterranean. . . . However, it is also a development which requires a great deal of wisdom, vision, and patience because of the fragile nature of the region and because decisions made today will affect many generations to come. . . . For us it was also important to make it clear to all our neighbors, and especially the ones with whom we had signed delimitation agreements, that agreements with one did not come at the expense of the other. We are delighted to note that this is a message that was well received by all three—Egypt, Lebanon and Israel—and that in practice, because we are perceived to be honest interlocutors, a positive attitude has dominated talks about other agreements necessary for the exploitation of the offshore wealth.[2]

Kozakou-Marcoullis recognized that the discovery of hydro-carbon reserves in the Eastern Mediterranean was a unique opportunity for Cyprus. But it was also fraught with peril, not least because of Cyprus's increasing strategic importance to Israel. The rift between Turkey and Israel has resulted in the strengthening of Israel's relationships with Cyprus and Greece in security, economic, and political matters. This rift began with Turkish Prime Minister Recep Tayyip Erdoğan's criticism of Israeli President Shimon Peres at the World Economic Forum at Davos in 2009. Erdoğan has continued to attack Israel verbally since then, and has ended the military arrangement between Israel and Turkey initiated in 1996 by Leon Fuerth, then Vice President Al Gore's national security advisor.

Although relations between Cyprus and Israel have dramatically improved since 2009, their good relationship goes back decades. In the mid to late 1940s, during Cyprus's occupation by the British, Greek Cypriots assisted Jewish refugees interned in Cyprus to get to Mandate Palestine. Kozakou-Marcoullis mused on the shared values and culture that form a sturdy foundation for trust between the two countries:

> There is . . . a dimension . . . which leads me to believe that the relationship between Israelis and Cypriots is being built on solid foundations of mutual appreciation and respect. I am referring to a mutual recognition that we share a common sphere, be it in terms of the synthesis called Mediterranean Culture, dating back several millennia, or in the values of democracy and freedom, or even in the fact that we are both small countries, with few resources and facing many challenges. These are . . . keys with which they can traverse into the worldview of the other, building trust, confidence and commitment.[3]

Beginning in 2009, Israel and Cyprus have exchanged presidential visits and visits by foreign ministers. In 2012, the Israeli Prime

Minister Benjamin Netanyahu visited Cyprus. The visits of Peres and Netanyahu were the first by an Israeli President and Prime Minister to Cyprus since Cyprus's independence in 1960. This high-level diplomatic activity reflects the increasingly close bond between the two countries now rooted in their careful management of recent gas and oil discoveries in the Eastern Mediterranean.

I have long contended that Greece and Cyprus are far more important strategically to Israel than Turkey is, and they are more reliable allies. Cyprus's location makes it particularly important to Israel. Greece has authorized Israel to use its air space for air force training. Both Greece and Cyprus have excellent relations with the Arab countries of the Middle East and North Africa, whereas Turkey is still regarded as a harsh former colonial ruler.

An article published July 3, 2013 by the respected Hudson Institute titled "Will U.S. Choose the Right Side in the Eastern Mediterranean?" by Seth Cropsey draws attention to the evolving three-way economic and security relationship among Israel, Cyprus and Greece. The article points out how the triangular relationship provides the United States with an opportunity "to bolster its waning influence in the Eastern Mediterranean Sea." The author details Turkey's moves away from the West under Prime Minister Recep Tayyip Erdogan whom he refers to as an Islamist. He discusses the merits of a "quadrilateral relationship—the U.S., Greece, Israel and Cyprus—based on economic and security interests."[4]

Ioannis Kasoulides, Minister of Foreign Affairs of Cyprus in the new 2013 government of Nicos Anastasiades, spoke at the Brookings Institution in Washington, D.C. on May 9, 2013, on "Geopolitics in the Eastern Mediterranean: A Cypriot Perspective." He discussed the strategic importance of Cyprus's geographic position in the Eastern Mediterranean and its relations with Egypt, Lebanon, Syria, Israel and Turkey. He discussed the energy resources in the waters south of Cyprus and maritime security. He discussed Turkey's role in the area and the proposals of his government regarding the Cyprus problem. He said that "the major difference is between Turkey and Cyprus, it's not between the two communities in Cyprus." Regarding his government's current position, he stated:

> We are open of lifting our own veto on . . . certain chapters of the accession negotiation of Turkey with the European Union, a win situation for Turkey; permit world trade, direct trade of the Turkish Cypriot community through the port of Famagusta under the supervision of the European Union, a win situation for the Turkish Cypriots; and we want that Turkey relinquishes the town of Famagusta, an empty town, a ghost town to its rightful inhabitants, which is a win situation for Cyprus.
>
> So a win, win, win situation. And I am saying that . . . such a big step will tremendously change the whole climate, and it will become the game changer if we want, during the negotiations to resolve the problem of Cyprus.[5]

Partly in recognition of its strategic importance in the Eastern Mediterranean, Cyprus gained admission as a full member of the European Union on May 1, 2004. Cyprus's current economic centrality in such a politically contested region is only part of the story. To understand the involvement of the United States in Cypriot affairs—and the duplicity of Henry Kissinger—we must briefly examine the interest of European powers in Cyprus, a history that stretches back to the British intervention of the late nineteenth century.

2

A Brief History and Background on the 1974 Crisis

The Convention of Defensive Alliance of 1878 between Great Britain and Turkey—known as the Cyprus Convention[1]—led to the eventual British annexation of Cyprus when Turkey entered World War I on the side of the Central Powers. In 1915, the British offered Cyprus to Greece as an inducement to enter the war on the Allied side. Although Greece did enter the war at a later date, the British refused to part with Cyprus, claiming that the offer had lapsed. Turkey recognized Britain's 1914 annexation of Cyprus in the Treaty of Lausanne of 1923, giving up all rights to Cyprus.[2] On March 10, 1925, Britain declared Cyprus a crown colony.[3]

Britain bears the original responsibility for the post–World War II calamities that have befallen Cyprus. After Greece entered World War II, Britain called for Greek Cypriot volunteers to fight for "Greece and Liberty." As colonial subjects, Greek Cypriots were not subject to conscription. Nonetheless, as many as 35,000 Greek Cypriots volunteered and fought in the British Army in World War II.[4] While other colonies were gaining their freedom after World War II, Cyprus was told it should abandon all hope of gaining its independence. The

British minister of state for colonial affairs Henry Hopkinson said, during a House of Commons debate in 1954, that "there can be no question of any change of sovereignty in Cyprus" and that "there are certain territories in the Commonwealth which, owing to their particular circumstances, can never expect to be fully independent."[5] For Great Britain, its own strategic and economic interests regarding its former colonial possessions in the Middle East trumped any commitment to self-determination for Cyprus.

Following Hopkinson's statement, Greece brought an application for self-determination on behalf of the people of Cyprus to the 1954 United Nations General Assembly session.[6] Because they were under colonial rule, the Cypriots had no standing to bring the application themselves. But even though the principle of equal rights and self-determination of peoples is enshrined in the United Nations Charter (which lists as among its founding purposes "To develop friendly relations among nations based on respect for the principle of equal rights and self-determination of peoples, and to take other appropriate measures to strengthen universal peace,") Britain continued to oppose self-determination for the Cypriots.

Britain claimed that the presence of the Turkish Cypriot minority population was an obstacle to a solution, despite the absence of any history of violence between the Greek and Turkish Cypriot populations and despite Turkey's having renounced all rights to Cyprus in the 1923 Lausanne Treaty. The Treaty states: "Turkey hereby renounces all rights and title whatsoever over or respecting the territories situated outside the frontiers laid down in the present Treaty and the islands other than those over which her sovereignty is recognized by the said Treaty, the future of these territories and islands being settled or to be settled by the parties concerned. The provisions of the present Article do not prejudice any special arrangements arising from neighborly relations which have been or may be concluded between Turkey and any limitrophe countries."[7]

The issue carried forward into the post-WWII years. A tripartite conference among Britain, Greece, and Turkey held in London in late August and early September 1955, to discuss the situation in the Eastern Mediterranean and Cyprus, ended in failure.[8] Nonetheless, Britain obtained its unacknowledged objective in convening the conference: greater Turkish involvement to blunt the Greek government's efforts to win self-determination for the people of Cyprus.[9] On August 24, 1955, C. L. Sulzberger wrote in the *New York Times:* "The British privately encouraged the Turks to express their interest. That was all Ankara needed. Ever since Turkey has been whipping itself into a frenzy over Cyprus. Instead of being dismayed, the British Foreign Office—which had taken over the hot potato from the colonial office—was pleased to cite Turkey's arguments as further excuse for doing nothing about changing the island's status."

To demonstrate its interest in Cyprus at the time of the tripartite conference, the Turkish government planned and organized riots on September 6–7, 1955, against its Greek citizens and residents in Istanbul. To make it appear as though Greeks were attacking Turks and thus foment a violent reaction from the Turks against Greek residents, on September 5 the Turkish government exploded a bomb in the Turkish Consulate in Salonika, Greece. The government spread a false report that Kemal Atatürk's birthplace had been bombed and destroyed.[10] Historian Speros Vryonis Jr. has detailed the Turkish government's pogrom against the Greek population of Turkey in his book *The Mechanism of Catastrophe: The Turkish Pogrom of September 6–7, 1955,* (2005). In 1955, there were more than one hundred thousand Greek citizens of Turkey living in Istanbul under the exchange of population agreement. Within ten years, the number had dropped dramatically; today, there are fewer than two thousand Greek Orthodox Christians left in Turkey.

Turkish actions precipitated diplomatic contact between Britain and Cypriot representatives, as London realized it could no longer ignore the issue of Cyprus's future, particularly in light of increasing tensions with Egypt. In fact, as future events in 1956 demonstrated, Britain wanted unfettered use of Cyprus as a military base against Egypt.[11] As a show of good faith, Ethnarch Archbishop Makarios of Cyprus and the British governor of Cyprus, Field Marshall Sir John Harding, entered into negotiations in October 1955 on the future status of Cyprus. Substantial progress was made. But London broke off negotiations in late February 1956 because it was unwilling to commit to majority rule and self-government for Cyprus.[12] Shortly thereafter, on March 9, 1956, Britain abducted the Archbishop and imprisoned him on the Seychelles Islands.[13] On October 29, 1956, Britain, France, and Israel invaded Egypt in what became known as the Suez Crisis.[14] After the invasion ended in a debacle, Britain decided that having a military base on Cyprus was a more feasible alternative than using Cyprus as a base.

Alan Lennox-Boyd, Britain's secretary of state for the colonies, continued Britain's "divide and rule" policy. In discussing possible self-determination in the House of Commons on December 19, 1956, he stated that it should apply equally and separately to Greek and Turkish Cypriots and "must include partition among the eventual options." The seeds of partition were thereby sown by Britain.[15] It was a distortion of the doctrine of self-determination. Partition is a synonym for a special form of apartheid.

The Greek government persisted in its application for self-determination for Cyprus, and Britain continued its opposition. In December 1957, the UN General Assembly passed a resolution stating the "earnest hope that further negotiations and discussions will be undertaken in a spirit of cooperation with a view to having the right of self-determination applied in the case of the people of Cyprus."[16] Although the resolution passed by a majority vote of 31 to 23, with 24 abstentions, it did not achieve the two-thirds majority vote required under the United Nations Charter to become a "recommendation with respect to the maintenance of international peace and security."[17]

Up to this point, there had been no history of interethnic violence on Cyprus. That changed in the summer of 1958. On the night of June 7, Turkish Cypriots, following Turkey's play-book from 1955, exploded a bomb at the Information Bureau of the Turkish Consulate in Nicosia, the capital of Cyprus, and then falsely blamed Greek Cypriots for the act. Turkish Cypriots began burning and looting Greek Cypriot shops and homes. The Greek Cypriots retaliated, and before long fighting had spread throughout the island. Twenty-six years later, Rauf Den-ktash, the longtime Turkish Cypriot leader, admitted on British television that a friend of his had set the bomb.[18]

On August 16, 1960, Cyprus gained limited independence from British colonial rule through the London–Zurich Agree-ments of 1959–1960, negotiated by Britain with Greece and Turkey and presented to the Greek and Turkish Cypriots as a package to be agreed to without modification.[19] The Agree-ments barred both union with Greece and partition. The Brit-ish were prepared to implement unilaterally the Macmillan partition plan of 1958 to divide Cyprus between Greece and Turkey if Archbishop Makarios refused to sign. Consequently, Archbishop Makarios signed for the Greek Cypriots and Fazil Kuchuck signed for the Turkish Cypriots. The constitution gave the 18 percent Turkish Cypriot minority veto power over all major governmental actions, legislative and executive, includ-ing taxation, defense, security, foreign affairs, and municipal matters, and contained a provision barring amendment of the basic articles. These undemocratic features of the constitution have been the major cause of the dispute between the Greek and Turkish Cypriots ever since.[20]

Predictably, it was not long before the divisive constitution led to problems between the two groups.[21] The Turkish Cypriot leadership, among other things, would not cooperate on tax legislation. On November 30, 1963, President Makarios submit-ted to the three guarantor powers (Britain, Greece, and Turkey) and to the Turkish Cypriots thirteen proposed amendments to the constitution intended to correct its undemocratic features.[22] Although Makarios thought he had the support of the British High Commissioner, Britain remained silent on Makarios's proposals for constitutional reform. Turkey rejected the proposals before the Turkish Cypriots made any response, and then the Turkish Cypriots followed suit.

In late December 1963, an incident of violence sparked the outbreak of intercommunal fighting, which led Turkey to threaten an invasion. There were several overflights of Nicosia by Turkish air force planes during the last week of December. In response to the fighting, the United Nations Security Council passed Resolution 186 on March 4, 1964, recommending mediation and the creation of a peacekeeping force. The resolution went into effect on March 27, but the intercommunal troubles continued. As tension mounted, Turkey again threatened to invade in June 1964, but was deterred by U.S. diplomatic efforts, including a letter from President Lyndon B. Johnson dated June 5, 1964, to the Turkish Prime Minister Ismet Inönü (discussed in chapter 8). Nevertheless, Turkey did bomb Cyprus on August 8 and 9, 1964, and the United Nations Security Council passed a resolution calling on Turkey to cease its bombing instantly. The next crisis occurred in November 1967, when President Johnson sent Cyrus Vance to Cyprus on a diplomatic mission to prevent the outbreak of further hostilities. Vance's mission was a success. Between 1968 and 1974, talks were held to achieve a new constitutional arrangement. But then the fateful events of 1974 precluded further discussion of a negotiated settlement.

In the decades before Turkey's invasion it was Britain's refusal to grant self-determination under the UN Charter to Cyprus, as well as its instigation of Turkish opposition to self-determination for Cyprus, that led to the situation in 1974. Secretary of State Henry Kissinger's actions and deliberate inactions in 1974 led directly to Turkey's aggression in 1974 and the illegal Turkish occupation of 37.3 percent of Cyprus, now in its 40th year in 2014.

Historian Perry Anderson has detailed the events immediately leading up to the 1974 crisis, including the 1974 coup against the Makarios government initiated by the Greek junta. This coup, "undoubtedly a breach of the [1960] Treaty of Guarantee," led to Turkish demands for British support in putting it down. As Anderson writes, these demands "settled the fate of the island. . . . Although Britain had not only a core of well-equipped troops, but overwhelming air-power on the island. . . [they] refused to lift a finger."[23] Two days after Turkish Premier Ecevit made his demands and Britain failed to act, Turkish forces began their invasion of Cyprus. As I discuss in more detail in chapter 8, the 1960 Treaty of Guarantee did not authorize the use of such force.

Anderson refers to Kissinger's role, including his desire to remove Makarios, as follows:

> The brutality of Turkey's descent on Cyprus, stark enough was no surprise. . . . Political responsibility for the disaster lay with those who allowed or encouraged it. The chief blame is often put on the United States. There by the summer of 1974, Nixon was so paralyzed by Watergate—he was driven from the office between the first and second Turkish assaults—that American policy was determined by Kissinger alone. . . . He wanted Makarios out of the way, and with Sampson in place in Nicosia, blocked any condemnation of the coup in the Security Council. Once Ankara had delivered its ultimatum in London, he then connived at the Turkish invasion, co-ordinating its advance directly with Ankara.[24]

Let us look more closely at the U.S. role in these tumultuous events that distorted the history of Cyprus.

3

Kissinger's Encouragement of Coup against Makarios

On November 25, 1973, Brigadier General Dimitrios Ioannides, who had been in charge of the military police, toppled the three-man junta of Greek colonels in a bloodless coup and assumed sole dictatorial powers in Greece.[1] During the first six months of 1974, the acrimony between Ioannides and Makarios increased. Ioannides was a fervent supporter of *enosis* and, more important, hated Cyprus's President, Archbishop Makarios, who Ioannides considered a communist. He determined to remove Makarios. On July 2, 1974, Makarios wrote to General Phaidon Gizikis, the President of Greece, accusing the Greek regime of trying to overthrow his government and demanding the removal of the roughly six hundred Greek military officers who commanded the Cypriot National Guard.[2]

On July 15, 1974, the Cypriot National Guard, acting on instructions from Ioannides and directed by officers from the Greek military, overthrew the government of Cyprus in a coup d'état and attempted to assassinate President Makarios. The Greek government installed Nicos Sampson, an ultra-rightist, as President of Cyprus on July 15.[3] Miraculously, Makarios survived and was flown by the British to Malta on July 16,[4] and from there to London, where he met with Prime Minister Harold Wilson and Foreign Secretary James Callaghan on July 17.[5]

The events of 1973–74 that resulted in the coup against Makarios were entirely satisfactory to the foreign policy of the United States—as it was conceived by Secretary of State Henry Kissinger. Kissinger had two aims regarding Cyprus. First, he wanted to oust the elected President, Archbishop Makarios, who had brought Cyprus into the Third World Non-aligned Movement. Second, he wanted to divide Cyprus between Greece and Turkey (see chapter 4), giving one-third of Cyprus to Turkey. As we shall see, others within America's diplomatic apparatus did not agree with these aims, which were, in fact, both unlawful and contrary to the best long-term interests of the United States.

Kissinger knew that Ioannides disliked Makarios and was making plans to oust him. He was aware of Makarios's letter to President Gizikis, which was made public in Cyprus on July 3, and reported in the *New York Times* on July 6. Yet Kissinger did nothing to prevent the July 15 coup against Makarios. Indeed, Kissinger's deliberate inaction, including his failure to make sure Ioannides was told that the United States opposed any action against Makarios, could only be interpreted by Ioannides as encouragement to move against Makarios. It furthered Kissinger's own aim to get rid of Makarios.

Thomas Boyatt's account

Thomas Boyatt, the director of Cypriot affairs at the State Department from 1971 to 1974, had "the initial responsibility for United States policy regarding the Cyprus problem" during the key period of 1974.[6] He became convinced that the Greek military was planning to overthrow Makarios and install a puppet government, and if it did so, Turkey would invade Cyprus. Judging that such developments would be counter to the foreign policy interests of the United States, Boyatt "began

the process of trying to convince my government to do something about the situation."[7] In 2010, he spoke on "The View of
the U.S. State Department in 1974" at a conference commem-
orating the fiftieth anniversary of the founding of the Republic of Cyprus. Boyatt recalled the resistance he encountered,
both from other departments and from other parts of the State
Department:

> It was extraordinarily difficult in terms of the interests of
> other parts of the United States government. The Defense
> Department took a position, as Bob [Keeley] outlined, of
> support for the junta, for a variety of their own reasons.
> Our friends in the CIA had had a close contact with the
> Greek military dating back to the Truman Doctrine 1947
> and 1948, when we assisted the Greek government against
> the Communist insurgency. And other elements of the U.S.
> government and parts of the State Department were equally
> opposed to an activist approach versus Greece with respect
> to the Cyprus problem.[8]

Meanwhile, the debate about policy toward Cyprus was
hampered by two major organizational problems within the
State Department. First, the Greek–Turkey–Cyprus division had
been transferred from the Near East Bureau to the European
Bureau in early 1974, and the European Bureau's leadership
had no understanding of or interest in the Cyprus problem. As
Boyatt put it, "They were basically more interested in the corn-
starch negotiations with the European Community or something
similar rather than the Cyprus problem."[9]

Second, and even more damaging, Henry Kissinger's management style was insular; it isolated him within an echo chamber. Boyatt recalled, "He surrounded himself with a group of
people that he knew and trusted. But it was almost by definition a small group. . . . But outside of that personal group, he
looked at everybody with a great deal of distrust, and with a

manifestation of the paranoia for which he is so justly famous. And I, of course, was an outsider."[10]

Boyatt and his colleagues, the country directors for Greece and Turkey and the several desk officers who worked for them, agreed that they had to act, regardless of the organizational difficulties and resistance they faced. Boyatt recounted the diplomatic impasse:

> On May 17th of 1974 the Department sent a cable to the Embassy in Athens and the Embassy in Nicosia, which said in pertinent part, we believe that you should get the message to General Ioannidis, that: "If the national guard and EOKA-B [the Cypriot paramilitary dedicated to *enosis*, political unification of Cyprus with Greece] succeed in getting rid of Makarios and installing a leadership responsive to Athens, a direct confrontation between Greece and Turkey would become inevitable." That was an official instruction to Ambassador Tasca. He disputed the instruction. . . . At one point in the debate we received a message through the intelligence channel from General Ioannidis in which he said that he was considering taking action against Makarios on Cyprus. We immediately sent another cable out to Embassy Athens, and it said . . . "It is evident that Ioannidis is seriously considering a way to topple Makarios from power, a move which could have disastrous consequences for U.S. interests in the Eastern Mediterranean as well as for the peoples of Cyprus, Greece, and Turkey. In our view . . ." that is to say the State Department's view, "the effort to remove Makarios by force contains unacceptable risks of chaos, eventually causing a Greco-Turk confrontation involving the Soviets in the Cyprus situation."[11]

Ambassador Tasca again resisted carrying out his instructions and the debate continued. In June 1974, Boyatt drafted a cable, which was never sent, setting forth clearly and unequivocally the view of the State Department staff on the ground who were intimately familiar with the situation and its ramifications. It read, in part,

> For several years the Greek military regime has maintained its litany that the Cyprus situation is composed of roughly equal parts of Makarios the Red Priest Devil theory, Cyprus as a Mediterranean Cuba threat, that *enosis* is the only acceptable solution view, and that Turkey is the hereditary enemy assertion. These views provide an extremely misleading and explosive background on which the Greek regime bases actions with respect to Cyprus. In opposition to Greek views the Department believes that Makarios is not pro-communist . . . , Cyprus is not on the verge of becoming a Mediterranean Cuba; in fact, Makarios' overwhelming democratic support in elections gives Cyprus a degree of stability not enjoyed by other countries in the area; *enosis* is not the solution to the Cyprus problem; the best interests of the West, the U.S., Greece are only served by cooperative relationships between Greece and Turkey. In short, the Department regards the views of the Greek regime/Greek military re Cyprus as factually inaccurate, analytically defective, and operationally dangerous as a rationale for Greek actions."[12]

This unambiguous statement of support for Cypriot independence did not comport with Henry Kissinger's vision for the Eastern Mediterranean. The cable was never sent. Instead, Undersecretary of State Joseph Sisco decided to deliver its contents by telephone. The message apparently was never delivered to Ioannides himself—and certainly not in the clear and unambiguous language required under the circumstances.[13]

These failures of communication occurred at the top leadership level of the State Department. As Thomas Boyatt convincingly argues, the professionals in the diplomatic service performed their functions well, gave clear and unambiguous warnings of the coming crisis in time to avert it, and proposed a strong, pragmatic policy solution that was in the best interests of the United States and upheld international law. The State Department leadership—meaning Secretary of State Kissinger and his small circle of advisors—failed to follow through and thus failed to protect U.S. foreign policy interests or to uphold international law.[14] In his memoirs Kissinger asserts, erroneously, that nobody really believed that Ioannides would attack Makarios and overthrow his government. Boyatt and his colleagues certainly did, and they vigorously warned the U.S. foreign policy leadership.

Boyatt went on to discuss the issue in the days following the junta-initiated coup and Sisco's mission to London, Athens, and Ankara to try to stop a Turkish invasion. In his judgment, Sisco "had no instructions from the upper levels of the State Department," and the mission's failure "was a failure of leadership."[15] After the Turkish invasion on July 20, Boyatt tried to convince Kissinger to limit the area of the invasion. He recommended that Kissinger use his influence with Turkey to convince them to remain in the territory they had overrun between the invasion on July 20th and the middle of August. Instead, the Turkish forces initiated the second and massive phase of its aggression on August 14–16, sundering the island in two. In Thomas Boyatt's account of those frustrating days, the "failure of leadership on the part of the U.S. government" has been "a bone in our throats" ever since. Boyatt himself was removed—by Kissinger—from his position as country director of Cypriot affairs. Although he continued to serve with distinction in the foreign service,[16] Boyatt's vision of a democratic Cyprus played no part in Henry Kissinger's plans.

Kissinger and the Greek Junta

Kissinger knew in advance of the junta's plans regarding Cyprus, and his efforts at the time were principally directed to shielding the junta from retaliation for the coup against Makarios. According to the late journalist, author, and Cyprus expert Christopher Hitchens, "It is, from Kissinger's own record and recollection, as well as from the record of the subsequent official inquiry, quite easy to demonstrate that he did have advance knowledge of the plan to depose and kill Makarios. He admits as much himself, by noting that the Greek dictator Dimitrios Ioannides, head of the secret police, was determined to mount a coup in Cyprus and bring the island under the control of Athens."[17] Kissinger admitted having seen Boyatt's June 1974 memorandum, "yet no demarche [warning Ioannides to desist] bearing his name or carrying his authority was issued to the Greek junta."[18] In the meantime, the U.S. ambassador to Greece, Henry Tasca, was in touch only with the figurehead President of Greece, General Phaidon Gizikis. Tasca did not and would not deal with the Greek dictator, Ioannides, whose primary American contact was the Central Intelligence Agency. Tasca has argued that he should not have dealt with the dictator Ioannides as a matter "of protocol or etiquette," but, as Christopher Hitchens reminds us, "Kissinger, in addition to his formal diplomatic eminence, was also head of the Forty Committee and supervisor of covert action, and was dealing in private with an Athens regime that had long-standing CIA ties."[19] Henry Kissinger's overarching power makes it clear that arguments attributing diplomatic failure to compartmentalization were inaccurate, to say the least.

Having been expelled from the Council of Europe and blocked from joining the European Economic Community, Ioannides was dependent on U.S. military aid and political backing. If, as was widely understood, Ioannides was determined to overthrow Makarios and had already tried to have him assassinated, the U.S. secretary of state and national security advisor could hardly have been in the dark about this client's plans.[20] The July 15, 1974 coup that overthrew the government of Archbishop Makarios was denounced by the British government and most governments throughout the world—except for the United States. Kissinger not only refused to denounce the coup, he also refused to enforce U.S. foreign military assistance and foreign military sales laws by immediately halting arms aid and arms sales to Greece. This should have been done not only as policy, to avoid supporting the coup, but also as a sanction against the junta's illegal use of U.S.-supplied arms to topple the Makarios government. Former U.S. ambassador to Greece and Cyprus and longtime State Department spokesman Robert McCloskey, Kissinger's advisor for the media and policy on his immediate staff, stated in an oral history that Kissinger's failure to denounce the coup was a major disappointment to him. McCloskey said that he had urged Kissinger to take a tough public stance condemning the Greek junta-initiated coup against Makarios and his government, but Kissinger rejected this advice.[21] Kissinger's real objective—to get rid of Makarios as President of Cyprus—had become clear.

Christopher Hitchens has accused Kissinger of being "an accomplice" to the Greek junta coup against Makarios and his government. He wrote:

> Even in the dank obfuscator prose of his own memoirs, he does admit what can otherwise be concluded from independent sources. Using covert channels, and short-circuiting the democratic process in his own country, he made himself an accomplice in a plan of political assassination which, when it went awry, led to the deaths of thousands of civilians, the violent uprooting of almost 200,000 refugees, and the creation of an unjust and unstable amputation of Cyprus which constitutes a serious threat to peace a full quarter-century later. His attempts to keep the record sealed are significant in themselves; when the relevant files are opened, they will form part of the longer bill of indictment.[22]

Kissinger's actions and deliberate inactions during the week of July 15, 1974 provide further evidence that he encouraged and supported the coup against Makarios, including the attempted assassination, initiated by the Greek junta dictator Ioannides through the Greek military officers who commanded the Cyprus National Guard. Because these issues also bear on his encouragement of Turkey's aggression against Cyprus on July 20, 1974, I discuss Kissinger's actions and inactions during this week more fully in the next chapter.

4

Kissinger's Encouragement of Turkey's Aggression

In the early hours of July 20, Turkey's armed forces invaded Cyprus by sea and air,[1] using U.S.-supplied arms and equipment in violation of U.S. laws, the United Nations Charter, the North Atlantic Treaty, and customary international law. Turkey's invasion was the tragic denouement to British and then American interference in Cypriot affairs. This tragic outcome culminated in Henry Kissinger's lawless, arrogant actions and inactions during the week of July 15th. We have seen that Kissinger refused to denounce the Greek junta–initiated coup against Makarios and his government on July 15th as Britain and most other nations of the world, including NATO and European nations, did. In addition, he failed to enforce U.S. laws by immediately halting shipments of arms to the Greek junta in response to its illegal use of American-supplied arms in the coup and the attempted assassination of Makarios. The refusal to halt arms shipments was a lost opportunity to stand against aggression and the use of force in ousting a democratically elected government (I discuss the legal implications of this refusal more fully in chapter 5).

Kissinger's machinations behind the scenes were even more significant. On July 15, Henry Kissinger directed the U.S. ambassador to the United Nations to postpone the UN Security Council emergency meeting on Cyprus from Monday, July 15, to Friday, July 19.[2] This had the effect of reducing worldwide publicity, downgrading the issue, and giving Turkey time to prepare to invade Cyprus. On July 16, he instructed the U.S. ambassador to Cyprus, Rodger Davies, to meet with the Sampson coup regime's foreign minister, Dimitrios Demetriou,[3] which could be considered *de facto* recognition of the regime. Finally, On July 17, Kissinger leaked to the *New York Times* that the United States was leaning toward recognizing the Sampson coup government over the legitimate Makarios government in Cyprus, although no final decision had been made. That leak by "high American officials" was the lead story on the front page of the *New York Times* the following day.[4] All of these items — the instructions, omissions, and delays — in effect gave the Turkish government, which strongly opposed the Sampson coup government, both the time to prepare and an excuse to invade Cyprus. By this time, Henry Kissinger had *de facto* control over U.S. foreign policy, and his actions and deliberate inactions during this crucial week exemplify his willful arrogance and diplomatic incompetence. By failing to obey and enforce U.S. laws against the Greek junta, Kissinger violated U.S. law. The dire consequences of these various machinations and diplomatic blunders would be readily apparent only days later, as Turkish forces continued to spread across Cyprus.

We have also seen that Kissinger rejected the recommendation of State Department specialists to denounce as illegal the intervention by Greek forces and to stand by Makarios. In the leaked story to the *New York Times* Kissinger transmitted his rationale for refusing to intervene or to disavow the Greek junta, actions that State Department staff hoped would serve as a lever to dislodge Ioannides from power: "The Secretary's rationale . . . was that the United States depended strategically on its air and sea bases in Greece and would do nothing to jeopardize them." In addition,

For years. . . the Nixon Administration has viewed Archbishop
Makarios as the "Castro of the Mediterranean," who turned
too readily towards Communist states for assistance . . .
"We think he is finished politically," a Kissinger aide said
of Archbishop Makarios. "He can't go back to Cyprus unless
General Ioannides is thrown out in Athens and even though
the junta has problems, that doesn't seem likely now."

Kissinger's rationale does not stand up to analysis. Getting
rid of the Greek junta would not jeopardize U.S. bases in
Greece. A democratic Greece would retain U.S. bases because it
would be in the interests of Greece to have them there. Actually,
Kissinger's failure to act against the Greek junta and apply U.S.
military aid and military sales laws to the junta damaged the
United States in the eyes of the people of Greece. But even that
did not result in the loss of the key U.S. naval and air bases in
Souda Bay, Crete, the most important U.S. bases in the Eastern
Mediterranean. Events continued to move quickly: on July 20,
only five days after the Greek junta's coup illegally established
a rightist government on Cyprus with Nicos Sampson as its figurehead, Turkey invaded.

That same day, July 20, 1974, the UN Security Council
adopted Security Council Res. 353, a resolution calling on "all
states to respect the sovereignty, independence and territorial
integrity of Cyprus."[5] Turkey had used the illegal Greek junta–
initiated coup on Cyprus as a pretext and cited the Treaty of
Guarantee under the London-Zurich Agreements of 1959-1960,
which established the Republic of Cyprus, as giving it the right
to invade.[6] (It is important to understand that Turkey had no
such right under the Treaty of Guarantee or otherwise, as I
discuss in detail in chapter 8.) The UN resolution called for a
cease-fire, demanded "an immediate end to foreign intervention" in Cyprus, and requested "the withdrawal without delay
from . . . Cyprus of foreign military personnel" except those

present under international agreement.[7] Although limited in scope, the resolution was a positive step.

By July 22, when the UN-sponsored cease-fire went into effect, Turkey had captured about 4 percent of the north of Cyprus, with a corridor from Kyrenia on the north coast to Nicosia. The cease-fire was soon violated by Turkish armed forces.[8] Robert McDonald wrote, "In the first wave some 6000 men with 30 tanks were landed by sea and parachute drop. . . . Despite having accepted the [UN] cease-fire, Turkey had reinforced its troop concentration and engaged in a series of advances to make its bridgehead more viable."[9]

On July 23, the Sampson regime fell.[10] Pursuant to the 1960 constitution, Glafcos Clerides, the President of the Cyprus House of Representatives, was installed as the acting President of Cyprus. Thus, on July 23, eight days after the coup and three days after the Turkish invasion, the legitimate government of Cyprus was restored, which reestablished the constitutional state of affairs prior to the coup. The right of "action" under the Treaty of Guarantee was for "the sole aim of re-establishing the state of affairs created by the present Treaty." Although this condition had already been met by the restoration of the legitimate government of Cyprus, Turkey had no intention of stopping its aggression against Cyprus.

Meanwhile, Britain, Greece, and Turkey entered into negotiations in Geneva. On July 30, 1974, the three nations ended the first phase of their talks and signed the Declaration of Geneva, which called for a second cease-fire, a halt to the expansion of occupied territory, and withdrawal of troops.[11] Once again, Turkey's armed forces violated the ceasefire agreement.[12] At this point, Turkey held about 6 percent of Cyprus.

On August 8, Britain, Greece, and Turkey began the second round of talks in Geneva. On August 13, Turkey issued an ultimatum to Greece and Britain to accept Turkey's proposal. This was tantamount to partition, for six separate Turkish Cypriot "cantons" in which an 18 percent minority would get 34 percent of the island nation, including its most productive areas.[13] The ultimatum was, in effect, an admission that the aim of its invasion of Cyprus had not been to reestablish "the state of affairs created by the present Treaty," in accordance with article IV of the Treaty of Guarantee, but rather to conduct a land grab in violation of international law.

That same day, August 13, although there was no evidence of any danger to the Turkish Cypriot community, the State Department spokesman Ambassador Robert Anderson issued a statement, cleared by Kissinger, that the Turkish Cypriots needed more security.[14] Kissinger's blatantly pro-Turkish position was not supported by the reality of the situation in Cyprus. This State Department release was a deliberate tilt toward Turkey, the aggressor. It was an irresponsible decision by Kissinger, a blunder and a clear example of arrogance. The *New York Times* headline stated: "U.S. Backs Turks in Cyprus but Warns against a War."[15]

On August 14, Kissinger had State Department Counselor Helmut Sonnenfeldt send him a self-serving "Secret/Eyes Only" memorandum recommending that Kissinger "privately assure Turks we will get them [a] solution involving one-third of island, within some kind of federal arrangement."[16] Such a recommendation was obviously illegal and in violation of numerous Security Council and General Assembly resolutions regarding the sovereignty, independence, and territorial integrity of Cyprus. Nevertheless, the process went forward.

On that day and following days, the UN Security Council passed resolutions reaffirming its Resolution 353 of July 20, 1974, in all its provisions, including its call "upon all States to respect the sovereignty, independence and territorial integrity of Cyprus," demanding a cease-fire, and recording "its formal disapproval of the unilateral military actions undertaken" by Turkey against Cyprus.[17] The UN urged compliance with its previous resolutions "including those concerning the withdrawal without delay from Cyprus of foreign military personnel present otherwise than under the authority of international agreements."[18]

Also on August 14, three weeks after the legitimate government of Cyprus had been restored, Turkey unilaterally broke off negotiations and launched a second more massive aggression from August 14 to 16. During this second assault, some forty thousand Turkish forces, equipped with two hundred tanks, occupied an additional 30 percent of Cyprus (for a total of 37.3 percent), and forcibly expelled more than 180,000 Greek Cypriots from their homes and other properties,[19] and 20,000 more in ensuing years."

Since the 1974 aggression, Turkey has continued to illegally occupy 37.3 percent of Cyprus. During this nearly four-decade occupation, Turkey has brought an estimated 200,000 settlers/colonists from Anatolia into Cyprus in violation of the Geneva Convention of 1949, Section III, Article 49, which prohibits colonization by an occupying power. The illegal colonists/settlers have been given homes and lands taken from Greek Cypriots and foreign nationals including American citizens. The Turkish Cypriot newspaper *Yeniduzen* reported on February 14, 1990, sixteen years after the invasion, that of the 160,000 persons who lived in the occupied area at that time, 80,000 were Turkish Cypriots and 80,000 were settlers from Turkey.[20]

In a report issued October 13, 1975, on the migration of Turks to the occupied part of Cyprus, the *Guardian* listed the rate of migration as 1,500 to 2,500 a month and asserted that the plan was "to implant as many as 80,000" settlers. Neither Kissinger nor anyone else at the State Department made any objection to Turkey's violation of the Geneva Convention of 1949 by colonizing Cyprus with Turkish nationals. Since the 1990 report in *Yeniduzen,* the steady flow of illegal settlers from Anatolia to Cyprus has continued. The government of Cyprus estimates that, as of 2012, 200,000 illegal Turkish settlers have been planted in occupied Cyprus.

Kissinger and Cyprus: In His Own Words

A Freedom of Information Act (FOIA) request to the State Department regarding Kissinger and Cyprus produced 148 transcripts of telephone conversations out of 3,568 searched from the Kissinger Transcripts. The telephone transcripts are heavily censored and key parts are blanked out. On July 19, 1974, at 8:51 PM, Kissinger had a conference call with Deputy Secretary Robert Ingersoll, Ambassador Robert McCloskey, and Wells Stabler. With the seven-hour time difference, it was July 20 in Turkey, and Turkey had started its invasion of Cyprus. In this telephone conversation, Kissinger mentioned a U.S. "double *enosis*" scheme to divide Cyprus between Greece and Turkey:

> KISSINGER: Now the other thing we have to keep in mind is to leave open the door to double *enosis*—but I think we better not start pushing that yet. . . . Now what is the judgment of the people about whether we should float the double *enosis* idea now?
>
> INGERSOLL: Some people think that is probably the practical thing with the Turks in place.
>
> KISSINGER: I think we should go to that after trying the Clerides [solution in which Clerides would be named acting president of Cyprus for six months, after which an election would be held]. It is too dangerous to come up with it now because it will run into massive Soviet opposition.[21]

Kissinger's reference to double *enosis* is evidence, first, that he had encouraged the Greek junta dictator to initiate a coup against Makarios, and second, that he was encouraging the invasion of Cyprus by Turkey.

Kissinger had several conversations with the Turkish Prime Minister Bülent Ecevit, his former student at Harvard. He never mentioned to Ecevit that partition of Cyprus was barred by the Treaty of Guarantee and that the United States opposed partition. This fact is to be compared to Kissinger's messages to the Greek junta and to Ecevit that the United States strongly opposed union with Greece.

Nor did he refer to the provisions of the UN Charter and the North Atlantic Treaty against "the threat or use of force." Furthermore, in his conversations with Ecevit, Kissinger never referred to the provisions of the U.S. laws that barred the use of American-supplied arms for aggression. Kissinger's own staff disagreed with this omission. Ambassador Robert McCloskey, Kissinger's media and policy advisor on his immediate staff, stated in 1989 that his second major disappointment regarding Kissinger was the continuation of arms shipments to Turkey after the beginning of the massive second phase of Turkey's aggression. McCloskey stated that during an August 14 meeting in Kissinger's office about how the State Department should respond to Turkey's second wave of aggression, Kissinger went around the room for comments and McCloskey said that he thought "that we should announce that from today, we will suspend any further deliveries of United States military equipment to Turkey. Well, he [Kissinger] exploded."[22]

The release of official documents proves that Kissinger knew ahead of time and, in effect, sanctioned the second phase of Turkey's aggression—its massive land grab. On August 13, 1974, the State Department's Bureau of Intelligence and Research issued a map of Cyprus, dated August 13, which depicted the lines of the land Turkey's forces would take on the following three days, August 14–16.[23] That map is shown on page vii to this book.

Even without a map, damning evidence though it is, it is not difficult to see that Henry Kissinger's actions—and inactions—added up to support of Turkish aggression. It was inaction on his part that fueled the Greek junta's coup against Makarios. Conversely, Kissinger actively moved in support of Turkey, making, as Christopher Hitchens puts it, "strict and repeated admonitions against any measures to block a Turkish invasion." Hitchens continues,

> Sir Tom McNally, then the chief political advisor to Britain's then foreign secretary and future prime minister, James Callaghan, has since disclosed that Kissinger "vetoed" at least one British military action to preempt a Turkish landing. But that was *after* the Greek colonels had collapsed, and democracy had been restored to Athens. There was no longer a client regime to protect.[24] . . . And, once Turkey had conducted two brutal invasions and occupied almost 40% of Cypriot territory, Kissinger exerted himself very strongly indeed to protect Ankara from any congressional reprisal for this outright violation of international law, and promiscuous and illegal misuse of US weaponry. He became so pro-Turkish, indeed, that it was as if he had never heard of the Greek colonels. (Though his expressed dislike of the returned Greek democratic leaders supplied an occasional reminder.)[25]

Kissinger cared nothing for the territorial integrity of Cyprus, or its independence. He went as far as openly supporting a policy of dividing Cyprus between Greece and Turkey. On August 13, in a meeting at the White House with President Ford, Kissinger said, "Some of my colleagues want to cutoff assistance to Turkey—that would be a disaster. There is no American reason why the Turks should not have one-third of Cyprus."[26] For Kissinger, what he perceived as *realpolitik* trumped international law.

My involvement in the Cyprus problem

This outcome is particularly disappointing to me because I was actively involved in the Cyprus problem from 1954 to 1959, supporting self-determination for Cyprus as in the best interests of the United States. I first met Archbishop Makarios in

December 1954, when he came to New York for the UN vote on self-determination for Cyprus. In 1971, there was an attempt to assassinate President Makarios. At that time I was assistant secretary of the U.S. Treasury Department in charge of several bureaus including the U.S. Secret Service, whose mission included protection of the president and vice-president. With the approval of the secretaries of state and treasury, I wrote to President Makarios and offered Secret Service assistance to review his protection procedures and make suggestions for improvement. Makarios thanked the U.S. government but noted that Britain had offered similar assistance and its advisors were already on site.

The events of July and August 1974 are vivid in my memory. In the early morning of July 15, an official from the Cyprus Embassy called to inform me about the coup and that Makarios was dead. I went to the embassy to pay my respects. Later that morning, we learned that Makarios was alive after all. On Tuesday, July 16, we learned that the British Royal Air Force had flown Makarios to Malta. On Wednesday, he was flown to London to meet with Prime Minister Harold Wilson and Foreign Secretary James Callaghan.

On Thursday, July 18, I met President Makarios at John F. Kennedy International Airport and went with him to the Carlyle Hotel in Manhattan. I arranged for James Vlasto, former press secretary to New York's governor Hugh Carey, to handle the media for Makarios, as he was front-page news. Makarios spent Thursday evening preparing his remarks for the meeting of the UN Security Council on Friday. The next day, July 19, he was received at the United Nations as the legitimate president of Cyprus and addressed the UN Security Council as head of state.

On Monday, July 22, I accompanied President Makarios to the State Department, where he met with Kissinger. At the July 18 daily briefing, the State Department had initially pointed out that Kissinger was not meeting Makarios as a head of state, additional evidence of Kissinger's view of Makarios; Kissinger was unilaterally rejecting his status as the elected president of the Cyprus government. At the last minute, on July 22, the State Department reversed its position and said that Kissinger would meet Makarios as a head of state.

While Makarios was meeting with Kissinger, I met with Ambassador-at-Large Robert McCloskey, Kissinger's media and policy advisor on his immediate staff. I knew McCloskey, as I did Kissinger, from my days as assistant secretary of the Treasury (1969–1973) during President Nixon's first term. McCloskey, a career foreign service officer with the State Department from 1955 to 1981, is best known as press spokesman for the department from 1964 to 1973.

During that visit with McCloskey on July 22, I specifically mentioned to him that, under U.S. laws, the United States had to stop sending arms to Turkey immediately. I said that Turkey's use of U.S.-supplied arms and equipment for aggression against Cyprus made Turkey "immediately ineligible" for further military aid and sales under the Foreign Assistance Act and the Foreign Military Sales Act. I told McCloskey that the language of the Acts was mandatory, not a matter of executive branch discretion. McCloskey replied that they would look into it, which in effect meant that he and his superiors would do nothing.

With that answer and Kissinger's failure during the ensuing days to publicly denounce Turkey's actions and to invoke U.S. laws against Turkey for the illegal use of U.S.-supplied arms in the invasion of Cyprus, I decided to press the issue. With American-made bombs dropping from American-made planes on my relatives, I decided to form an organization with a full-time professional staff and an office in Washington, DC for lobbying, research, and think-tank purposes dealing with U.S. relations with Greece and Cyprus. I incorporated the American Hellenic Institute on August 1, 1974, and rented office space at 1730 K Street, N.W., in downtown Washington. That organization led the successful effort by the Greek American community to lobby the Congress to pass the rule of law arms embargo legislation against Turkey.

5

Kissinger's Violations of U.S. and International Laws

Arms Aid and Sales and U.S. Law

Turkey's use of American-supplied arms and equipment in its aggression against Cyprus and the Greek junta's use of American-supplied arms in its coup against the elected government of President Makarios in Cyprus were in flagrant violation of the purposes of the Foreign Assistance Act of 1961 as amended (FAA) and the Foreign Military Sales Act (FMSA). Section 502 of the FAA limits the use of such assistance to internal security, legitimate self-defense, and regional and collective defensive arrangements. Furthermore, Turkey and the Greek junta did not seek or obtain the requisite formal consent from the United States to use American-supplied arms for purposes not provided for in the FAA and FMSA. Thus, Turkey and the Greek junta were acting in violation of Section 505(d) of the FAA and Section 3(c) of the FMSA and became "immediately ineligible" for further military assistance and sales.

Kissinger, as Secretary of State, was the primary official responsible for implementing Section 505(d) of the FAA and

Section 3(c) of the FMSA.[1] Except for the president, Kissinger had final authority regarding these particular laws.[2] But instead of adhering to law, he continued to authorize arms shipments to Turkey and failed to declare Turkey "immediately ineligible" for further military assistance and sales as required under the FAA and the FMSA.

In his confirmation hearing in September 1973, in a colloquy with Senator Frank Church, Kissinger stated:

> If what I have said to this Committee is to have any meaning, then it would be totally inappropriate for me as Secretary or as an advisor to the President to behave like a sharp lawyer and to try to split hairs and find some legal justification for something clearly against the intent of the law. So I think the better answer to you, Senator, is to say that when the law is clearly understood—and it will be my job to make sure that I clearly understand the intent of Congress—we may disagree with it, but once the intent is clear we will implement not only the letter but the spirit.[3]

Kissinger lied to the members of the Senate Foreign Relations Committee in that statement. He not only failed to enforce the clear provisions of the FAA and the FMSA but actually tried to alter the substance of the legal opinion of the State Department lawyers in the Office of the Legal Adviser.

Because of Kissinger's refusal to halt arms shipments to Turkey, legislation was introduced in the House and Senate in September 1974, to enforce the law by embargoing arms to Turkey. From September to December 1974, there were more than a dozen votes in the House and Senate culminating in a rule of law arms embargo on Turkey enacted in December 1974.[4] Throughout the congressional battle, Kissinger fought the legislation, personally lobbying congressional representatives and senators.[5]

After the rule of law arms embargo went into effect on February 5, 1975, Kissinger immediately undermined its force by publicly announcing that legislation would be introduced to repeal it. On February 26, Kissinger had a bill introduced in Congress that would authorize the president to lift the rule of law arms embargo on Turkey.[6] The administration, led by Kissinger, mounted a massive drive to overturn the embargo and scuttle mandatory sanctions against Turkey for violating the U.S. policy against aggression. Kissinger partially succeeded, as the embargo was lifted on October 2, 1975, for items paid for by Turkey and already in the pipeline.[7]

Kissinger's decision to overturn the arms embargo instead of supporting the rule of law in international affairs by pressing Turkey to remove its armed forces and settlers/colonists from Cyprus was irresponsible and a prime example of his contempt for our democracy and the rule of law. By not enforcing the penalty provisions of the FAA and the FMSA against Turkey, Kissinger violated laws that go to the very heart of U.S. foreign policy. This policy, that weapons and aid from the United States are not to be used for offensive strikes, not only is fundamental to American foreign policy but also is central to the purposes underlying the UN Charter and the North Atlantic Treaty. Both call for disputes to be settled peacefully and not by "the threat or use of force."

Kissinger, Cyprus and International Law

The United States has long been an exemplar of democracy—a beacon demonstrating the rule of law and freedom from oppression. To that end, the U.S. was a prime mover in the series of sweeping modern agreements intended to extend the rule of law, as conceived by Western democracies, worldwide. In the case of Cyprus, Henry Kissinger ignored all of these—the North Atlantic Treaty that created NATO, the

Geneva Conventions, and the UN Charter itself—not to mention the UN's resolutions on Cyprus. If the United States had joined Britain and the other members of the Security Council in immediate condemnation of the July 15 coup, as well as the Council's support of Makarios as the elected leader of Cyprus, the Sampson government would have fallen before the end of that week. This would have removed any possible excuse for Turkey to invade Cyprus. If the United States had actively opposed Sampson, Turkey's aggression would have been prevented. But that was not Kissinger's aim. He wanted to get rid of President Makarios and to partition Cyprus by giving one-third to Turkey.

A fundamental purpose of the United Nations, as set forth in its Charter, is to keep the peace and to prevent aggression, that is, to settle problems peacefully. Article 1, paragraph 1 of the Charter states that one purpose of the United Nations is "to maintain international peace and security, and to that end: to take effective collective measures for the prevention and removal of threats to the peace, and for the suppression of acts of aggression or other breaches of the peace, and to bring about by peaceful means, and in conformity with the principles of justice and international law, adjustment or settlement of international disputes or situations which might lead to a breach of the peace." Article 2, paragraphs 3 and 4, which set forth the principles to be acted on to achieve the purposes proclaimed in article 1, state:

(3) All Members shall settle their international disputes by peaceful means in such a manner that international peace and security, and justice, are not endangered.

(4) All Members shall refrain in their international relations from the threat or use of force against the territorial integrity or political independence of any state, or in any other manner inconsistent with the Purposes of the United Nations.

In the matter of the Greek military coup and Turkey's invasion of Cyprus, the United States was not only implicitly rejecting the UN Charter's general purpose to maintain international peace, it was also ignoring the specific territorial integrity of a sovereign state. In his interactions with the United Nations, Kissinger had twisted the purposes of that peace-making body beyond all recognition.

Even more specific to the peace of Western Europe and the Mediterranean, Kissinger astonishingly ignored the North Atlantic Treaty Organization. NATO is a regional alliance created under article 52 of the UN Charter for collective defense against aggression. The fundamental principles, objectives, and purposes of the North Atlantic Treaty are to deter aggression and to support democratic government. Signatories to NATO promised:

> . . . to safeguard the freedom, common heritage and civilisation of their peoples, founded on the principles of democracy, individual liberty and the rule of law. . . [and] to promote stability and wellbeing in the North Atlantic area.

Article 1 of the NATO treaty states:

> The Parties undertake, as set forth in the Charter of the United Nations, to settle any international dispute in which they may be involved by peaceful means in such a manner that international peace and security and justice are not endangered, and to refrain in their international relations from the threat or use of force in any manner inconsistent with the purposes of the United Nations.

Kissinger failed to uphold the provisions of the North Atlantic Treaty against Turkey's aggression in Cyprus, an aggression that threatened to destabilize the Eastern Mediterranean as it thumbed its nose at international peace.

Moreover, the Geneva Convention of 1949, Section III, article 49 prohibits colonization by an occupying power. Article 49 states in its last paragraph: "The Occupying Power shall not deport or transfer parts of its own civilian population into the territory it occupies." Turkey brought into its occupied territory in Cyprus illegal settlers/colonists from Anatolia from the beginning of its occupation on July 20, 1974, in violation of the Geneva Convention of 1949. Kissinger did nothing to stop this.

Demonstrating his pro-Turkish bias, Kissinger went even further in support of Turkish aggression. He did nothing to ensure the success of the Geneva negotiations, nor did he try to prevent further use of force by Turkey. In fact, he encouraged it. He continued arms assistance to Turkey and rejected Britain's proposal to use the threat of British air strikes to stop Turkey's continuing violations of the July 30 Geneva Declaration cease-fire and bring a halt to any further advances. Despite the lack of any evidence that Turkish Cypriots were threatened, Kissinger told the world on August 13 that their position required "considerable improvement and protection." Because of Kissinger's actions and inactions, the Turkish government had no incentive to negotiate a reasonable and fair solution.

After the Turkish invasion of Cyprus, Ioannides' junta dictatorship in Greece fell on July 23. The former Prime Minister, Constantine Karamanlis, was recalled from self-imposed exile in Paris and was sworn in on July 24 to head a unity government. In November 1974, he was elected to head the Greek government. Instead of working for a settlement between the restored democratic government in Greece under Prime Minister Karamanlis and the military-dominated government in Turkey,[8] Kissinger tilted fully toward Turkey. Kissinger's failure to work with the Karamanlis government to achieve a negotiated settlement with Turkey based on democratic values and the rule of law is a blatant example of both diplomatic incompetence and irresponsibility.

In particularly perceptive editorials on September 14 and 26, and October 13, 1974, the *New York Times* put the responsibility for the events in Cyprus on Kissinger's shoulders and condemned him for failing to apply the law mandating the cutoff of military aid to Turkey in response to its aggression in Cyprus. The editorials stated in part:

> Cutting off American military aid to Turkey may, as Secretary of State Kissinger contends, be "ineffective and counterproductive" so far as getting the Turks to roll back their occupation of Cyprus is concerned; but it is mandatory under the law. In pretending for nearly a month to be studying this question, the State Department is clearly stalling, as it has stalled at every point since the outset of the Cyprus tragedy when action was called for to demonstrate this country's disapproval of aggression.

Senator Thomas F. Eagleton had charged that Kissinger was keeping even President Ford in the dark about his abrogation of American laws regarding the "mandatory cutoff for Turkey" of American military aid. But instead of the "erroneous policy judgments" Eagleton thought this misinformation was designed to protect, the *Times* laid the blame directly on Kissinger's doorstep: "But it has been not so much the State Department bureaucracy that has so bungled American policy in the Cyprus crisis as Mr. Kissinger himself." The *Times* continued:

> The stalling on the aid cutoff, in violation of the laws, is of a piece with Washington's earlier unwillingness to condemn Greece's disintegrating junta for the coup against the legal Government of Cyprus—*a reluctance that encouraged Turkey to intervene on the island.* It is also consistent with Washington's refusal to condemn Turkey's subsequent massive occupation of a third of Cyprus in flagrant breach of solemn cease-fire pledges . . . [9]
> The virulent White House opposition to efforts by decisive majorities in both houses of Congress to suspend military aid

aid to Turkey has no basis in either law or logic. President Ford's repeated threats to veto a bill requiring such a cut-off can only be seen as an attempt to block Congress from a meaningful role in the shaping of foreign policy and a move to fend off a blow at the prestige of Secretary of State Kissinger. . . . [T]he law is clear and it should be obeyed. Congress should stick to its guns on the military aid issue— veto or no veto.[10]

The *Times* editorial board put the issue clearly and forcefully: that the American government was more concerned with the "prestige" of its foreign policy chief than with obeying its own laws.

Graham Hovey, a member of the *New York Times* editorial board, in an August 27, 1974, op-ed analysis article, blamed Kissinger for the Cyprus tragedy:

> Once a shaky military regime in Athens had staged a putsch against President Makarios, clearly aimed at *enosis*—the union of Cyprus with Greece—there was only one way to prevent Turkish intervention: to demonstrate that Greece would not be allowed to get by with it, Washington could have made the point by backing Britain in refusing to recognize the new Cyprus regime and in demanding that Athens recall the Greek officers who had directed the coup.
>
> Instead, the United States gave Turkey and the world every reason to believe it accepted the coup. Washington refused to pin responsibility for it on the Greek dictatorship. . . .
>
> Turkey's initial invasion of July 20 was the inevitable result.

What could the U.S. have done instead? In congressional testimony approximately one year after the invasion by Turkey, Cyrus Vance, former deputy secretary of defense under President Lyndon B. Johnson and future secretary of state under

President Jimmy Carter, offered a possible answer. He stated: "I would have acted differently than the Government did under these circumstances. It seemed to me that once the legitimate constitutional government of Cyprus was overthrown by a coup that the first and clear step that the United States should have taken was to denounce that action and to state very clearly that it expected the constitutional government to be restored. This would have been in conformity with what Great Britain had publicly stated and with what our other NATO allies had said."[11] Former undersecretary of state George Ball testified before Congress on August 20, 1974, that the U.S. government should have publicly denounced the Greek coup against Makarios and told Greece: "You have got to unscramble this coup and restore constitutional government," while saying to Turkey, "You've got to hold off while we work this situation out."[12]

It should be apparent to any observer that Henry Kissinger violated his constitutional oath of office to "defend the Constitution of the United States," to "bear true faith and allegiance to the same," and to "well and faithfully discharge the duties of the office on which I am about to enter." The duties of his office included enforcing the FAA and the FMSA. Kissinger never informed Turkey that the FAA would be invoked and aid to Turkey would cease if Turkey invaded Cyprus. Instead, Kissinger's actions and deliberate inactions kept the Sampson government afloat long enough for Turkey to prepare and execute its invasion of Cyprus. Turkey's blitz killed several hundred (331) with 1,288 missing, displaced some 200,000, sowed new seeds for protracted intercommunity strife, provoked Greece into pulling its forces out of NATO, and increased instability in the Eastern Mediterranean and the Middle East. It also dealt a heavy blow to U.S. credibility and the reputation of Henry A. Kissinger.[13]

6

Kissinger's Account in His Memoirs

The third and final volume of Henry Kissinger's memoirs, *Years of Renewal* (1999), has a forty-eight-page chapter titled "Cyprus, a Case Study in Ethnic Conflict."[1] It is a clumsy attempt to rewrite history to cover up Kissinger's violations of U.S. laws and his responsibility for the Cyprus tragedy of 1974. In this chapter, he brazenly attempts to portray Turkey's aggression against Cyprus not as a land grab using American-supplied arms but as an ethnic conflict. Careful reading of the chapter in the context of history reveals not only Kissinger's arrogant violations of U.S. and international laws but also an inherent incompetence, which resulted in a U.S. foreign policy debacle. As the former U.S. senator and presidential advisor Daniel Patrick Moynihan put it, "Everyone is entitled to his own opinion, but not his own facts."

Kissinger's main purpose was not to give an accurate account of events but to salvage his own reputation. In reviewing *Years of Renewal*, the distinguished historian John Lewis Gaddis commented that "historians are likely to regard this book as an elaborate smokescreen designed to conceal what really happened" during Kissinger's tenure.[2] Jussi M. Hanhimäki,

President Makarios, with Soviet Foreign Minister Andrei Gromyko and Henry Kissinger, May 7, 1974 in Nicosia, Cyprus.

President Makarios with British Prime Minister Harold Wilson at No. 10 Downing
Street in London, July 17, 1974.

President Makarios with British Foreign Secretary James Callaghan at the Foreign Office, London, July 17, 1974.

President Makarios at the United Nations Security Council in New York, July 19, 1974.

President Gerald Ford, President Makarios, Secretary of State, Henry Kissinger and Under Secretary to the President of Cyprus, Patroclos Stavrou at the Conference on Security and Cooperation in Europe in Helsinki, August 1975.

Secretary of State Henry Kissinger with President Makarios at the State Department in Washington, October 2, 1974.

President of Cyprus Archbishop Makarios addresses a rally at the Archbishopric on his return to Cyprus, December 7, 1974.

Senator Thomas Eagleton, (D-MO) and President Makarios in Nicosia, Cyprus, December 28, 1975.

author of *The Flawed Architect: Henry Kissinger and American Foreign Policy,* wrote that Kissinger "with greater hindsight" made the final volume of his memoirs "a more blatantly revisionist account" even than the earlier volumes.[3]

Robert G. Kaiser, former associate editor and foreign correspondent of the *Washington Post,* in a book review of *The Kissinger Transcripts—The Top Secret Talks with Beijing and Moscow* (1999), edited by William Burr, states that "this [Burr's] volume demonstrated irrefutably that, alas, Kissinger's own version of the story is unreliable."[4] Kaiser points out that "Burr has done some preliminary detective work" that reveals where "Kissinger ignored entire meetings or moments within meetings that didn't suit his narrative line as he wrote his inevitably self-serving memoir." He adds that "there is room for more detailed detective work by future Kissinger biographers to see just how he distorted the record."[5]

Kissinger's Cyprus chapter contains numerous false or misleading statements as well as omissions of fact. He attempts to shift the blame for the Cyprus tragedy from himself to others, particularly President Makarios of Cyprus, Prime Minister Constantine Karamanlis of Greece, Foreign Secretary James Callaghan of the United Kingdom, and the U.S. Congress. In the conclusion to his chapter, incredibly, Kissinger claims success in achieving his "most important objective: the eastern flank of NATO, though strained, remained intact." In reality, Kissinger permanently damaged NATO's eastern flank.

Kissinger's chapter on Cyprus reveals his disregard for American values and for democracy. He does not believe in the separation of powers or checks and balances, concepts that are basic to our system of government. Nowhere does he call for majority rule, the rule of law, and protection of minority rights for Cyprus. His disdain for Congress and its constitutional role in foreign affairs and policy is evident throughout the chapter.

As I have shown in previous chapters, the Cyprus tragedy was directly caused:

1. by Kissinger's encouragement of the Greek junta dictator Dimitrios Ioannides' planned coup against President Makarios—his failure to tell Ioannides, as requested by State Department professionals in the region, not to take any action against Makarios;
2. by his failure to condemn the coup on July 15, 1974;
3. by his failure to uphold U.S. policy and enforce U.S. laws that mandated the immediate halt in arms aid and sales to the Greek junta;
4. by his encouragement of Turkey's illegal aggression against Cyprus on July 20;
5. by his failure to condemn this aggression;
6. by his failure once again to enforce U.S. laws, which mandated an immediate halt in arms aid and sales to Turkey;
7. by his encouragement of Turkey's second, massive wave of aggression on August 14–16;
8. by his failure to condemn this second phase of aggression; and
9. by his failure, following this second phase of aggression, to enforce U.S. laws calling for the immediate halt in arms aid and sales to Turkey.

In "Cyprus, a Case Study in Ethnic Conflict," Kissinger sets forth his views on a variety of subjects surrounding his involvement in Cyprus. Besides framing the issue as fundamentally an ethnic conflict between Greek and Turkish Cypriots, he discusses President Makarios of Cyprus, as well as the roles of Turkey and Greece in the conflict—from his biased perspective. He also covers the role of Britain, especially that of Foreign Secretary James Callaghan, and NATO as a whole, as well as U.S. involvement—in particular, the role of Congress. In the following sections I will examine each of Kissinger's positions.

The Cyprus problem as an ethnic conflict between Greek and Turkish Cypriots

The title of Kissinger's chapter, "Cyprus, a Case Study in Ethnic Conflict," reveals his Orwellian aim up front, namely: to portray the invasion and occupation of Cyprus, not as aggression and a land grab by Turkey, but rather as an ethnic conflict whose "origins went back centuries; the passions ran so deep as to be almost beyond the comprehension of anyone not belonging to either of the two ethnic groups."[6]

Kissinger's portrayal of Greek and Turkish Cypriot relations is fundamentally flawed. From 1571, when the Ottoman Empire conquered Cyprus, to 1878, when Britain gained control, to 1960, when Cyprus was forced to accept its fettered independence, Greek and Turkish Cypriots lived peaceably in mixed villages. This was the situation for nearly four hundred years, except for the few years in the 1950s when Britain instigated trouble between the Greek and Turkish Cypriots. Kissinger claims that decolonization made civil conflict between Greek and Turkish Cypriots "inevitable," but this claim is both false and disingenuous, designed to distract attention from his own role in aiding and abetting those who fomented civil conflict between ethnic groups that had peacefully coexisted for centuries.

Even today, after decades of partition and Turkish inciting of ethnic tension, civil conflict between Greek and Turkish Cypriots is not "inevitable." In April 2003, the Turkish Cypriots (led by Rauf Denktash, first President of the Turkey-backed Turkish Republic of Northern Cyprus) opened, in the Turkish barbed wire fence dividing Cyprus, one crossing point in Nicosia for Turkish and Greek Cypriots to use.[7] Since then, five more crossing points have been opened. To date there have been more than fifteen million crossings of Greek and Turkish Cypriots without serious incident. Today, about six thousand

Turkish Cypriots cross daily to work in the free area of Cyprus.[8] These facts and others belie Kissinger's claim that the Cyprus problem was an ethnic conflict.

Kissinger's "learned" essay on ethnic conflict and its relation to the Cyprus problem is replete with misleading or false statements and omissions of basic facts. He attempts to evade the issue of the rule of law, especially his own refusal to enforce American law, and tries to whitewash his mistakes in his dealings with Cyprus. For example, he ignored the advice of the Cyprus Desk officer Thomas Boyatt and his colleagues to demand that the Greek dictator Ioannides halt any efforts to remove President Makarios and his elected government. If Kissinger had accepted Boyatt's advice there would have been no Cyprus crisis in 1974.

Kissinger omits several key turning points in Cyprus' history, points that are crucial to understanding ethnic relations between Greek and Turkish Cypriots. These events do not fit his narrative. He fails to mention the Treaty of Lausanne of 1923, in which Turkey renounced all rights to Cyprus. He fails to discuss British colonial rule of Cyprus from 1878 to 1960, and Britain's attempts to maintain its colonial rule over the island by opposing majority rule and self-determination and by inciting Turkey in 1955 to voice its objections to self-determination for Cyprus. He fails to note that Britain, along with France and Israel, used Cyprus in 1956 as a base for aggression against Egypt, in retaliation for President Gamal Abdel Nasser's legal expropriation of the Suez Canal Company. And he fails to state that Britain forced the fettered independence of the 1959–1960 London–Zurich Agreements, under threat of the Macmillan partition plan of 1958. The London–Zurich Agreements gave the eighteen percent Turkish Cypriot minority veto power over all major decisions of the executive branch and legislature, the major factor that prevented Cyprus's democratic government from functioning.

Kissinger is making up his own facts when he claims, "Three hundred years of Ottoman domination starting in 1571 . . . had ensconced a Turkish minority in the northern part of the island closest to Turkey."[9] The Turkish minority in Cyprus, which grew to about eighteen percent during the three centuries of Ottoman rule from 1571 to 1878, was not concentrated "in the northern part of the island" but was spread throughout the island in ethnically mixed villages. Kissinger uses this falsehood to rationalize his support of Turkey's aggression against Cyprus and a subsequent policy of apartheid.

This apartheid is masked by Kissinger's portrayal of an American policy that he says was neutral, a false and self-serving stance. He writes, "Fearful of weakening the strategically crucial eastern flank of the Atlantic Alliance, the United States tried to do justice to the concerns of both sides and, in the process, often earned their opprobrium."[10] In fact, the evidence is clear that Kissinger at every stage supported Turkey and the Turkish Cypriot minority over the Greek Cypriot majority, and against the rule of law. As Laurence Stern wrote, "One of the most important keys to an understanding of the Cyprus muddle is the realization that the United States, far from being a disinterested broker to the disputes of the past was a deeply involved participant."[11]

Given his evident sympathy for the Turkish position, Kissinger's protestation that "the classic fault lines of ethnic conflicts" prevented true democracy in Cyprus is disingenuous. To Kissinger, the "concerns" of Greek and Turkish Cypriots were "unbridgeable. . . . The Greek majority insisted on a unitary state, which, by turning the Turkish population into a permanent minority, in effect disenfranchised the Turks. The Turkish minority demanded a federal structure and multiple vetoes, which, given the ethnic animosities, amounted to partition."[12] The passage reveals Kissinger's lack of understanding of democracy and what majority rule, the rule of law, and the protection of minority rights mean. His "unbridgeable" concerns are a straw man. The key problem since 1974 has been not "the classic fault lines of ethnic conflicts" (whatever that means) but instead the refusal of the Turkish government and Turkish military to agree to a democratic solution based on majority rule, the rule of law, the protection of minority rights, and the principle of one person, one vote. Kissinger is simply wrong in asserting that the Greek Cypriot majority and the Turkish Cypriot minority could not arrive at a negotiated democratic, just, and viable solution.

Kissinger's claim that in a "unitary state" the Turkish Cypriot population is turned "into a permanent minority" and "in effect disenfranchised" further reflects his misunderstanding of democratic norms. In a unitary state reflecting a democratic Cyprus (including a federal unitary state) Turkish Cypriots would be a permanent minority but would not be disenfranchised. They would have the standard democratic rights of freedom of speech, press, assembly, and religion. The Turkish Cypriots would have the same individual civil, human, and religious rights as the Greek Cypriot majority.

Kissinger on President Makarios

Kissinger devotes three pages to "Makarios: The Wily Archbishop" in which he both extols Makarios and sharply criticizes him. He ludicrously calls Makarios "the proximate cause of most of Cyprus's tensions" and then says that he "was also the best hope for a long-term peaceful solution,"[13] although Kissinger never used him as such. The claim that Makarios was the "proximate cause" of tension in Cyprus is dealt with appropriately by Christopher Hitchens:

> Makarios was the democratically elected leader of a virtually unarmed republic which was at the time an associate member of the European Economic Community (EEC), [a member of] the United Nations and the Commonwealth. His rule was challenged, and the independence of Cyprus was threatened, by a military dictatorship in Athens and a highly militarized

government in Turkey, both of which sponsored right-wing gangster organizations on the island, and both of which had plans to annex the greater or lesser part of it. In spite of this, "intercommunal" violence had been on the decline in Cyprus through the 1970s. . . . Several attempts had been made on the life of President Makarios himself. *To describe his person as "the proximate cause" of the tensions is to make a wildly aberrant moral judgment.*[14]

Kissinger misleadingly states, without citing any evidence, that Makarios was "distrusted by Turkey, where he was considered to be . . . a dedicated and effective opponent of rights for the Turkish minority."[15] In actuality, Makarios was a proponent of full rights for the Turkish, Armenian, and Maronite minorities.

Kissinger also claims, "To protect himself against interference from Greece and pressure from Turkey, Makarios tended to follow the path of Egypt's Gamal Abdel Nasser and Libya's Muammar Qaddafi by allying himself with the radical elements of the Non-aligned Movement."[16] This reveals Kissinger's real annoyance with Makarios, namely, his joining the Third World Nonaligned Movement. But Makarios did not align Cyprus with "the radical elements of the Nonaligned Movement." Further, Kissinger should have had the common sense to realize that Makarios's membership in the Nonaligned Movement could be used to the advantage of America and the West.

In his memoirs, the former Soviet foreign minister Andrei Gromyko writes that in a meeting with Kissinger in May 1974, he asked whether Kissinger supported Cyprus's independence and territorial integrity. He recounts Kissinger's response: "He was evasive, but his answer boiled down to the admission that Washington would basically be happy to see the division of the island into two parts, Greek and Turkish—that is, the creation of two separate states. He also made a number of sarcastic remarks about Makarios. Although he refrained from a direct attack, his veiled and sugar-coated gibes made it plain that he personally, and the U.S. administration, regarded Makarios as an anomaly, a church man who would be better sticking to church affairs."[17]

Kissinger writes, "My attitude toward Makarios reflected the general ambivalence. . . . I considered Makarios more of a nuisance than a menace. At no time during my period in office did we take any measure to reduce his hold on power."[18] This last sentence is demonstrably false, as Kissinger took a number of actions (and deliberate inactions) to undermine Makarios's legitimacy, encourage the Greek junta to overthrow his government, and legitimize the Sampson coup.

Kissinger's portrayal of the Turkish Cypriot minority's position under Makarios's leadership is equally false. He makes two misleading charges, citing no evidence or sources for either. First, he writes that "Makarios would not grant any sort of meaningful autonomy to the Turkish minority for fear that it might secede; the Turkish minority continued to equate majority rule with disenfranchisement." Second he misrepresents Makarios's 1963 proposal to amend the constitution, charging that the Cypriot leader "broke the deadlock by imposing thirteen amendments to the constitution." According to Kissinger, these imposed amendments "effectively established a unitary state with majority rule."[19] In actuality, the Turkish Cypriot minority had equal political, civil, human, and religious rights with the Greek Cypriot majority. Even more, the Turkish minority had undemocratic veto rights over all major executive branch and legislative matters, the main cause of the problems between the two communities, a crucial fact that Kissinger leaves out of his analysis entirely. Neither did Makarios *impose* amendments to the constitution. On November 30, 1963, Makarios submitted to the Turkish Cypriots and the three guarantor powers Britain, Greece, and Turkey, *for their consideration* thirteen *proposed* amendments to the constitution to correct its undemocratic features.

Incredibly, Kissinger blames Makarios for the Greek junta–initiated coup against his government, but not the Greek dictator Ioannides or himself. He writes:

> What drove the situation on Cyprus out of control was not so much mistakes in Washington as actions by Makarios, who was once again testing his dexterity on the high wire—this time with disastrous results. On July 2, he informed the president of Greece that he was reducing the size of the National Guard, and he demanded the withdrawal of the Greek officers who controlled it. These two steps would greatly reduce, if not eliminate Athens's influence in Cyprus and enable Makarios to rely even more on the local Communist Party internally and on the Nonaligned Movement internationally.[20]

Kissinger also erroneously and shockingly implies that the coup initiated by Ioannides against the Makarios government, including the attempted assassination of Makarios, was authorized "to implement its [Greece's] right as a guaranteeing power to enforce the London–Zurich Agreements."[21] President Makarios, who was attempting to build the groundwork for democratic rule, was in Kissinger's eyes a crypto-communist agitator. The *coup d'etat* by Ioannides was transformed by Kissinger into a legitimate act of governance. On the matter of Cyprus, Henry Kissinger seems to think day is night.

Turkey

Kissinger's leak to the *New York Times* on July 17, 1974 (intimating that the U.S. would recognize the Sampson government over the legitimate Makarios government), was part of his overall effort that week to remove Makarios as President of Cyprus. It was also intended to encourage Turkey to invade

Cyprus. His actions gave Turkey both time to prepare and the purported excuse to invade, namely the Sampson coup regime, which Turkey strongly opposed.

In the last paragraph of his section "Greek–Turkish Minuets," Kissinger states, "Turkey had never abandoned its demands for an autonomous Turkish region and had never forgiven the humiliations of 1964 and 1967."[22] Throughout the chapter, Kissinger supports Turkey's views by failing to challenge them. For example, here he refers to Turkey's "demands for an autonomous Turkish region" for the Turkish Cypriot minority without challenging the validity of such demands. Turkey had no legal right to make such a demand. It had renounced all rights to Cyprus in the 1923 Treaty of Lausanne. Similarly, he writes, "All these frustrations heightened Turkey's resolve to vindicate its claims by force at the next opportunity." He does not disclose what "claims" Turkey had or their legitimacy, if any. Nor does he observe that Turkey's use of force would violate the UN Charter, the North Atlantic Treaty, and customary international law. For Kissinger, the rule of law is utterly irrelevant to the behavior of nations.

One of the most important decisions that led to the tragedy of Turkey's dismemberment of Cyprus was Kissinger's refusal to enforce U.S. laws that prohibit the use of American-supplied arms and equipment for non-defensive purposes such as aggression. Kissinger believed Turkey's importance to the U.S. as a strategic ally overrode any other consideration, writing, "In the first four months of the Ford presidency, Congress cutoff military aid to Turkey, a strategically indispensable ally and host to twenty-six surveillance installations from which the United States was monitoring Soviet missile and nuclear testing."[23] As we will see later, Turkey was never "a strategically indispensable ally," and the twenty-six surveillance installations were not needed because the United States had better installations elsewhere, including in Cyprus. Even more important, by 1974 Turkey had already made an accommodation with the Soviet

Union and had actively aided the Soviet military on several occasions. I discuss Turkey's collaboration with the Soviet military and its unreliability as an ally in chapter 9.

As I demonstrated in chapter 4, Kissinger encouraged the Turkish invasion of Cyprus on July 20, 1974. Kissinger denies this, stating that "Contrary to the mythology that the United States encouraged the Turkish invasion—or even colluded with it—our strategy during the first week concentrated on removing Turkish pretexts for military action."[24] In reality, if Kissinger had joined Britain and other countries in denouncing the coup and had announced a halt in arms shipments to Greece, the junta would have fallen and the Sampson regime along with it. This would have deprived Turkey of the pretext to invade Cyprus. Kissinger's "strategy" for removing pretexts for Turkish aggression was little in evidence. Furthermore, following the coup, Kissinger states, "we sought to remove pretexts for military action by any of the parties." As discussed before, however, Kissinger's aim was to divide Cyprus between Greece and Turkey through "double *enosis*." The very last thing Kissinger wanted was to "remove pretexts for military action by any of the parties." Indeed, his actions that week were perfectly designed to create pretexts and encourage Turkey to take military action.

Military action was just what Kissinger expected from the Turks. He disingenuously claims, "We did not expect the outbreak of another round of fighting,"[25] in the period leading up to Turkey's massive second phase of aggression. Yet Kissinger's own words belie that claim. On Gerald Ford's first full day in office, August 10, 1974, Kissinger told him, "The Turks want a quick result leading to partition of the island. . . . They have about 15 percent of the island and want 30 percent. They might try to grab it."[26] Even more damning evidence has arisen in classified documents revealed since 1999, when *Years of Renewal* was published. These documents demonstrate that Kissinger not only knew ahead of time about Turkey's planned second wave of aggression, he also was prepared to offer Turkey one-third of Cyprus. On August 13, the day before the beginning of the second, massive phase of aggression, the State Department's Bureau of Intelligence and Research published a map of Cyprus (printed on page vii of this book) showing the land grab Turkey would make starting the next day, August 14, 1974.[27] In keeping with his complete disregard for the rule of law and his partiality for Turkey, on August 13, Kissinger told President Ford, "There is no American reason why the Turks should not have one-third of Cyprus."[28]

It should be noted that in his presentation of the situation to Ford on August 10, 1974, Kissinger never mentioned that Turkey's aggression against Cyprus meant that, according to the U.S. Foreign Assistance Act (FAA) and the Foreign Military Sales Act (FMSA), the United States was required to immediately halt all arms assistance and sales to Turkey. He also failed to inform Ford that Turkey's aggression also violated the Treaty of Guarantee, the UN Charter article 2(4) and the North Atlantic Treaty article 1. He further failed to inform Ford that since the legal government was restored on Cyprus on July 23, 1974, Turkey's invasion forces should have been removed from Cyprus.

In one of his few references to the FAA in his memoirs, Kissinger makes two misleading and erroneous statements—one pertaining to the aim of the Act and the other to its supposed "legal ambiguities." He writes: "A provision of the Foreign Assistance Act prohibited the use of American weapons for purposes other than national self-defense, the aim being to preclude domestic repression or civil war being carried out with American assistance. But, to Turkey, Cyprus involved key issues of international security. I believed that Congress and the executive branch would, given the stakes involved, find some means of dealing with the legal ambiguities."[29] He omits to state that a key aim of the Act is to prohibit the use of American-supplied weapons for aggression.

His reference to "legal ambiguities" regarding the relevant provisions of the FAA is also specious—there are no relevant legal ambiguities in the FAA. Turkey's use of U.S.-supplied arms for aggression against Cyprus was a clear violation of the FAA and FMSA and the U.S.-Turkish agreement under those laws. During the congressional debates on an arms embargo against Turkey, all sides agreed that Turkey's invasion with U.S. arms and equipment violated U.S. laws. In fact, Laurence Stern points out that during these debates, Kissinger and the administration did not raise the argument about "legal ambiguities" or question the fact that Turkey had violated U.S. laws by its invasion of Cyprus: "The legal case . . . was sufficiently compelling so that Kissinger never, in the course of the harshest conflict he experienced with the Congress, chose to defend his policies on legal grounds."[30] The only ambiguity, it seemed, was a moral one.

On August 13, although there was no evidence of any danger to the Turkish Cypriots, Kissinger had the State Department issue a statement that the "Turkish community on Cyprus requires considerable improvement and protection." The statement was designed to disassociate Kissinger from Turkey's renewed military operations. Kissinger recounts:

> I had the State Department issue a statement on August 13 that sketched the ideas I had put to Ford. It supported greater autonomy for the Turkish community in Cyprus — a hint that the United States favored a change to that effect in the London–Zurich Agreements. But signaling that we were not endorsing Turkey's insistence on justifying a single contiguous area with access to the sea, we spoke of negotiations regarding one or more autonomous areas and said nothing about access to the sea. And we rejected any attempt at a military solution, clearly dissociating ourselves from renewed military operations by Turkey:
>
> > "The avenues of diplomacy have not been exhausted and therefore *the U.S. would consider a resort to military action unjustified.*" (Emphasis not

in original which was delivered at the noon briefing
August 13, 1974.)[31]

Even apart from the mixed signals inherent in this statement, how was Turkey supposed to react to U.S. support for
greater Turkish Cypriot autonomy combined with a weakly
stated protest against what sounded like a foreordained division? It should be noted that Kissinger did not rule out the use
of force. The implication is that if the avenues of diplomacy
have been exhausted the use of force is justified. This is not and
should not be part of U.S. foreign policy, and it would violate
the UN Charter and the North Atlantic Treaty. Kissinger should
have informed Turkey in that statement of August 13 that if it
resumed military action with U.S.-supplied arms it would be
in violation of U.S. laws and he would immediately halt arms
assistance and sales to Turkey. That he did not do so, further
demonstrates his true motives. In fact, the August 13 statement
as a whole reveals Kissinger's views and policy throughout the
crisis—his support of Turkey and its aggression against Cyprus
and his lack of support for the rule of law.

Greece

When parsed, Kissinger's presentation in his memoirs of
his dealings with Greece during the Cyprus crisis, both
with the junta government of Ioannides and with the government of former Prime Minister Constantine Karamanlis which
replaced it, reveal his fundamental sympathy for Turkey. Any
concern for the sanctity of democratic government in Greece,
much less in Cyprus, was secondary. Kissinger cloaks this sympathy with his stated concern for Greece's position and legitimacy as a NATO signatory. He writes that he "had rejected
a policy of isolating and humiliating Greece—whatever my
reservations about its government—because I considered it to
be an essential pillar of our NATO strategy."[32] An attack on the

Greek junta calling for its removal and the return of democracy to Greece would not be "a policy of isolating and humiliating Greece" and could only strengthen Greece's role in NATO. In any case, Kissinger had little interest in promoting democracy through accepted international law in Greece or Cyprus.

Kissinger's memoirs are replete with references to "constitutional solutions" and "independence" for Cyprus, but this veneer is shallow indeed. This becomes apparent as he narrates his instructions to diplomatic subordinates on the ground in Greece. On July 16, 1974, the American ambassador in Athens, Henry Tasca, "was instructed to see Ioannides, who refused to receive Tasca on the ground that. . . Ioannides held no official position. . . . Tasca thereupon sent a trusted emissary to the junta leader, who warned Ioannides that the United States supported the independence of Cyprus and the existing constitutional arrangements—in other words, that we would oppose *enosis*." Kissinger states that Ioannides "accepted our view."[33] Note that Kissinger is dealing with the Greek junta on the basis of *de facto* recognition of the Sampson coup government.

The aforementioned "constitutional solution" was a U.S. proposal which Undersecretary Sisco was instructed on July 17, 1974 to put forward on his trip to London, Athens and Ankara:

> . . .[It was] dubbed the 'constitutional solution'—constitutional because it would elevate Glafkos Clerides, speaker of the Cyprus parliament . . . to acting President for a period of six months. After this time, an election would be held in which Makarios would be free to run. In the interval, a new communal arrangement would be negotiated between the Greek and Turkish populations. Clerides had the reputation of being more moderate then Makarios and therefore provided a possible face-saving interim solution for both Athens and Ankara. The reasoning behind this proposal was that affirming the constitution ended the prospect of *enosis*, while

making Clerides caretaker would avoid the need for Athens
to deal with Makarios in the communal talks.[34]

Again we see Kissinger's concern to avoid upsetting the
Greek junta dictator Ioannides in general, and his desire to
remove Makarios as president in particular. Kissinger also fails
to mention Makarios's speech to the UN Security Council on July
19, 1974, in which he castigates the Greek junta for the coup
it initiated against his government through the Greek officers
attached to the Cypriot National Guard. Makarios was received
at the UN as head of state. Kissinger's "constitutional solution"
was primarily an effort to get rid of Archbishop Makarios as
president of Cyprus, which did not work, and to bolster the
Greek junta.

Sisco met with British Foreign Secretary James Callaghan
"concerting policy," as Kissinger put it, in London on July 18,
then traveled to Athens on July 19 for talks with Greek ministers. July 19 found him in Ankara, where he met with Prime
Minister Ecevit. During this time, Kissinger was at San Clemente,
California, the summer White House, with Richard Nixon from
July 18 to 20, 1974. He writes "Having received ominous reports
of Turkish military preparations for an invasion of Cyprus, I
instructed the State Department from San Clemente" to have
Sisco deliver a "sharp warning" to Ecevit. The instructions
stated in part that Sisco was: "to point out to the Turkish government that the U.S. would take the gravest view of Turkish
military moves *before all diplomatic processes are exhausted.*"[35]
(Emphasis added.)

The Kissinger instructions to the State Department were
hardly a "sharp warning." By stating that "the US would take
the gravest view of Turkish military moves *before all diplomatic
processes are exhausted,*" Kissinger, in effect, is stating that
"military moves" are acceptable after "all diplomatic processes
are exhausted." That statement fails to acknowledge the UN
Charter, the North Atlantic Treaty and customary international

law all of which oppose "the threat or use of force" except in the case of self-defense.

The phrase "before all diplomatic processes are exhausted," coupled with Kissinger's failure to state that the United States would enforce the provisions of the FAA and the FMSA and the U.S.–Turkey agreements under those acts, makes Kissinger's "sharp warning" a hollow and self-justificatory formulation for his memoirs. He also failed to mention in the instructions the UN Charter and the North Atlantic Treaty provisions against "the threat or use of force."

After the outbreak of hostilities, Kissinger remained solicitous of the Greek dictator Ioannides. His "principal goal," he states in his memoirs, "was first to prevent an outbreak of war between two NATO allies; next to obtain a cease-fire on Cyprus; and, finally, to start negotiations between the parties."[36] Sisco was instructed on July 20, 1974 to call on Ecevit with a message which stated in part:

> The United States, for its part, is prepared to support a constitutional solution and a level of forces which existed before the [Sampson] coup. The only way, in our view, to restore constitutional government is through the legitimate succession of Clerides. No other solution is possible or acceptable to the Greeks.[37]

Underlying this message was Kissinger's fundamental hostility toward the Makarios government and sympathy with the aims of the Greek military junta, which also wanted Makarios out. Kissinger instructed Sisco to then return to Athens and "to urge the same solution there, where the junta was reeling from the loss of prestige incurred by its increasingly obvious failure in Cyprus."[38] Kissinger was trying to protect the Greek dictator and keep the junta in power.

Kissinger continued to attempt to prop up Ioannides' militarist government through backstage machinations in Washington.

On Sunday, July 21, 1974, he vetoed Secretary of Defense James Schlesinger's proposal to the Washington Special Action Group (WSAG) to cutoff "all military aid to Greece."[39] On that same day the *Washington Post* headlined the Defense Department's position, obviously leaked to them. It was a lawless decision and a blunder by Kissinger. His reasons were flimsy, at best: namely, that it "would surely whet Turkey's appetite," and that "I wanted to uphold the principle that the territorial integrity of the eastern flank was a vital and continuing American interest."[40] Clearly, the rule of law was not a "vital and continuing American interest" for Kissinger.

Finally Kissinger, joined by Foreign Secretary Callaghan and backed by the French Foreign Minister Jean Sauvagnargues, tried to push through a cease-fire. He writes:

> Greece, the weaker, was the more ready, provided it could obtain the *status quo ante*. Ecevit too professed to be willing, provided he was handed what he wanted without war, which happened to be a drastic change of the status quo. Pending that, he refined procrastination into a high art.[41]

A cease-fire was achieved on July 22, 1974, which Turkey promptly violated. Kissinger writes: "The cease-fire proved to be the junta's final act."[42] On July 22, 1974, midnight Greek time, the Greek junta fell. Ambassador Tasca telephoned Kissinger "at 5:00 p.m., July 22, or midnight Athens time" with the news. On the morning of July 23, 1974, former "Greek Prime Minister, Constantine Karamanlis, was recalled from his Paris exile, and the curtain fell on the first act of the Cyprus crisis."[43] Despite Kissinger's best efforts, the junta of Dimitrios Ioannides had fallen.

In spite of widespread approval—even celebration—at Karamanlis's return from exile, the situation was obviously not to Kissinger's liking. In his memoirs, he criticizes Karamanlis for not making concessions to the aggressor Turkey and falsely states "Karamanlis and his colleagues. . . persisted in the basic nationalist position of the junta."[44] Kissinger stated the following about Karamanlis's options:

> Once back in power, Karamanlis had the choice of either blaming his predecessors for the mess and, with our support, settling quickly for the best terms available or, in order to stave off nationalist criticism, seeking shelter behind the junta's traditionalist nationalist position.[45]

Kissinger's reference to Karamanlis "seeking shelter behind the junta's nationalist position" is demagogic. The junta's position in support of *enosis* was contrary to the Treaty of Guarantee, which Karamanlis supported and to which he was a signatory. Trying to tie Karamanlis to the Greek junta is a shocking distortion of the facts. And Kissinger doesn't mention that Karamanlis had another choice: namely, to support the rule of law against Turkey's aggression and violation of the terms of the Treaty of Guarantee, which barred the partition sought by Turkey.

In Kissinger's mind, Karamanlis's situation was intractable: "he had not only the Greek opposition to worry about but also Makarios, equally insistent on a restoration of the precise *status quo ante*. That was beyond anyone's diplomatic capabilities; it could be achieved only by military force."[46] This assertion is highly questionable and also very revealing. In his interactions with Greece and Turkey, we have seen many of Henry Kissinger's real goals for those two countries, and for Cyprus itself. Asserting that a solution to the Cyprus crisis was, by July 23, already impractical through diplomatic means says much about Kissinger's overall views, policies, and outlook. In Kissinger's worldview, the rule of law is not to be considered. The aggressor, in this case Turkey, is to be rewarded, because Turkey is, according to Kissinger, "indispensable" for United State interests in the Middle East, in the former Soviet Union and Europe. A resolution to a tense situation "restoring the *status quo ante"* on Cyprus was not attainable without force. And most fundamentally, international law in the form of the UN Charter and the North Atlantic Treaty were not relevant. Throughout this section of his memoirs, Kissinger studiously avoided referring to them.

Ironically, the long-term result of Kissinger's support for the junta dictator Ioannides is still evident in Greece today. Kissinger's support for the dictator Ioannides, his failure to denounce him and the Sampson coup government, and his failure to seek their removal resulted in anti-American sentiments by the Greek people for the first time. It should be further noted that throughout the ensuing decades of democratic governments in Greece, including the problems with Andreas Papandreou and his anti-American rhetoric in the 1980s, the United States had full use of the naval and air bases in Souda Bay, Crete, the key bases for the projection of U.S. power in the Eastern Mediterranean. Kissinger's concerns about the continuation of American influence in the region turned out to be phantoms.

British Foreign Secretary James Callaghan

Britain's long history and continuing influence in Cyprus made it an important power broker in the region. Henry Kissinger had to work in tandem with Foreign Secretary James Callaghan, whose shortcomings Kissinger was careful to detail in his memoirs. Kissinger's actions at the time failed to support Britain's views on the crisis as expressed by Callaghan. Britain, a guarantor power and former colonial ruler of Cyprus (1878–1960), denounced the Greek junta-initiated coup against the Makarios government, as did most nations of the world, including European and NATO countries[47] — but the United States did not. Kissinger refused to denounce the coup. Further, and of key importance, Kissinger rejected Callaghan's request for U.S. support for Britain's proposal to back up diplomatic efforts with Turkey with the threat of British air strikes against any further Turkish violations of the July 30, 1974 Geneva Declaration cease-fire.[48] Britain believed it would have prevented the second and massive phase of Turkey's aggression.

As he did with Makarios, Kissinger first extolled Callaghan and then sets forth his alleged shortcomings. Regarding Callaghan he said "it was his first exposure to crisis diplomacy," and his "principal experience had been in ministries concerned with domestic British problems where mediators are generally dealing with willing parties that start from the premise that a compromise will emerge."[49] Kissinger then contrasts Callaghan's experience with his own: "Unlike Callaghan, my experience in mediation came from Middle East diplomacy; hence I took the pronouncements of the parties less literally, and my expectations for rapid progress were correspondingly lower."[50] He also states that his and Callaghan's "initial approaches to the crisis differed." Callaghan was "strongly anti-Greek junta. During the first week, my views were dominated by the desire not to add to Turkish incentives to invade, which an all-out dissociation from Athens might invite."[51] There is no substance to Kissinger's views. The demise of the Greek junta would not "add to Turkish incentives to invade." How could it? It would result in a democratic government in Greece, which would maintain its NATO ties for a number of reasons, including as a protection against Turkey. Democratic Greece's ties with NATO would be far stronger then the junta's ties.

Kissinger claims in his memoirs that he was not in favor of Turkish intervention. He writes:

> I was as eager to get rid of Sampson as Callaghan and end the attempt to bring about *enosis*. But my tactics were tempered by the desire to keep Greece in the Alliance and provide Turkey no pretext for invasion.[52]

Kissinger's actions demonstrate brazen falsity of this statement. While Britain and most other nations denounced the coup of July 15, 1974, Kissinger refused to do so. He failed to immediately stop arms aid and sales to Greece as required by U.S. laws. He directed our representative at the United Nations to postpone the emergency UN Security Council meeting on Cyprus of Monday, July 15 to Friday, July 19, 1974, which downgraded the issue, substantially reduced world publicity and gave Turkey time to prepare to invade Cyprus. The next day, July 16, 1974, he instructed our ambassador in Nicosia, Roger Davies, to meet with the coup government's Foreign Minister Dimitrios Demetriou. This was arguably a form of *de facto* recognition of the coup regime. Finally, on July 17, 1974, he leaked to the *New York Times* information that the United States was leaning toward recognizing the Sampson coup regime over the duly elected Makarios government, although no final decision had been made on the issue. That leak by "high American officials" was the lead story in the July 18, 1974, *New York Times,* appearing on page A1, column 8. It gave Turkey the excuse to invade because Turkey strongly opposed the Sampson coup regime. Further, it was well-known that Kissinger wanted to get rid of Makarios as president of Cyprus. Contrary to his statement in his memoirs, maintaining relations with the junta government had more to do with ousting Makarios than with keeping Greece in the NATO Alliance. It would have been in the interests of a democratic Greece to stay in the Alliance. A Greece under the rule of law would have been a stronger and more welcome member of NATO than the junta-led Greece.

As Kissinger was pursuing these machinations in Washington and New York in mid-July, Callaghan put forward three propositions, with the support of "all the countries in the Nine [the European Community] and NATO." Those three propositions were: (1) the refusal to accept Sampson; (2) "the withdrawal of Greek officers serving with the Cyprus National Guard;" and (3) "the return of Makarios" to Cyprus.[53] Kissinger's reaction—an erroneous one—was that "The Europeans now had declared objectives for the attainment of which they had neither a strategy nor the means."[54] The Europeans clearly had a strategy: pressure Greece to get rid of the Sampson regime. They had the means to accomplish this—economically, diplomatically and militarily. Obviously, if the United States had joined in pressuring Greece on Britain's three propositions, success would have been assured. But Kissinger declined because his objectives, to oust Makarios and partition Cyprus, were not the same as Britain's and the European Community and the European members of NATO.

Kissinger stated that "Congressional thinking ran along the same lines," namely, against the Greek junta, and quoted Senate Majority Leader Mike Mansfield and the Chairman of the Senate Foreign Relations Committee, Senator William Fulbright to that effect.[55] Unsurprisingly, Kissinger was against Callaghan's three propositions:

> I was trying to navigate American policy to preserve the eastern flank of NATO and keep both Greece and Turkey in the Alliance. This, in my view, precluded an all-out identification of the United States with one of the parties—a view I maintained when the dominant mood took a 180-degree turn, and Turkey became the target.[56]

Kissinger's argument is, to be frank, sophomoric. The demise of the Greek junta and return of democracy to Greece with or without U.S. help would only have resulted in a strengthened Greek relationship with NATO. If it was done with U.S. help, the United States would earn plaudits from the Greek people and government. The suggestion that a democratic Greece would leave NATO has no merit. The demise of the Sampson coup government, the removal of the Greek officers serving with the Cyprus National Guard, and the return of Makarios and the *status quo ante* to Cyprus would have made it more difficult for Turkey to invade Cyprus or even to consider it further.

Britain, a guarantor power, was not about to threaten or take military action against Turkey without American support, even though such action was lawful. Callaghan so states in his memoirs, citing Britain's collaboration with France and Israel in the disastrous invasion of Egypt in 1956 regarding the Suez Canal.[57] President Dwight D. Eisenhower opposed the action as a violation of the rule of law and effectively forced them to evacuate from Egypt.

Kissinger rejected "Callaghan's request to support the threat of a British air strike against Turkish cease-fire violations. . . [In] the first days in office of a nonelected President [we were not] in a position to consider military moves of our own."[58] These words are a sad commentary on Kissinger's leadership. He is stating, in effect, that our government (or rather he, Kissinger) was paralyzed during a presidential transition—"in the first days in office of a nonelected President." Kissinger should have supported Callaghan's threat of an air strike by Britain "against Turkish cease-fire violations." Britain, a guarantor power, had a responsibility to stop Turkey's invasion. Instead of supporting Britain, Kissinger instructed Arthur Hartman to reject Callaghan's request in the following language:

> [I]t is out of the question to be asking a president in the first 48 hours of his administration to consider supporting military action. . . . We will do everything we can to assist in keeping the talks going, but we will have little room for maneuver if he [Callaghan] continues to rattle the saber.[59]

Thus Kissinger rejected out of hand even the threat of peace-keeping airstrikes, even as he was secretly in favor of Turkey's military action. Britain's desire to back up diplomacy with the threat of air strikes in response to Turkey's violations of the July 30, 1974 Geneva Declaration cease-fire — a potentially effective method to forestall further Turkish advances — was sacrificed to Kissinger's sympathy toward Turkish aggression.

Just how effective the threat of Western military intervention could be was illustrated by the Nicosia International Airport incident in August 1974, which Kissinger fails to mention in his memoirs. In early August 1974 Turkey's armed forces threatened again to breach the July 30, 1974 Geneva Declaration cease-fire by advancing and seizing the Nicosia International Airport, which was under UN control. Callaghan responded by stating that if Turkey attacked it would be met by British troops, the 16/5th Lancers and British planes. Turkey backed down. James Callaghan discusses his disagreement with Kissinger over this incident at length in his memoirs, *Time and Chance* (1987). Kissinger took the position that diplomacy was sufficient, but Callaghan strongly believed that it was necessary to back up diplomacy with the threat of British military action against Turkey's cease-fire violations. The incident at Nicosia International Airport only strengthened his conviction; if Britain and the United States were "sufficiently resolute the Turks would at the last moment back off." He continues:

> I reported to the Prime Minister and also explained my thinking to Arthur Hartman, the American Assistance Secretary of State, who had accompanied me to Geneva at Henry Kissinger's request. . . . I asked Arthur Hartman to convey to Washington my misgivings and proposals, and ask that prudent forethought be given to possible Turkish military intentions so that the attitude of both our countries could be decided before a response was needed.
>
> At noon on Sunday 11 August 1974 he returned with the Administration's reply. . . . [H]e informed me stiffly that the United States was not happy with Her Majesty's Government's approach. . . . Hartman added that the Secretary of State would react very strongly against any further announcement of British military activities.

Callaghan told Hartman "that Dr. Kissinger was mistaken" regarding future Turkish actions and that we needed to respond "on both the diplomatic and military level."

> I told Hartman that . . . I would repeat the warning to the Turks . . . but I must be assured of American support if I were to do so, and in the light of our conversation this would apparently not be forthcoming.

> * * * *

> I fired off a telegram to Henry Kissinger, saying that these important differences were impairing our mutual confidence. I reiterated that it was not sufficient to approach the Turks solely through the medium of diplomacy. The correct policy was to tackle them on parallel lines, namely to convince them that we were in earnest on both the diplomatic and the military level. This was the most likely way to achieve results. As to his complaint that the British had introduced a military dimension, I reminded him that the reality was that this dimension was constantly hanging over the heads of the British troops who were heavily outnumbered by up to twenty-five thousand Turkish soldiers.

> * * * *

> I was convinced that more would be needed on this occasion. The only thing that might deter the Turks was the conviction that they would face military opposition if they attempted to advance further.[60]

Kissinger was not to be swayed. By August 12, Callaghan recounts, "matters had reached an impasse. . . . There was no prospect of a determined stand by the United Nations, the United States, and Britain." Kissinger's reluctance to negotiate in strength had taken priority, even after evidence to the contrary at Nicosia International Airport.

The North Atlantic Treaty

Kissinger's reluctance to support Callaghan's three proposals, as well as the use of force against repeated Turkish incursions, was rooted in his absurd fear that the eastern flank of NATO would collapse if the Western alliance even threatened further repercussions. This argument cannot withstand analysis. We recall Callaghan's three proposals: (1) attack the Greek junta and the Sampson coup government; (2) call for the removal of the Greek officers serving with the Cyprus National Guard; and (3) call for the return of Makarios. Any of these actions would potentially have ameliorated the situation; all three together might have defused the crisis altogether. The demise of the Greek junta and return of democracy to Greece with or without U.S. help could only result in a strengthened Greek relationship with NATO. The suggestion or implication that a democratic Greece would leave NATO has no merit. The demise of the Sampson coup government, the removal of the Greek officers serving with the Cyprus National Guard, and the return of Makarios to Cyprus and the *status quo ante* to Cyprus would have made it more difficult for Turkey to invade Cyprus or even to consider it further. As usual, Kissinger failed to acknowledge that the North Atlantic Treaty article 1, opposes "the threat or use of force."

A basic policy that Kissinger voiced several times is that: "It must remain an objective of US policy that both Greece and Turkey remain members of the NATO structure."[61] This is a truism. What Kissinger failed to understand is that a democratic Greece in NATO was far preferable to the alternative: a militarist government led by the dictator Ioannides. Furthermore, the junta's blunder in its coup against the Makarios government gave the United States, Britain, and the other members of NATO an important opportunity to get rid of the Greek junta government. But Kissinger of course had other objectives, namely, (1) to get rid of Makarios as president of Cyprus, (2) to support tacitly Turkey's invasion of Cyprus, and (3) if possible achieve "double *enosis*"—the formal division of Cyprus between Greece and Turkey. It could be that Kissinger also preferred a junta-led Greece since he had such difficulty dealing with democracies, particularly European democracies.

It is interesting to note that Kissinger states that in addition to Congress and the media, "much of the bureaucracy" favored a "cut-off of military aid to Greece" because of its coup against the democratically elected government of Makarios.[62] Kissinger states that he:

> resisted pressures from Congress, the media, and much of
> the bureaucracy to cutoff military aid to Greece because,
> in our view, military aid to a NATO ally was an expression
> of the long-term interest of the Atlantic Alliance and not an
> expediency to be manipulated.[63]

Kissinger was evidently not interested in the form of government that a NATO ally took, or whether it was even legitimate. To Kissinger, the rule of law and the terms of the North Atlantic Treaty against "the threat or use of force" had no meaning or relevance.

One might think that his own government's successful intervention in an almost identical situation might be proof of its effectiveness in Kissinger's mind, but this was not so. A decade before the 1974 crisis, Turkey had also threatened Cyprus with invasion. This prompted a letter from then-President Lyndon Johnson reminding Turkey of the previous agreements regarding military assistance. The strongly worded letter read in part: "Under Article IV of the Agreement with Turkey of July 1947, your Government is required to obtain United States consent in the use of military assistance for purposes other than those for which assistance was furnished." The letter successfully forestalled Turkish action. But in his memoirs, Kissinger turns this successful precedent on its head, attacking the Johnson letter as damaging to NATO:

> By casting doubt on these crucial premises [i.e., guaranteed military aid to NATO members], Johnson's letter transformed the NATO guarantee from a strategic necessity into a whim of American policy.[64]

Kissinger's statement is inaccurate and misleading. The NATO guarantee was not transformed. It still remained valid against any threat of invasion of a NATO member. Kissinger fails to acknowledge that Turkey's threats to invade Cyprus in 1964 and thereafter violated not only the UN Charter Article 2, paragraph 4, but also the North Atlantic Treaty Article 1, which prohibits "the threat or use of force." The Johnson letter strengthened NATO by setting a precedent against aggression by a NATO member and strengthened the stated purpose of the North Atlantic Treaty.

Kissinger's position, in effect, is that the North Atlantic Treaty applies only to aggression against a member country and not to aggression by a NATO member against a third party non-member. He is obviously wrong; this interpretation is inconsistent with the plain meaning and purposes of the North Atlantic Treaty. The Preamble of the Treaty, in the most general terms, declares that it is an instrument firmly bound to uphold universal democratic principles:

> The Parties to this Treaty reaffirm their faith in the purposes and principles of the Charter of the United Nations and their desire to live in peace with all peoples and all Governments. . . . They are determined to safeguard the freedom, common heritage and civilisation of their peoples, founded on the principles of democracy, individual liberty and the rule of law.

Article 1 is more specifically targeted to the settlement of international disputes, cautioning NATO members to "settle any international dispute in which they may be involved by peaceful means . . . and . . . to refrain in their international relations from the threat or use of force in any manner inconsistent with the purposes of the United Nations." Henry Kissinger apparently failed to remember the text of the North Atlantic Treaty or was hoping no one else would.

Congress

As we have seen, it was not only NATO partners who disagreed with Kissinger about the Cyprus situation. He also had to deal with a recalcitrant Congress. Kissinger's memoir attacks the role of Congress in foreign policy, complaining that "congressional micromanagement" had limited "presidential discretion in foreign policy."[65] He says the Cyprus issue set in motion a pattern that was followed by:

> in short order: the Jackson-Vanik and the Stevenson Amendments in December 1974, severely restricting trade and credits to the Soviet Union; the cutoff of aid to Indochina in March 1975; the prohibition against assistance to groups in Angola resisting a Cuban expeditionary force in December 1975; and a host of restrictions on various other activities. The trend to limit presidential discretion in foreign policy has continued—if not accelerated—in the interval.[66]

Kissinger equates Congress upholding the rule of law with a "trend to limit presidential discretion in foreign policy." Here Kissinger's lack of commitment to American constitutional government, which had been proven over two centuries and forged in the fire of internecine conflict and two world wars, is laid bare. He passes over Congress's constitutional role in foreign affairs without a thought; nor does he support the rule of law and democratic values in foreign affairs. Throughout his career in government, he blamed Congress for his foreign policy failures, including those in Vietnam, Chile, Cyprus, Bangladesh, East Timor and elsewhere.

Kissinger attempts to portray congressional action in the matter of Cyprus as a response to ethnic politics instead of a necessary part of Congress's constitutional role. He makes the highly questionable assertion that "congressional pressures did the Greek cause far more harm than good."[67] To Kissinger, congressional resistance had to be about ethnic tension, not the rule of law. He continues on this theme when discussing the American response to the return to power of Constantine Karamanlis: "From the moment Karamanlis was restored the Greek American community brought massive pressure to bear on Congress to legislate its preferred outcome,"[68] This false statement corresponded to his feeble attempt to depict Turkey's aggression and land grab into an intractable ethnic conflict.

In fact, the organized efforts of the Greek American community did not start until after the second and massive wave of Turkey's aggression on August 14–16, 1974, well after Karamanlis was sworn in as prime minister on July 24, 1974. Without pretext, the Turkish military seized an additional 30 percent of Cyprus three weeks after the legitimate government of Cyprus had been restored and the *status quo ante* achieved. Turkey forced 180,000 Greek Cypriots from their homes and property in July and August 1974 and 20,000 more in the ensuing years, and committing war crimes and crimes against humanity, as I set forth in chapter 8. This was hardly something to which the Greek American community could turn a blind eye, but it had little to do with the restoration of Karamanlis.

As it happens, I was part of the Greek American community's effort to stop the outrages occurring on Cyprus. On August 20, 1974 the House Foreign Affairs Committee held hearings on the Cyprus problem. On August 29, 1974 Congressman

John Brademas, (D-IN), Deputy Majority Whip, and three col-
leagues, Paul Sarbanes (D-MD), Gus Yatron (D-PA) and Peter
Kyros (D-ME) wrote to Secretary of State Henry Kissinger that
U.S. laws required an immediate halt in arms to Turkey. That
letter was based on my memorandum of August 28, 1974 to
Brademas on the rule of law and Cyprus. Fundamentally, the
efforts of the Greek American community were about enforcing
U.S. laws which mandated an immediate halt in arms aid and
sales to Turkey, not "legislat[ing] its preferred outcome." Greek
Americans were concerned with the rule of law on Cyprus, not
with perceived ethnic tensions.

Congressional action in the Senate started with Senator
Thomas Eagleton's remarks on the Senate floor on September 5,
1974, in support of the rule of law in enforcing U.S. laws against
Turkey for its illegal use of U.S.-supplied arms in its aggression against Cyprus.[69] It focused U.S. and worldwide attention
on Turkey's aggression. I had also contacted Eagleton's office
on August 26, 1974, and sent to him and his legislative assistant, Brian Atwood, a copy of my August 28, 1974, memorandum to Brademas (for excerpts from Eagleton's speech, see
chapter 7). Throughout late 1974, other members of Congress
pushed back against Kissinger's strategy for Cyprus. From
September through December 1974 there were over a dozen
votes in the House and Senate and two presidential vetoes of
an arms embargo. On October 17, the House came within two
votes of overriding the second veto. The Ford administration
capitulated, informing Congressmen John Brademas, Benjamin
Rosenthal, Ed Derwinski, Paul Sarbanes, and Dante Fascell,
and Senator Thomas Eagleton, that the White House would
not oppose or veto the next version of the cutoff of arms to
Turkey, presumably because they believed the House would
override another veto. Congressional concern helped prevent
further military action by Turkey in Cyprus and new military
action in the Aegean, where Turkey had an armada of land-
ing ships. Turkey had made claims (and still does) to one-half

of the Aegean Sea, despite the treaties establishing maritime boundaries in that part of the Mediterranean.

All of these efforts in Congress were anathema to Kissinger's preference for secretive, extra-constitutional maneuvering. He falsely asserts in his memoirs that "Congress shed these restraints and prescribed the tactics of Cyprus policy."[70] Congress did not do that. It insisted on the rule of law—an immediate halt in arms to the aggressor, Turkey, in accordance with U.S. laws. He cites as tactical interference the language of the House bill introduced in late September cutting off aid to Turkey "until the president certifies to Congress that substantial progress towards agreement has been made regarding military forces in Cyprus." That is not prescribing tactics, but supporting the goal of the rule of law by the removal of Turkey's invasion and occupation forces. He neglects to include the language of the Senate bill which cutoff aid "until Turkey is in compliance with United States laws." The final rule of law arms embargo legislation melded both the House and Senate language.

Regarding Congress, Kissinger writes "Turkish actions on Cyprus were held not to constitute self-defense under the provisions of the Foreign Assistance Act."[71] Turkey's violation of our laws was clear-cut; it was not just Congress who took this position. The Comptroller General and the Law Library of Congress issued opinions that Turkey violated our laws by its use of U.S. arms to invade Cyprus. It was certainly not an issue of "self-defense." During the more than twelve votes and congressional debates from September through December 1974, Kissinger and the administration did not question Turkey's violations of our laws.

In his recollection, Kissinger blames Congress for the lack of progress in securing Turkish concessions, saying "The legislation set up a vicious circle." He asserts without citation, details, or evidence that "The Ford Administration had already committed itself to encourage significant concessions from Turkey. But once Congress appointed itself as the arbiter of what constituted progress, its definition would go beyond the capacities of diplomacy."[72] In effect, Kissinger is stating that aggression pays and the United States should seek "concessions" from the victim, Cyprus, and not insist on the rule of law. We did not do that with Iraq's invasion of Kuwait (as I point out in chapter 10). We should not have done that with Turkey in 1974 and we should not continue to appease Turkey today.

It is clear that Kissinger does not believe in any significant role for Congress in foreign policy. His statement that "The American style of government works best when Congress concentrates on overall supervision of long-range policy without attempting to second-guess day-to-day tactics" is a twisted interpretation of Congress's constitutional role in foreign policy.[73] Our government would not "work best" if Congress only concentrated "on overall supervision of long-range policy." In fact, the Congress has a constitutional duty to oversee the country's foreign policy. Kissinger's interpretation of Congress's appropriate role is especially misleading when applied to the Cyprus issue. Congress was not second-guessing day-to-day tactics. It was insisting on enforcement of the fundamental policy enacted by Congress and signed into law by the president over a decade earlier; American-supplied arms cannot be used for aggression.

The following tale related by Kissinger in his memoirs illustrates his view of the appropriate spheres for congressional and executive action:

> The difference between the congressional and executive branch perspectives became apparent when I showed a week's worth of cables to and from Ankara to the three congressional leaders most identified with the Greek cause. The purpose was to demonstrate to John Brademas, Benjamin Rosenthal, and Paul Sarbanes that they were risking a vital alliance without advancing the prospects of a Cyprus settlement. . . . The congressional mind-set was on justifying a single legislative act; mine was on managing a continuing

process. The Congressmen were dealing with absolutes; I sought to accumulate nuances. My congressional interlocutors wanted me to challenge each point raised by the Turkish government; I thought it wiser to conserve whatever capital of trust we still had in Ankara for the negotiating process rather than squandering it on debating points.[74]

Several problems become apparent when we delve a little deeper into this tale. First, Turkey is not a "vital" ally, as I discuss in chapter 9. Kissinger fails to state in his chapter on Cyprus that Turkey had already made an accommodation with the Soviet Union and had actively assisted the Soviet military on several occasions during the Cold War, to the detriment of the United States and the West. Second, he refers to the "Greek cause" instead of the American cause in support of the rule of law in international relations. Third, he denigrates Congress and the rule of law and, in effect, supports aggression by stating "The congressional mind-set was on justifying a single legislative act; mine was on managing a continuing process." And fourth, he falsely states in that same paragraph that the "congressional interlocutors wanted me to challenge each point raised by the Turkish government." That was not what Congress was calling for. What Kissinger calls "absolutes," Congressmen Brademas, Rosenthal, and Sarbanes would have more accurately portrayed as an entirely appropriate concern with the enforcement of U.S. laws, and a desire to prevent American arms being used by a foreign country for an aggressive land grab.

Kissinger does not understand, or simply refuses to acknowledge, Congress's role in the formulation of U.S. foreign policy. And he pointedly omits mention of Congress's budget, appropriations, and oversight responsibilities regarding foreign policy and its execution and implementation. He fundamentally disagrees with the role of Congress in our constitutional system and simply does not understand the importance of the separation of powers and a system of checks and balances.

Kissinger was determined to overturn the arms embargo, stating on February 5, 1975, that legislation would be introduced to achieve this goal. Such legislation was indeed introduced on February 26, 1975. Thus, he scuttled the impact of the embargo legislation and openly opposed fundamental U.S. policy in support of the rule of law in international affairs. All of this Congressional maneuvering was because Kissinger believed, erroneously, that the congressional cutoff of arms to Turkey, which the White House said it would not oppose, "removed flexibility from both sides:"

> For the Greek government, the congressional intervention was a deus ex machina that enabled it to sidestep the concessions which its more thoughtful members must have recognized to be necessary. For its part, Turkey greeted the aid cutoff with a combination of outrage and relief: outrage that its key ally should have turned the American-Turkish security alliance into a form of blackmail; relief because it also provided it with the pretext to ask me to postpone my trip to Ankara designed to discuss Turkish concessions.[75]

Kissinger seems to think that there were only two possible pretexts for Turkish concessions: a steady flow of American arms, and his own personal presence on the scene. Readers can perhaps judge for themselves the accuracy of this remarkable contention.

Kissinger's approach to the crisis in Cyprus undercut the influence of the United States and NATO in the Eastern Mediterranean. In the remainder of 1974 and throughout 1975, he used congressional action as an excuse to do nothing regarding pressuring Turkey, and he repeatedly attacked and blamed Congress for the situation during the remaining two years of the Ford administration. Thus, from February 5, 1975, to the end of the Ford administration in January 1977, Kissinger did not pressure Turkey to remove its troops and settlers from Cyprus.

In fact he did nothing to pressure Turkey from July 20, 1974 when Turkey initiated its aggression against Cyprus. And he spent most of 1975 overturning the congressional rule of law arms embargo legislation. In fact, the introduction on February 26, 1975 of legislation to overturn the embargo had the effect of freezing the Turkish position in Cyprus in place. Kissinger's actions are not only a key example of his arrogance and wrong-headed approach to the Turkish invasion of Cyprus, they also demonstrate his lack of belief in American values.

In terms of NATO's position after the Cyprus crisis, Kissinger's approach also did more harm than good. His rather equivocal contention that "In the end, the Ford Administration did achieve its most important objective: the eastern flank of NATO, though strained, remained intact," is erroneous. The eastern flank, Greece and Turkey, was not simply "strained," it was cracked and permanently damaged. Kissinger asserts that "preserving the general peace and the structure of the Western Alliance . . . were important objectives in their own right. And those objectives the Ford Administration did achieve in the Cyprus crisis of 1974." To the contrary: Greece's relations with the United States after the junta fell were not "friendly." They were cool rather than friendly and, because of Kissinger's support of the Greek junta, anti-Americanism took root in Greece for the first time. The crisis also resulted in putting Greece and Turkey at odds, which has certainly damaged NATO's unity and moral stature to this day. The two countries are still at odds and will remain so until Turkey removes its 43,000 occupation troops from Cyprus and returns the 200,000 illegal Turkish colonists/settlers from Cyprus back to Anatolia.

What policy could the Ford Administration have followed instead? Kissinger's contention that "the parameters of the issue had been established before Ford entered office" is in error since the second and massive phase of Turkey's aggression occurred on August 14–16, 1974, six days after Ford took office. An alternate course of action is not difficult to outline in retrospect. During those six days, Ford could have and should have: (1) agreed to the British air strikes against Turkish cease-fire violations recommended by Callaghan and rejected by Kissinger; (2) informed Turkey that he was stopping all arms shipments to Turkey in accordance with U.S. military assistance and sales laws and U.S.–Turkish agreements under those laws; (3) supported the Treaty of Guarantee and the Treaty of Establishment, which barred both partition and union with Greece, by calling on Turkey to adhere to the terms of the treaties; and (4) stressed to Turkey that the *status quo ante* had been restored on July 23 with the swearing in of Clerides as acting president and that Turkey should promptly remove its invasion and occupation forces from Cyprus.

Much more important than NATO's position in the Eastern Mediterranean or America's political standing with Greece was the harm done to the rule of law in international affairs and the physical trauma and tragedy meted out to the people of Cyprus. Kissinger's position, refusing to use the congressional arms embargo legislation in any negotiation with Turkey, rewarded Turkey for its aggression. He damaged and downgraded the rule of law in international affairs and the role of the United Nations. (I compare President George H. W. Bush's actions in support of the rule of law and the UN Charter regarding Iraq and Kuwait with Kissinger's actions regarding Turkey and Cyprus in chapter 10.) Kissinger's position on the arms embargo illustrates Kissinger's basic views of foreign policy, his disdain for the Congress and its constitutional role, his lawlessness and responsibility for the Cyprus tragedy of 1974.

Cyprus, thanks to Henry Kissinger, was and remains a U.S. foreign policy debacle. The 48-page text of Kissinger's chapter on Cyprus indicts Kissinger as an intellectual fraud who created his own set of facts, omitted key facts and subjects, and distorted the record. His version of what happened is deeply flawed. Additionally, I believe his actions make Kissinger an accessory and an accomplice to Turkey's war crimes, crimes against humanity, and cultural cleansing, including the religious cleansing of the occupied north.

In the TV documentary "Cyprus Still Divided: A U.S. Foreign Policy Failure," which aired on Detroit Public TV on September 13, 2010, and Maryland Public TV on October 17, 2011, Christopher Hitchens summed up Kissinger's role in the Cyprus tragedy: "It's difficult to encapsulate the wickedness of Kissinger's role in a sentence, but if you wanted to try for an epigram, it would be to support the Greeks as long as they were fascists, then to turn against them when they were democrats; to support the Turks only when they were aggressors and to end up with a country ruined and partitioned, which I have to believe was in fact the objective of the policy in the first place."

7

The Arms Embargo Battle in Congress

We saw part of the story of congressional action in 1974 regarding Cyprus in the last chapter, through the lens of Henry Kissinger's memoirs. Since it speaks so powerfully to Kissinger's innate disdain for the rule of law, including the legislative role of the United States Congress itself, it is worth taking a closer look at this episode. It is also here that I became most personally involved in the American reaction to the Turkish invasion of Cyprus. Congress's pushback against Kissinger's policies *vis-à-vis* Cyprus, Greece and Turkey was one of deep frustration because Kissinger did all he could to overturn the arms embargo and subvert the will of Congress and its constitutional role in foreign policy. He was partially successful as discussed below. However, it cannot be said the episode had no consequences for the Secretary of State. In my view, the rule of law arms embargo battle in the Congress against the Ford administration led by Kissinger was the beginning of the public's disenchantment with him and the decline of his high public opinion rating.

In September through December 1974, the Congress of the United States upheld the rule of law and the integrity of the

Foreign Assistance Act and the Foreign Military Sales Act in over a dozen votes, including two near overrides of presidential vetoes. Congress finally enacted Public Law 93-559 signed by President Ford on December 30, 1974, a law which contained provisions imposing an embargo on all military assistance and military sales to Turkey starting February 5, 1975, until "the President determines and certifies to the Congress that. . . . Turkey is in compliance with the Foreign Assistance Act, the Foreign Military Sales Act, and any agreement entered into under such Acts, and that substantial progress toward agreement has been made regarding military forces in Cyprus."[1]

The course of the congressional debate and the Administration's comments reveal the polarity of their positions on the issue of further aid to Turkey. On August 14, 1974, Congressmen John Brademas (D-IN), Peter Kyros (D-ME), Gus Yatron (D-PA), Paul Sarbanes (D-MD) and Skip Bafalis (R-FL) introduced House Resolution 1319 expressing the sense of Congress "that all U.S. economic and military assistance and military sales to Turkey should immediately be stopped until all Turkish armed forces have been withdrawn from Cyprus."[2] The language did not state, as it would shortly, that Turkey was "immediately ineligible" under existing law for further arms aid or sales.

On August 19, 1974, Kissinger held a press conference during which reporter James McCartney asked Kissinger "whether the Foreign Assistance Act did not require the cut-off of American aid to Turkey as a result of its aggression in Cyprus."[3] Kissinger replied "I will have to get a legal opinion on that subject, which I have not done."[4] Kissinger's evasive reply fooled no one—the language of the act was clear. The next day, an arms embargo gained an important ally when George Ball, former undersecretary of state (1961–1966), testified before the House Foreign Affairs Subcommittee on Europe that he would support legislation calling for a halt in military assistance to Turkey until an agreement acceptable to all parties was reached regarding the presence of foreign military forces on Cyprus.[5]

On August 26, 1974, I called Congressman John Brademas, who was Deputy Whip for the Democrats, and told him that military aid and military sales to Turkey had to stop "immediately" under the Foreign Assistance Act and the Foreign Military Sales Act. I informed him that the law was mandatory, and that it was not a matter of Executive Branch discretion. He asked me to send him a memorandum on the matter, which I did on August 28, 1974 in the form of a draft letter to Kissinger. That draft letter was the basis of the letter that Congressmen John Brademas, Peter Kyros, Gus Yatron and Paul Sarbanes sent to Kissinger on August 29, 1974.

Brademas called me on August 29, 1974, and said he and Paul Sarbanes had signed the letter to Kissinger and asked me to arrange for the other signatures and its delivery. Gus Yatron and Peter Kyros responded quickly and authorized their offices to sign the letter. Skip Bafalis was out on a fishing boat off the Florida coast and could not be reached. My messenger picked up the letter from Brademas's office, got the other signatures and delivered the letter to Kissinger at the State Department and a copy to the White House. Thus, on August 29, 1974, four of the five sponsors of House Resolution 1319 wrote to Secretary Kissinger that Turkey had violated U.S. laws and was "immediately ineligible for further assistance."[6] That letter, in effect, started the rule of law arms embargo fight in the House of Representatives, although it was not until September 24, 1974 that the bipartisan Pierre DuPont (R-DE) –Ben Rosenthal (D-NY) amendment was attached to the continuing resolution on appropriations, H.J. Res 1131, by a resounding vote of 307 to 90. The amendment suspended military assistance and sales to Turkey "until the President certifies to Congress that substantial progress towards agreement has been made regarding military forces in Cyprus."[7]

During August 1974 I had one employee at the American Hellenic Institute and hired a second in September. I initiated and led the nationwide lobby effort in the Greek American community from late August through December 1974 which culminated, after twelve votes in the House of Representatives and two presidential vetoes, in the rule of law arms embargo against Turkey in December 1974 effective February 5, 1975. I developed a basic numbering system of one to six with Congressmen John Brademas (D-IN) and Ed Derwinski (R-IL) in the House and with Thomas Eagleton (D-MO) in the Senate to gauge the positions of members of the House and Senate on our arms embargo legislation. A rating of one meant the member was committed to vote for our position; a rating of two meant the member would probably vote for our position; three meant he or she was leaning in our direction; four meant leaning against; five meant probably against; and six meant a vote against our position. This numbering system was transmitted to the Greek American community with the results going to Brademas, Derwinski and Eagleton: thus we had an organizational tool that we hoped would enhance our lobbying efforts.

On August 26, 1974, I also called Sam Nakis, a leading member of the Order of AHEPA, the largest Greek American fraternal organization. Mr. Nakis, a resident of St. Louis, put me in touch with Senator Thomas Eagleton's (D-MO) office. On August 28, 1974, I sent my memorandum on the rule of law to Eagleton and his legislative assistant, Brian Atwood. On September 3, 1974, a State Department official confidentially informed Senator Thomas Eagleton's chief foreign policy aide, Brian Atwood, "that the legal study of the Turkish military aid question had been completed in the Office of the Legal Advisor" and that "its conclusion was that by no stretch of the statutes or the legal imagination of the State Department's attorneys could military aid to Turkey be continued."[8] The official said:

> he could not understand why the highest level of government could still not obey the law [and] that pressure was being applied at the top of the department to modify the conclusions more to the tactical requirements of Kissinger

by returning the unsatisfactory opinion to the staff for revision. The message, as read by Eagleton's staff, was that an attempt was being made to fiddle with the legal opinion and the State Department staff was holding firm to its position.[9]

There was, apparently, dissent within the State Department — Kissinger's manipulation had not gone unnoticed. It was doubly troubling that his manipulation was in the service of what was obviously an act of international aggression.

On September 5, 1974, Eagleton initiated in the Senate the rule of law debate regarding Turkey by a statement he delivered on the Senate floor. His remarks were reported in the *New York Times* on September 6, 1974. He also introduced S. Res. 1897, a non-binding sense of Congress resolution that military aid and sales to Turkey be immediately suspended until Turkey complied with U.S. laws. Eagleton's remarks at this crucial point deserve to be quoted at length:

> Mr. President, throughout our history Congress in fulfilling its constitutional responsibilities has sought to provide the Executive with maximum flexibility in the conduct of foreign affairs. It was, of course, the intention of the framers that the President be allowed to negotiate with foreign governments with as little statutory restriction as was deemed by Congress to be in the national interest. This scheme has served the United States well even in this era of foreign entanglements.
>
> But one area where Congress felt the national interest was best served by restrictive legislation—by keeping the Executive on a short leash—was the area of military assistance. Recognizing the inherent danger of providing arms to foreign governments by grants or sales, Congress passed legislation carefully circumscribing the use of those arms. And we carefully limited the President's discretion in continuing military assistance to a recipient nation when that nation is in violation of the applicable statutes.

> For the past month the Government of Turkey has been in violation of the provisions of section 505 of the Foreign Assistance Act and chapter 1, section 4 of the Foreign Military Sales Act. Whether or not it suits the policy of the executive branch at this time, these laws state categorically that a violating nation "shall be immediately ineligible" for further assistance.

* * * *

> It seems apparent that the law is either being ignored or openly abridged in order to accommodate an ill-perceived short-range gain—ill-perceived because we have gained nothing and lost much in our "tilt toward Turkey."

Significantly, Eagleton stipulates the importance of Congress's allowance for Executive Branch flexibility in foreign policy. This only served to highlight Kissinger's twisting of this tacit principle; his constant manipulation was flexibility run rampant, to the point of "ignor[ing] or openly abridg[ing]" American law. Eagleton then punctuated this troubling state of affairs by contrasting it to an earlier confrontation, in which the Executive branch stood firm against the Turks: Lyndon Johnson's 1964 letter to the Prime Minister of Turkey, warning him of the consequences of the use of American arms to intervene in Cyprus. Eagleton continued:

> What are the purposes for which we furnish a nation with weapons under military assistance programs? Subsection (b) of sections 505 of the Foreign Assistance Act addresses that question directly when it requires the President to determine that each of the four following conditions be met:
> "(1) that such country conforms to the purposes and principles of the Charter of the United Nations;
> "(2) that such defense articles will be utilized by such country for the maintenance of its own defensive strength, or the defensive strength of the free world;

"(3) that such country is taking all reasonable measures, consistent with its political and economic stability, which may be needed to develop its defense capacities; and

"(4) that the increased ability of such country to defend itself is important to the security of the United States."

Mr. President, the words "immediately ineligible" strongly imply that the President must make an expeditious determination that these four conditions have been met. Now, more than a month after the invasion of Cyprus, it is obvious that Turkey has clearly violated conditions one and two. It cannot, in my opinion, legitimately be argued that the administration has acted in good faith to expeditiously implement the provisions of this law.

The Foreign Military Sales Act is equally specific in defining the purposes for which military sales are authorized.

* * * *

Mr. President, even the wildest imagination could not construe the Turkish invasion of Cyprus as conforming to the purposes and principles of the U.N. Charter. Turkish troops have actually engaged U.N. peacekeeping forces on Cyprus. Certainly the aggressive actions of Turkey cannot be interpreted as "legitimate self-defense"—or "internal security"—or "public works"—or "helpful to the economic and social development" of Cyprus. Those are quotations from the aforementioned statute.

It is clear, therefore, that the action of Turkey is in direct violation of the 1947 bilateral agreement and, consequently, in violation of the legal authority under which that country receives military aid. The President in this rare instance has virtually no discretion under the law—he must determine that Turkey is immediately ineligible for military grant assistance and military sales.

Mr. President, the legal provisions I have cited apply directly to the Cyprus situation.

Impatient with Kissinger's prevarications, Eagleton lays out the legal terrain in decisive terms. Turkey's "direct violation" of diplomatic agreements gave the U.S. government little choice in the matter. Eagleton next turned to Kissinger and the Executive branch:

> Secretary of State Henry Kissinger stated that he would seek a legal opinion on the issues I have discussed today. He also strongly implied that it would not be in our interests to terminate military aid to Turkey at this time.
>
> Mr. President, it is always in the interest of the United States to assure that our laws are faithfully executed. I would rather believe that the delay in receiving a legal opinion on military assistance to Turkey is unrelated to the State Department's perception of the best policy to follow in the Cyprus matter. Yet, the implication is inescapable. There is no excuse for the failure to implement what is a clear requirement of law.
>
> It is my personal belief that a cutoff of military aid to Turkey would indeed serve to inspire accommodation among the warring factions on Cyprus. If such action is taken immediately, as is required, it will present a tangible expression of concern to Greece—an expression which might save U.S. bases in that country and hopefully stem the tide of anti-Americanism. And it may demonstrate to Turkey that, although it has won a military victory, that victory cannot be sustained over time unless it is transformed into political accommodation.
>
> . . . I am sure that it is not President Ford's intention to ignore the law in this instance. I have greatly admired his efforts to restore confidence in the law during his brief tenure as President. But it is my belief that he is being ill-advised or being kept uninformed of the legal ramifications of his inaction in the Cyprus matter in order to protect erroneous policy judgments made by the foreign affairs bureaucracy.

I call upon the President to make the inescapable determination he is required to make under the statutes I have
cited today. He has no choice but to declare Turkey ineligible to receive further military assistance. Such action will
not only conform the administration's actions with the law;
it will begin to correct the grievous errors our Government
has made in sacrificing relations with Greece in favor of a
nation which has committed aggression.

Eagleton's dramatic speech on the Senate floor brought full day-
light to what had been diplomacy conducted in the shadows,
behind the scenes. His intimation that the President himself had
been "ill-advised" and "uninformed" laid down the gauntlet to
Kissinger.

On September 19, 1974 Kissinger appeared before a Senate
Democratic Caucus at his request to argue against Senate
Resolution 1897. However, "during an exchange with Senator
Eagleton . . . [Kissinger] admitted that the 'dominant interpretation within my legal department' agreed with Eagleton's contention that aid to Turkey is illegal since its invasion of Cyprus
employed U.S.-supplied weapons which, under the aid legislation, can only be used for defensive purposes."[10] Kissinger
added that in his view there were times in world history when
diplomats had to act outside the law.[11] The non-binding resolution passed by a vote of sixty-four to twenty-seven.

On September 24, 1974, the House of Representatives voted
307 to 90 to attach the bipartisan DuPont-Rosenthal amendment to the continuing resolution on appropriations, H.J. Res.
1131. The amendment suspended military assistance and sales
to Turkey "until the President certifies to Congress that substantial progress toward agreement has been made regarding
military forces in Cyprus."

On September 30, 1974, the Senate voted 57 to 20 for an
amendment to H.J. Res. 1131 suspending military assistance and
sales to Turkey until Turkey was in compliance with U.S. laws

and mandating that the Executive Branch apply the statutory penalty to any nation using American arms for purposes other than for which they were granted.[12] President Ford announced he would veto the continuing resolution on appropriations if it contained language halting military assistance and sales to any country.[13]

Despite requests from the Congress, Kissinger refused to transmit a copy of the State Department's legal opinion to the Congress. He ordered the State Department to withhold the release of a departmental legal ruling on whether Turkey was in violation of the Foreign Assistance Act and the Foreign Military Sales Act with respect to Turkey's use of U.S.-furnished arms in its invasion and occupation of 37.3 percent of Cyprus. Senator Eagleton, Congressman Ben Rosenthal and others requested copies of the State Department's legal opinion to no avail. According to Laurence Stern:

> The legal study became a major point of contention in the recurrent jousts between the press office and the news media. Five months after the State Department's legal opinion was completed, the Department's spokesman Robert Anderson still found himself floundering with the issue.
>
> "What is the justification," one reporter asked in a heated exchange in February 1975, "for keeping secret the results of a study that was ordered to determine whether or not a foreign government was in compliance with American law?"
>
> "The study is not going to be made public," Anderson said.[14]

In addition, Kissinger initially refused to allow the Cyprus Desk Officer, Thomas Boyatt, to testify before congressional committees. Boyatt did testify in executive session to avoid being cited for contempt of Congress, but Kissinger refused to send to Congress a copy of Boyatt's memorandum in which he took issue with the direction of State Department policy on Cyprus.

The Comptroller General of the United States also concluded that Turkey had violated Section 505(d) of the Foreign
Assistance Act of 1961 and Section 3(c) of the Foreign Military
Sales Act.[15] In his opinion the violation lay in the diversion
of U.S.-supplied military assistance for use in Cyprus without
obtaining the prior formal consent of the United States, which
was required by article IV of the July 1947 United States-Turkey
bilateral agreement on Aid to Turkey.[16]

The Comptroller General held that Subsection 505(d) of
the Act also required a determination that the violations were
"substantial" in order to render a country "immediately ineligible for further assistance."[17] He then stated that any diversion
of a substantial amount of military supplies would "constitute
a 'substantial' violation of Section 505(d)" and that he believed
"Turkey had diverted substantial quantities of military assistance items."[18] He continued:

> . . . . The purposes and use to which the diverted mili-
> tary assistance is applied would certainly also be relevant
> to the gravity of the violation. If such purposes and use
> [are] in contravention of the explicitly stated policies and
> purposes of the Foreign Assistance Act of 1961, the viola-
> tion would undoubtedly be "substantial." It is our impression
> that Turkey has diverted substantial quantities of military
> assistance items furnished by the United States, although we
> have no official information as to the types and quantities
> of defense articles which are involved. In addition, as noted
> hereinbefore the particular purposes for which the items
> were diverted and the uses to which they were applied may
> well be in contravention of the policies and purposes of the
> Foreign Assistance Act of 1961.

By this point, the legal situation had become clear. There
was no convincing argument by Administration supporters
that Turkey had not violated the law. In fact, Laurence Stern

wrote that "the legal case . . . was sufficiently compelling so that Kissinger never, in the course of the harshest conflict he experienced with Congress, chose to defend his policies on legal grounds."[19] Instead, the Administration emphasized the strategic importance of Turkey and pressed for a suspension of the cutoff of aid to Turkey to give Kissinger time to negotiate. In asking for additional time, leading supporters of the Administration such as Senate Majority Leader Mike Mansfield and Congressman John Anderson, admitted that the law had been broken. As Majority Leader Mansfield stated on the Senate floor:

> The position of the distinguished Senator from Missouri (Mr. Eagleton) which has won the overwhelming approval of Congress, is clear: These laws as applied to the hostilities on Cyprus require a cutoff of aid to Turkey. The foundation of this judgment is incontrovertible: This is a Nation of laws and not of men and when the law is clear, it must be followed whether it seems expedient or not at the time.[20]

> * * * *

> The joint resolution suspends until December 15 the application of the cutoff of funds prescribed in the Foreign Military Sales Act and the Foreign Assistance Act of 1961 as amended. . . . But in doing so, it acknowledges that these laws clearly prescribe a cutoff.[21]

This appeared to be another end run around the letter of the law, giving Kissinger time and room to maneuver although he had no intention of pressuring Turkey. The Mansfield motion, S.J. Res. 247, passed narrowly on October 9, by a vote of 40 to 35.[22] However, the House rejected the Joint Resolution two days later, 187 to 171.[23]

The President and Congress continued to press the embargo issue back and forth during October. On the 14th, Ford vetoed

H.J. Res. 1131 (Fiscal Year 1975 Continuing Resolution on Appropriations), which contained an amendment banning military aid to Turkey until the president certified to Congress that "substantial progress" has been made toward agreement regarding military forces in Cyprus, and that Turkey was in compliance with the Foreign Assistance Act.[24] The next day an attempted override of this veto failed, 223 to 135, falling 16 votes short of the two-thirds needed, and thus requiring a new continuing resolution on appropriations for the fiscal year 1975.[25] The House again passed embargo legislation on the 16th, in the form of a new amendment to H.J. Res. 1163 (Continuing Resolution on Appropriations) calling for a cutoff of military aid to Turkey.[26] On the same day the Senate rejected, by a vote of 40 to 27, the Mansfield Amendment, which would have allowed the President to delay the aid cutoff to Turkey until December 10, 1974. President Ford promptly vetoed the continuing resolution on appropriations for the second time (H.J. Res. 1163 was the second resolution) insisting that such action was detrimental to U.S. national security interests in the Mediterranean and would cause a deterioration of the political situation in Cyprus.[27]

Meanwhile, Kissinger was also being forced to defend himself in the court of public opinion. In a series of editorials in September and October of 1974, the *New York Times* condemned Kissinger's failure to apply the law mandating the immediate cutoff of military aid to Turkey in response to its aggression against Cyprus. Even prior to Kissinger's appearance before the Senate Democratic Caucus on September 19, the *Times* had warned of foot-dragging in the State Department on the embargo question: despite the clarity of America's legal position:

> Cutting off American military aid to Turkey may, as Secretary of State Kissinger contends, be "ineffective and counterproductive" so far as getting the Turks to roll back their occu-

pation of Cyprus is concerned; but it is mandatory under the law. In pretending for nearly a month to be studying this question, the State Department is clearly stalling, as it has stalled at every point since the outset of the Cyprus tragedy when action was called for to demonstrate this country's disapproval of aggression.[28]

The *Times* emphasized public disapproval of the Turkish invasion two days after the House's vote on the DuPont-Rosenthal amendment on September 24: "the overwhelming (307 to 90) approval by the House of a binding cutoff in military aid to Turkey until 'substantial progress' is made toward a Cyprus settlement dramatizes American revulsion against the massive Turkish aggression on the island. The action was also aimed at forcing Administration compliance with laws that mandate such a cutoff. . . ."[29] By October 13, the Administration's intransigence had prompted another blast from the *Times:*

> The virulent White House opposition to efforts by decisive majorities in both houses of Congress to suspend military aid to Turkey has no basis in either law or logic. President Ford's repeated threats to veto a bill requiring such a cutoff can only be seen as an attempt to block Congress from a meaningful role in the shaping of foreign policy and a move to fend off a blow at the prestige of Secretary of State Kissinger. . . . [T]he law is clear and it should be obeyed. Congress should stick to its guns on the military aid issue— veto or no veto.[30]

On October 17, 1974, the House of Representatives, in a vote of 161 to 83, fell just two votes short of overriding the second presidential veto of legislation containing provisions to cutoff aid to Turkey.[31] Following that close vote, the White House called Brademas and Eagleton and agreed to the rule of law arms embargo with a December 10, 1974 cutoff date to facilitate possible negotiations with Turkey. Brademas called me to attend a meeting in his office to discuss the White House's proposal. At the meeting were Congressmen Brademas, Paul Sarbanes, Ed Derwinski, Ben Rosenthal and Dante Fascell, Chairman of the House Foreign Affairs Committee, and Senator Eagleton. We agreed to accept the White House's proposal and we requested, at my initiative, $25 million in humanitarian aid for the Greek Cypriot refugees which the Congress approved.[32]

With that agreement, H.J. Res 1167 passed in the House, 191 to 33, and by voice vote in the Senate. It provided for a cutoff of military aid to Turkey until the president certified to the Congress that Turkey was in compliance with American foreign aid laws and that substantial progress has been made regarding military forces in Cyprus. However, it also contained a provision that postponed the ban on military aid to Turkey until Dec. 10, 1974, unless Turkey violated the Cyprus cease-fire, increased its forces on Cyprus, or transferred any American "implements of war" to that island prior to that date.[33] President Ford signed the bill into Public Law 93-448 the next day.[34] On December 4, the Senate passed the Humphrey amendment to the Foreign Assistance Act of 1974 to delay the cutoff of military aid and sales to Turkey until Feb. 5, 1975.[35]

A week later, the House of Representatives followed suit (by a vote of 297 to 98), passing the DuPont-Rosenthal amendment to the Foreign Assistance Act of 1974. The amendment was the same as the amendment in the continuing resolution on appropriations.[36] Finally, on December 17, 1974, Congress passed the Foreign Assistance Act of 1974 with an amendment requiring the president to suspend all military assistance or sales of defense articles, as well as the issuance of any licenses for transportation of arms, ammunition and implements of war to Turkey. A provision authorized the president to resume assistance if he determined that the government of Turkey is in compliance with the Foreign Assistance Act of 1961, as amended, the Foreign Military Sales Act, and any agreement entered into under such acts, and that substantial progress is made toward an agreement regarding military forces on Cyprus. The amendment was the same as the amendment in the continuing resolution on appropriations. Congress authorized the president to suspend the effective cutoff date until February 5, 1975 if he determined that such suspension could further negotiations for a peaceful solution to the Cyprus conflict. Twenty-five million dollars in humanitarian assistance was authorized for Cyprus.[37] This was signed into law by the President on December 30.[38] Military aid and sales to Turkey had been cutoff—at least for the time being.

The Administration announced on February 5, 1975, the date the rule of law arms embargo legislation went into effect, that it would introduce legislation to overturn it, which it did on February 26, 1975.[39] This action reflected Kissinger's desire to supply arms to Turkey regardless of its acts of aggression. Kissinger had moved quickly again to restrict Congress's role in foreign policy to long-range advice. The move illustrated once more Kissinger's arrogant and irresponsible disdain for the rule of law. In addition, the Administration initiated an amendment to Section 505(d) that removed the mandatory nature of the sanction in the Foreign Assistance Act for misuse of U.S.-supplied defense articles,[40] instead allowing presidential discretion and then a congressional vote if the president refused to act. That amendment weakened the role of Congress in foreign policy.

Cyrus Vance (who was later to become Secretary of State in the Carter Administration) and George Ball testified jointly on July 10, 1975 before the House International Relations Committee[41] against the Administration-backed bill aimed at modifying the embargo that Congress had enacted in the fall of 1974.[42] Ball and Vance believed that Turkey had violated the Foreign Assistance Act and the Foreign Military Sales Act, as well as the bilateral agreement under those Acts. Their testimony included this statement:

> Our one safeguard is that most of these arms are provided under explicit conditions that they will be used only for the purposes for which they are explicitly provided, which are solely for internal security, legitimate self-defense and to permit the recipient country to participate in collective security. . . . But that raises the central question: How can we preserve the credibility of these conditions if we are prepared to ignore them in the case of Turkey in a *highly visible* situation which all the world is watching?
>
> That Turkey used the arms we provided in violation of the relevant American laws and of the express language of the bilateral agreement that governed their transfer is not in dispute. . . . The question now is: Should the Congress wipe out the penalties of violation which, in express terms, would render Turkey ineligible for further American weapons until the Turkish Government takes steps *to purge itself* by some serious move to settle its dispute with Greece and to remove its troops from Cyprus? To do so might dangerously undercut the conditions we have imposed on the use [of] . . . the arms we have provided. . . . Finally, and in many ways this is the most important point, we are seriously concerned that this so-called compromise would create a widespread impression that no nation that has acquired arms from the United States need any longer pay attention to the conditions on which those arms were made available but would be free to use them in pursuit of its own interests in local conflicts.[43]

Expressing deep concern that a precedent was being set for other nations to disregard the conditions of our military assistance, they urged action to reinforce the fundamental principles of our programs, namely, that our arms are to be used for defensive purposes only and not for aggression.[44] They proposed a three-month lifting of the embargo and its reimposition indefinitely if satisfactory progress had not been made to resolve the problem.[45]

After persistent pressure from the Administration, led by Kissinger, Congress partially lifted the embargo on October 2, 1975 for arms paid for and in the pipeline, estimated at $125–150 million. In August 1978, the remaining restrictions were lifted[46] by the Carter Administration, after advice to that effect from long-time presidential advisor Clark Clifford. Carter reneged on his campaign pledges and previously stated policy. Cyrus Vance, by now Secretary of State in the Carter Administration, reluctantly acquiesced and arms once again flowed to Turkey. Was America's position in the world strengthened by this policy? In so far as America's role in the world depends upon moral as well as military force, the nation was weaker.

Anthony Lewis, noted *New York Times* columnist, accurately characterized Kissinger regarding Congress and the rule of law. On July 30, 1973 he wrote:

> The fundamental that Mr. Kissinger has never understood is respect for the institutions of democracy. The foreign policy of which he has been a principal author has operated too often with open contempt for Congress and law.[47]

8

Turkey the Rogue State

Turkey's barbaric invasion of Cyprus is only one example of its troubled, unstable and lawless nature. Its behavior toward international organizations, its neighbors, its own minorities, its journalists and media has also been consistently contrary to the norms of civilized nations. Turkey is a rogue state.

Turkey's violations of United States laws

The Foreign Assistance Act of 1961 as amended,[1] and the Foreign Military Sales Act[2] set forth the purposes, terms and conditions of U.S. military assistance and military sales programs to foreign countries. The U.S.–Turkish bilateral agreement under those acts is designed to make sure that the recipient country understands and agrees to the purposes and conditions that accompany U.S. arms transfers.

The language of both statutes is clear and unambiguous regarding the use of U.S.-supplied arms. The Foreign Assistance Act proclaims the fundamental policy of the United States against aggression and against the use of force except for defensive purposes. The Act states in part:

The Congress of the United States reaffirms the policy of the United States to achieve international peace and security through the United Nations so that armed force shall not be used except for individual or collective self-defense. The Congress hereby finds that the efforts of the United States and other friendly countries to promote peace and security continue to require measures of support based upon the principle of effective self-help and mutual aid. It is the purpose of this part to authorize measures in the common defense against internal and external aggression, including the furnishing of military assistance, upon request, to friendly countries and international organizations.[3]

The provisions of Section 505(d) of the Foreign Assistance Act and Section 3(c) of the Foreign Military Sales Act are similar. Basically, these acts proclaim that U.S. military equipment can only be used for defensive purposes. Any country that violates these acts is "immediately ineligible" for further assistance and arms sales. Section 505(d) of the Foreign Assistance Act provided in 1974 that:

Any country which hereafter uses defense articles or defense services furnished such country under this Act, the Mutual Security Act of 1954, as amended, or any predecessor foreign assistance Act, in substantial violation of the provisions of this chapter (22 U.S.C. 2311 *et seq.*) or any agreements entered into pursuant to any of such Acts shall be *immediately ineligible for further assistance.*[4]

Both laws reiterate this again and again—arms furnished are only for defense and peacekeeping. Section 502 of the Foreign Assistance Act sets forth the purposes for which our assistance can be used:

Defense articles and defense services to any country shall be furnished *solely* for internal security, for legitimate self-defense, to permit the recipient country to participate in regional or collective arrangements or measures consistent with the Charter of the United Nations, or otherwise to permit the recipient country to participate in collective measures requested by the United Nations for the purpose of maintaining or restoring international peace and security. . . .[5]

Subsection 505(a) requires consent of the President for use of defense articles for any other purpose:

In addition to such other provisions as the President may require, no defense articles shall be furnished to any country on a grant basis unless it shall have agreed that - (1) it will not, without the consent of the President. . . . (C) use or permit the use of such articles for purposes other than those for which furnished.[6]

Finally, Section 3(c) of the Foreign Military Sales Act provided:

[A]ny foreign country which hereafter uses defense articles or defense services furnished such country under this Act, in substantial violation of any provision of this Act or any agreement entered into under this Act, shall be immediately ineligible for further cash sales, credits, or guarantees.[7]

The language in these two acts is clear and unequivocal. Violation, including use of arms for offensive purposes, stops the flow of arms—immediately.

The basic facts of Turkey's actions in 1974 are not in dispute. Cyprus is an island separated from Turkey by forty miles of sea. There is no question of a disputed border or border incident. Nevertheless, Turkey transported its troops equipped with U.S.-supplied arms to Cyprus, via ship and air, while its U.S.-supplied planes bombed military and civilian targets in Cyprus using U.S.-supplied bombs. American-supplied arms and equipment were used by Turkey in the initial aggression of July 20,

1974, and the renewed massive aggression on August 14–16, 1974, three weeks after the coup government had collapsed and the legitimate government of Cyprus and the *status quo ante* was restored. Turkey did not use these arms for "internal security," "legitimate self-defense," or "to participate in regional or collective arrangements or measures consistent with the Charter of the United Nations."

Turkey used U.S.-supplied arms for aggressive purposes by invading a sovereign nation. Because Turkey's action did not come within any of the purposes set forth in Section 502 of the Foreign Assistance Act of 1961, Turkey was in violation of that Act, and under Section 505(d) of that Act, was on July 20, 1974 "immediately ineligible for further assistance." Also as a result, under Section 3(c) of the Foreign Military Sales Act, Turkey was "immediately ineligible for further cash sales, credits, or guarantees."[8] There is no legal distinction between the aggression of July 20, 1974 and the renewed aggression of August 14, 1974. Both involved unauthorized use of U.S. military arms and equipment and Turkey is culpable in each instance.

But Turkey's agreements with the United States go beyond the Foreign Assistance Act and the Foreign Military Sales Act, going back in fact to the immediate post-Second World War period and the Truman Doctrine. The Agreement on Aid to Turkey of July 1947 was entered into pursuant to the act of May 22, 1947. This act is a "predecessor foreign assistance act"[9] under Section 505(d) of the Foreign Assistance Act of 1961. Therefore, military assistance to Turkey under the 1947 agreement was subject to the terms of Section 505(d). Violation of the agreement would render Turkey immediately ineligible for further assistance, as would violation of the Act itself.

The 1947 agreement required U.S. consent for any use of military assistance outside the specific purposes for which assistance was given. Thus, U.S. consent was required for Turkish deployment in Cyprus of U.S. military assistance in 1974.[10] The United States and Turkey entered into another agreement by an exchange of notes dated May 16, 1960 and June 16, 1960, in which the United States consented to a Turkish request to use certain American-supplied military assistance program materiel for Turkey's 650-man military force in Cyprus.[11] The agreement clearly established that Turkey cannot use or deploy American military assistance in Cyprus without the formal consent of the United States.[12] Consent was granted, limited to specified types and quantities of defense articles. The U.S. ambassador's note of May 16, 1960 added: "The materiel to be deployed initially to Cyprus has been agreed upon . . . and is listed in the attached schedule and any Military Assistance Program materiel Turkey may subsequently wish to deploy to Cyprus will have to be the subject of a separate request."[13]

As we have seen, the provisions of this act were put to the test in 1964, when Turkey's threat to intervene militarily in Cyprus led to a written response from President Lyndon Johnson to the Turkish prime minister:

> I wish also, Mr. Prime Minister, to call your attention to the bilateral agreement between the United States and Turkey in the field of military assistance. Under Article IV of the Agreement with Turkey of July 1947, your Government is required to obtain United States consent in the use of military assistance for purposes other than those for which assistance was furnished. Your Government has on several occasions acknowledged to the United States that you fully understand this condition. I must tell you in all candor that the United States cannot agree to the use of any U.S.-supplied military equipment for a Turkish intervention in Cyprus, under present circumstances.[14]

It is interesting to note that following this letter, Turkey did not intervene militarily in Cyprus in 1964.

In his legal opinion of the status of the Turkish action in Cyprus in 1974 under U.S. law, the Comptroller General noted

that Turkish use of U.S. military assistance was not provided
for under either the 1947 or 1960 agreements or the Foreign
Assistance Act of 1961.[15] Therefore, he concluded, such use
constituted a diversion of assistance from its intended purpose
for which consent was required prior to deployment.[16] The
fact that consent was neither sought nor granted rendered the
Turkish use of U.S. assistance in Cyprus in violation of the 1947
and 1960 agreements as well as the Foreign Assistance Act of
1961 because its use went beyond that authorized by the 1960
agreement.[17] The violation, believed by the Comptroller General
to be substantial in terms of quantity and purpose, fell clearly
within the scope of the penalty clause of Section 505(d) of the
Foreign Assistance Act.[18]

The illegal Turkish use of U.S. military equipment was
underscored by an advisory legal opinion in 1974 by the
Congressional Research Service, as well as by the public's and
the United Nations' responses to Turkey's aggression. The
Congressional Research Service of the Library of Congress,
in response to an inquiry from Congressman John Brademas
(D-IN), concluded that Section 505(d) of the Foreign Assistance
Act was mandatory in nature and that while "Congress provided
little or no guidance for clearly distinguishing between" defensive and aggressive purposes, "it is not unlikely that Congress
had common sense standards in mind, i.e., general notions
of the differences between offense and defense."[19] Turkey's
aggressive actions were "highly visible," as George Ball and
Cyrus Vance stated in their testimony, and fully reported in the
media to the world community.

Additional support for the proposition that Turkey's use of
force in Cyprus was illegal came from United Nations Security
Council resolutions such as those passed on July 20, 1974,
the day of Turkey's initial aggression against Cyprus, and on
August 14, 1974, the date of the second and massive phase of
Turkey's aggression, calling for the recognition of the sovereignty, independence and territorial integrity of Cyprus and for

the immediate withdrawal of all foreign troops not authorized by international treaty. Although these resolutions deal with the UN Charter and not U.S. laws, they do pertain to the question of the illegal use of force.

The violations by Turkey of U.S. laws were clear, blatant and "highly visible." The problem that needs to be addressed is how to enforce our laws in the realm of foreign affairs as efficaciously as we do in domestic matters.

Turkey's violations of international laws

A fundamental purpose of the UN Charter is to keep the peace and to prevent aggression: that is, to settle problems peacefully. The preamble of the UN Charter states in part that the basic aims of the organization are:

> to reaffirm faith in fundamental human rights, in the dignity and worth of the human person, in the equal rights of men and women and of nations large and small, and to establish conditions under which justice and respect for the obligations arising from treaties and other sources of international law can be maintained, and . . . to ensure, by the acceptance of principles and the institution of methods, that armed force shall not be used, save in the common interest.

Paragraph 1 of article 1 on the purposes of the UN Charter states that one purpose is:

> (1) To maintain international peace and security, and to that end: to take effective collective measures for the prevention and removal of threats to the peace, and for the suppression of acts of aggression . . . and to bring about by peaceful means, and in conformity with the principles of justice and international law, adjustment or settlement of international

disputes or situations which might lead to a breach of the peace . . .

Article 2, paragraphs 3 and 4 of the Charter, which set forth the principles to be acted upon to achieve the purposes proclaimed in article 1, state:

(3) All Members shall settle their international disputes by peaceful means in such a manner that international peace and security, and justice, are not endangered.

(4) All Members shall refrain in their international relations from the threat or use of force against the territorial integrity or political independence of any state, or in any other manner inconsistent with the Purposes of the United Nations.

Article 51 of the Charter deals with individual and collective self-defense and states in part:

Nothing in the present Charter shall impair the inherent right of individual or collective self-defense if an armed attack occurs against a Member of the United Nations, until the Security Council has taken measures necessary to maintain international peace and security.

Turkey's use of military force to invade and occupy a large part of Cyprus directly violated the plain meaning of these provisions of the UN Charter, especially the sections that call for peaceful methods of dispute resolution without resort to the use of force. Turkey's actions could not be interpreted as individual self-defense under article 51 since, of course, Turkey was not attacked, nor was she under threat of attack. Similarly, collective self-defense was inapplicable. Furthermore, the principle of self-defense does not allow for defense of foreign nationals. The Turkish Cypriots were and are citizens of Cyprus and Turkey cannot legally justify the invasion on the grounds of protecting them.

Similarly, article 53 of the Charter, which permits the Security Council to use regional arrangements for enforcement action, is not available to Turkey. Even if the London–Zurich Agreements among Britain, Greece and Turkey were to be considered a regional arrangement, article 53 states that "no enforcement action shall be taken under regional arrangements or by regional agencies without the authorization of the Security Council." Turkey, of course, never attempted to obtain such authorization for its actions in Cyprus, and continues to this day to be in violation of the UN Charter, whose key precepts are universally accepted as preemptory legal norms. In 1980, Sir David Hunt, former British High Commissioner in Cyprus, formulated Turkey's rogue action in no uncertain terms:

> But the rule of law, as both philosophers and practical states-men agree, can only be established when there are institutions to formulate it and maintain it. Almost as essential is for it to be universally recognized. These conditions have now prevailed for thirty-five years. The basis of international law is formulated in the Charter of the United Nations; and the same document provides for the organs to enforce it. All the sovereign nations of the world have voluntarily undertaken to observe the obligations which the Charter lays on them: that disputes are to be settled by peaceful means; that members undertake not to use force or the threat of force in contravention of the purposes of the United Nations; and that each member must assist the organisation in any action it takes under the Charter.
>
> * * * *
>
> [T]here is a rule of law in the world and the guarantee of it is the United Nations. Applying these principles to the case of Cyprus it is clear and undeniable that the government of Turkey, by invading with military force the territory of the Republic of Cyprus, is in open and deliberate breach of the Charter.[20]

There is not the slightest question that Turkey abrogated international law and acted in direct contradiction to the UN Charter, a document to which it had promised adherence. The only question, as ever with the United Nations, was: could, or would, the international community actually enforce its dictates?

The United Nations Security Council and General Assembly passed a number of resolutions following Turkey's invasion of Cyprus. In summation, the resolutions called upon all states to respect the sovereignty, independence, and territorial integrity of Cyprus, demanded an immediate end to foreign intervention, and requested that foreign military forces withdraw without delay.[21] The resolutions are either explicitly or implicitly premised on the judgment of the Security Council and General Assembly that Turkey is in violation of the UN Charter.

The 1964 crisis on Cyprus, which was partially defused, as we have seen, by Lyndon Johnson's stern letter to the Turkish Prime Minister, prompted action from the UN Security Council. Since 1964, more than 120 UN Security Council resolutions involving Cyprus have been passed dealing with substantive matters and with periodic extensions of the United Nations Peace-Keeping Force. During the crisis in 1964, two resolutions were particularly important: Resolution 186 (March 4, 1964) and Resolution 193 (August 9, 1964). The first of the two was passed on March 4, 1964, two-and-a-half months after the intercommunal fighting started. It referred to the relevant provisions of the Charter, quoted in full article 2, paragraph 4 that proscribes the "threat or use of force," and recommended the creation of a United Nations Peace-Keeping Force in Cyprus and the designation of a mediator.[22] A United Nations Force was created, which became operational on March 27, 1964, and a mediator was appointed. Resolution 193, passed five months later, reiterated the "urgent appeal to the Government of Turkey to cease instantly the bombardment of and the use of military force of any kind against Cyprus, and to the Government of Cyprus to order the armed forces under its control to cease firing immediately. . . ." and called for an "immediate cease-fire by all concerned."[23]

Security Council action continued following Turkey's invasion in 1974. Resolution 353,[24] adopted July 20, 1974, the day of Turkey's invasion, called "upon all states to respect the sovereignty, independence and territorial integrity of Cyprus," called for a ceasefire, demanded "an immediate end to foreign military intervention" in Cyprus and requested "the withdrawal without delay . . . of foreign military personnel" except those present under international agreement. Resolution 354 (July 23, 1974) demanded immediate compliance with Security Council Resolution 353, paragraph 2, which called for a cease-fire; Resolution 357 (August 14, 1974) deplored the resumption of Turkey's military action, once again demanded a cease-fire and called for resumption of negotiations; Resolution 358 (August 15, 1974) deplored the noncompliance with Resolution 357 and "insist[ed] on the full implementation" of its resolutions 353, 354 and 357 "with the immediate and strict observance of the cease-fire." Resolution 359 (August 15, 1974) discussed casualties in the United Nations Peace-Keeping Force in Cyprus; Resolution 360 (August 16, 1974) in which the Security Council "recorded its formal disapproval of the unilateral military actions" by Turkey against Cyprus and urged compliance with previous resolutions "including those concerning the withdrawal without delay . . . of foreign military personnel" except those present under international agreements; finally, Resolution 361 (August 30, 1974) covered "the plight of the refugees," urging "appropriate measures to provide for their relief and welfare and to permit persons who wish to do so to return to their homes in safety," and noting that the United Nations High Commissioner has already been appointed as Coordinator of United Nations Humanitarian Assistance for Cyprus. Turkey continued its invasion and occupation despite these Security Council Resolutions.

The General Assembly of the United Nations added its voice in the late fall, as the situation on Cyprus continued without change. General Assembly Resolution 3212[25] was unanimously passed on November 1, 1974. Among other things, Resolution 3212 "[c]all[ed] upon all states to respect the sovereignty, independence, territorial integrity and non-alignment of . . . Cyprus" and "[u]rge[d] the speedy withdrawal of all foreign armed forces and foreign military presence and personnel from. . . Cyprus, and the cessation of all foreign interference in its affairs." The Security Council endorsed General Assembly Resolution 3212 by Security Council Resolution 365 of December 13, 1974, calling on "the parties concerned to implement [Resolution 3212] as soon as possible" in the "Question of Cyprus." Again, these Resolutions were ignored by Turkey. To date, Turkey has failed to comply with any of these United Nations Security Council and General Assembly resolutions and continues to violate them.[26]

The North Atlantic Treaty Organization (NATO) is a regional alliance created under article 52 of the UN Charter for collective defense against aggression under article 51 of the Charter. The fundamental principles, objectives and purposes of the North Atlantic Treaty are to deter aggression and to support democratic government. According to the preamble and article 1 of the treaty:

> The Parties . . . reaffirm their faith in the purposes and principles of the Charter of the United Nations. . . They are determined to safeguard the freedom, common heritage and civilisation of their peoples, founded on the principles of democracy, individual liberty and the rule of law . . . The Parties undertake, as set forth in the Charter of the United Nations, to settle any international dispute in which they may be involved by peaceful means in such a manner that international peace and security and justice are not endangered, and to refrain in their international relations from the threat or use of force in any manner inconsistent with the purposes of the United Nations.

As is readily apparent, the NATO treaty explicitly reinforces the dictates of international law laid down by the UN Charter. Turkey not only ignored the latter, but, as a signatory to NATO, violated the former treaty by failing "to settle" the Cyprus problem "by peaceful means in such a manner that international peace and security and justice are not endangered" and by her "use of force . . . inconsistent with the purposes of the United Nations." Turkey rejected the spirit of these international agreements: the fundamental policies against aggression and in support of "democracy, individual liberty and the rule of law" set forth in the preamble and underlying the North Atlantic Treaty. In its naked grab for political and economic power on Cyprus, it also violated the letter of these agreements to which it was a signatory. Although some may argue that the North Atlantic Treaty applies to aggression against a member country only and not to aggression by a NATO member against a third party non-member, this interpretation is inconsistent with the plain meaning and the purpose of the North Atlantic Treaty. Article 1 prohibits the use of force in "any international dispute." But the question remained: would anyone hold Turkey's feet to the fire?

At a minimum, NATO should have suspended Turkey until its aggression in Cyprus had been "purged." "Purged" is the word used by George Ball and Cyrus Vance in their testimony to Congress on July 10, 1975.[27] Instead, NATO assisted in supplying arms to Turkey after Congress enacted the rule of law arms embargo in 1974. NATO Secretary General Joseph Luns met with Turkish officials to discuss their defense requirements following the U.S. arms embargo. Luns said that West German arms had begun to compensate for the cutoff in American supplies. Luns stated: "I assure you and your government that an important number of NATO countries have undertaken to meet the arms shortage which was the result of Congress' decision."[28]

Furthermore, NATO's Secretary General Joseph Luns joined the Administration's lobbying effort to persuade the Congress to lift the embargo against Turkey. In Washington, D.C., Luns "expressed his concern about Turkey's disaffection with the United States as the result of the arms cutoff."[29] Luns was in Washington, D.C. and met with President Ford when Congress was considering the repeal of the embargo.[30] Although Turkey continues to violate the North Atlantic Treaty by its presence in Cyprus, NATO has ignored the transgression. Turkey's aggression against Cyprus is a stain on NATO's history and honor and will remain until Turkey ends its illegal occupation of Cyprus.

Turkey's aggression against Cyprus

Here are the bare facts. Turkey invaded Cyprus on July 20, 1974, and resumed its aggression with offensive operations between August 14 and 16. Turkey seized 37.3 percent of the territory of Cyprus in this period. Its troops, in excess of forty thousand of them, used American-supplied arms in violation of U.S. laws and agreements under those laws. Turkey also violated the UN Charter preamble and article 2 paragraph 4 and the North Atlantic Treaty preamble and article 1, against "the threat or use of force," customary international law, and the London-Zurich Agreements of 1959–1960, including the Treaty of Guarantee and the Treaty of Establishment. Turkey violated more laws in its aggression against Cyprus than Iraq did in its invasion of Kuwait in 1990. How does Turkey justify its blatant aggression?

Turkey has stated she had the right to invade Cyprus under article IV of the Treaty of Guarantee,[31] one of the three treaties under the London-Zurich Agreements of 1959-1960. Before discussing the validity of Turkey's contention, it is important to note that the U.S. Foreign Assistance Act and the Foreign Military Sales Act make no exception for, and are not subject to, the provisions of the Treaty of Guarantee. Whether or not Turkey had the right to use force in Cyprus under article IV of the Treaty of Guarantee, Turkey nevertheless violated U.S. laws and the bilateral agreements under those laws in its aggression against Cyprus with the illegal use of U.S.-supplied arms and equipment. Similarly, the UN Charter and the North Atlantic Treaty do not permit an exception for the Treaty of Guarantee.

The 1959-1960 London-Zurich Agreements comprise three treaties: (1) the Treaty of Establishment between Britain and Cyprus that transferred sovereignty over the island from the United Kingdom to Cyprus itself, except for ninety-nine square miles retained by Britain to be used for military purposes (known as The Sovereign Base Areas); (2) the Treaty of Alliance among Cyprus, Greece and Turkey, which established a tripartite headquarters and authorized the presence of 950 Greek troops and 650 Turkish troops on Cyprus; and (3) the Treaty of Guarantee among Britain, Greece, and Turkey, which banned both union with Greece and partition.

Article IV, the final article of the Treaty of Guarantee, is the article relied on by the Turkish government to justify its use of force and invasion of Cyprus. It reads:

> In the event of a breach of the provisions of the present Treaty, Greece, Turkey and the United Kingdom undertake to consult together with respect to the representations or measures necessary to ensure observance of those provisions.
>
> Insofar as common or concerted action may not prove possible, each of the three guaranteeing Powers reserves the right to take action with the sole aim of re-establishing the state of affairs created by the present Treaty.[32]

According to Sir David Hunt, Britain's High Commissioner in Cyprus from 1965 to 1966, the second sentence was added at the insistence of Turkey.[33]

It might seem immediately evident to the reader that this clause seems rather weak as a rationale for Turkey's aggression. Indeed, not only did the London-Zurich Agreements not authorize Turkey's use of armed force to invade Cyprus, but, as

I will show, the Treaty of Guarantee, on its face, indicts Turkey. Turkey's argument that the Treaty of Guarantee, and in particular article IV, gave her the right to intervene in Cyprus with the use of armed force is untenable for a number of reasons. The first is contained in the language of the clause: Article IV of the Treaty of Guaranty did not authorize "armed force" when it authorized "action." There is no mention of the words "armed force" or the word "force" in the Treaty.

Second, when Cyprus became a member of the United Nations in 1960, all provisions of the London-Zurich Agreements in conflict with or inconsistent with the Charter of the United Nations became null and void pursuant to article 103 of the UN Charter. Article 103 states: "In the event of a conflict between the obligations of the Members of the United Nations under the present Charter and their obligations under any other international agreement, their obligations under the present Charter shall prevail." Even if an interpretation of Article IV of the Treaty of Guarantee could be made to justify the use of armed force, this interpretation would be in conflict with, and inconsistent with, article 103 of the UN Charter and, consequently, would be void *ab initio*.

Article 2(4) of the UN Charter states that member states "shall refrain. . . from the threat or use of force." Article 51 of the Charter authorizes the use of force for purposes of self-defense only; Turkey cannot avail herself of this article since she was not attacked nor was she threatened with attack. Additionally, while the use of force is permitted under the Charter in Article 53 in the chapter on Regional Arrangements, Article 53 is also not available to Turkey since the Treaty of Guarantee is not a regional arrangement as specified under this article. Even if the Treaty of Guarantee is considered a regional arrangement, article 53 states that "no enforcement action shall be taken under regional arrangements . . . without the authorization of the Security Council."

Professor R. St. J. Macdonald concludes that Article IV "to the extent that it purports to authorize the use of armed force, is inconsistent" with the UN Charter and void.[34] His analysis deserves to be quoted at length:

I thus reach the following conclusions: that obligations imposed by Article 2(4) have not been discharged on the basis of frustration, that by virtue of Article 103, Charter obligations prevail over treaty rights as well as treaty obligations, and that for one obligation to prevail over another inconsistent obligation is for it to render the latter invalid or void. Therefore, subject to what is said below on Article 51, Article 4 of the Treaty of Guarantee, to the extent that it purports to authorize the use of armed force, is inconsistent with Article 2(4) of the Charter and does not fall within the Article 53 exception. Even if the 1974 invasion was in compliance with Article 4, such compliance was not sufficient to render it legal.[35]

* * * *

Conclusion On The Legality Of The Turkish Invasion: On the basis of the following reasoning, I conclude that the 1974 invasion of Cyprus was in contravention of international law: for an invasion to be legal, it must be consistent with the provisions of the United Nations Charter, whether express or implied; compliance with a treaty, on its own, is insufficient to render an invasion consistent with Article 2(4) of the Charter; the 1974 invasion was not in compliance with Article 53 of the Charter on regional arrangements, as it is doubtful that a regional arrangement was in being, and, in any event, prior authorization of the Security Council was not obtained for an enforcement action; there is no implied exception to Article 2(4) in regard to quasi-regional arrangements according to which enforcement action may be taken until the Security Council states otherwise; there is no implied exception to Article 2(4) in regard to the right to protect "legitimate interests;" that is, no implied right of self-help; the invasion was not in compliance with Article 51 on individual self-defense, as there was no armed attack on Turkey; if the customary right of anticipatory self-defense or the right to protect nationals are implied exceptions to Article 2(4), the factual requirements for the exercise of such rights were not satisfied; the invasion was not in compliance with Article 51 on collective self-defense as the Republic of Cyprus did not request Turkish aid; if there are implied exceptions to Article 2(4) in regard to the right of humanitarian intervention or the right to aid a people to achieve self-determination, they are not appropriate rights to invoke to justify the 1974 invasion, which was prompted not by international strife but by the Greek *coup d'état*. In reaching the conclusion that the 1974 invasion contravened international law, it should be emphasized that reliance has been placed on the provisions of the Charter rather than on any specific resolutions of the General Assembly or the Security Council.[36]

Sir David Hunt also takes the position that the language and provisions of the Charter prevail over the Treaty of Guaranty. He said:

There is, however, a more fundamental objection to be brought against the Turkish thesis than an argument based on the wording of this one particular article and its interpretation. This is that the Treaty of Guarantee lacks all legal validity.

[T]his argument . . . rests on the principle that the obligations which all nations have accepted voluntarily on their accession to the United Nations are superior to all other obligations. Where there are conflicts between them the Charter is a *Jus Cogens*, laying down peremptory norms of international law from which no derogation is permitted.

* * * *

There is therefore no escape from the two-pronged argument: first that Article 4 of the Treaty of Guarantee did not authorize the use of force; secondly that if force was sanctioned under that article, then the Treaty was void *ab initio* as inconsistent with the Charter.[37]

The legal conclusion is clear. Turkey's argument that Article IV of the Treaty of Guarantee authorizes force is false. And even if that Article had authorized force, it was void in any case because of Turkey's UN membership.

The third reason Turkey had no right to intervene with force on Cyprus was that, on its face, the Treaty of Guarantee only authorized action to restore the *status quo ante.* Article IV states that the right to take action is for "the sole aim of re-establishing the state of affairs created by the present Treaty." Throughout the past forty years, Turkey has demonstrated that she never had any such intention. As Hunt states:

> The parties announced that they reserve the right to take action. The nature of the action is undefined—there is certainly no reference to the use of force—but its purpose is defined, in restrictive terms, as having the sole aim of re-establishing the state of affairs created by the treaty. But neither in 1974 nor at any time since have the Turkish government either professed or practised this aim. They have on the contrary presented as their aim a form of settlement wholly contrary to the one defined in the treaty, and specifically excluded by it: territorial partition and the creation of a separate Turkish-Cypriot state.[38]

It should be noted that American diplomats, despite Henry Kissinger, were not averse to supporting this conclusion: Taylor G. Belcher, a former U.S. ambassador to Cyprus, concurred in this view.[39] Turkey's actual goal was made clear during the

crisis: on August 13, 1974, three weeks after the legitimate government of Cyprus had been reinstated, Turkey issued a thir-
ty-six hour ultimatum to Greece and Britain to accept Turkey's
proposal for six separate Turkish Cypriot "cantons" covering a
third of Cyprus. The proposal was not aimed at "re-establishing
the state of affairs created by the treaty," but was tantamount to
partition, which was barred by the Treaty of Guarantee.

The fourth reason Turkey's use of force was unjustified
was that it acted unilaterally, in violation of the terms of the
Treaty of Guarantee. Although Turkey apparently consulted
with Britain, Turkey did not consult with Greece and therefore
did not meet the requirements of article IV.[40] Fifth, the United
Nations had already preempted such aggressive action ten years
earlier. The Security Council passed Resolution 186 on March
4, 1964, following the outbreak of intercommunal fighting in
December 1963. Resolution 186 led to the creation of a United
Nations Peace-Keeping Force in Cyprus[41] and the designation
of a mediator. Nevertheless, Turkey bombed northern Cyprus
in August 1964.[42] The Security Council then authorized the
Secretary-General "to make an appeal to the Government of
Turkey to cease instantly the bombardment of and the use of
military force of any kind against Cyprus. . . . "[43]

Sixth, the Treaty of Alliance only allowed Turkey a force
of 650 on Cyprus. This was certainly a far cry from an aggressive invasion force of more than forty thousand, armed with
American weapons.

The seventh reason Turkey's interpretation of Article IV
of the Treaty of Guarantee was (and still is) unjustified will be
familiar to legal scholars. A normal rule of statutory interpretation is to choose the interpretation which preserves the legality
of the statute. Since the use of force by United Nations member
states to settle disputes is so clearly contrary to the Charter, it
is reasonable to assume that the parties did not mean to put an
interpretation on the word "action" in the treaty contrary to a
fundamental purpose of the Charter.

Thus we see that Turkey's interpretation of the Treaty of Guarantee is false in a number of different ways. These reasons alone should be enough to force Turkey to a Cypriot rapprochement. But what is even more damning is Turkey's record of human rights violations and cultural destruction during the forty years of the forced partition of Cyprus. Let us turn next to these offenses.

We have seen that the forced colonization of Cypriot territory by Turkish migrants was one of Turkey's aims during its 1974 invasion. Therefore, Turkey has been and remains in violation of the Geneva Convention of 1949, Section III, article 49, which prohibits colonization by an occupying power. Generally, Section III of the convention deals with Occupied Territories. Article 49 states in its last paragraph: "The Occupying Power shall not deport or transfer parts of its own civilian population into the territory it occupies." Turkey has brought an estimated 200,000 illegal settlers/colonists from Anatolia to Cyprus in an attempt to change the demographics of Cyprus. The Turkish Cypriot newspaper *Yeniduzen* reported on February 14, 1990, that of the 160,000 persons who live in the occupied area, 80,000 are Turkish Cypriots and 80,000 are settlers from Turkey. The *Guardian*, in a report on October 13, 1975, on the migration of Turks to the occupied part of Cyprus, listed the rate of migration as 1,500 to 2,500 a month and asserted that the plan was "to implant as many as 80,000" settlers.[44] Currently, the government of Cyprus has estimated the number of illegal colonists at 200,000. The Turkish Cypriots have been a minority in the occupied north for many years. Over 30,000 Turkish Cypriots have gotten passports from the government of Cyprus and emigrated to other countries in the EU, particularly Britain, leaving only about 80,000 Turkish Cypriots in the occupied north.

It is not only the Geneva Convention under which Turkey has committed human rights violations on Cyprus, however. Human rights considerations have become an integral part of U.S. foreign policy and are clearly set forth in our military assistance and military sales statutes. Section 116 of the Foreign Assistance Act has been in effect since 1975.[45] While this provision, and Section 502B of the Foreign Assistance Act were not in force at the time of Turkey's aggression against Cyprus in 1974, their terms apply to the continuing occupation of Cyprus, the continuing detention of persons, the continuing forcible seizure and use of Greek Cypriot and Greek American homes and property, the continuing prevention by armed force of the return of people to their homes and property, the deprivation of freedom of movement, and other violations. Section 116 states that no assistance may be provided:

> to the government of any country which engages in a consistent pattern of gross violations of internationally recognized human rights, including torture or cruel, inhuman, or degrading treatment or punishment, prolonged detention without charges, causing the disappearance of persons by the abduction and clandestine detention of those persons, or other flagrant denial of the right to life, liberty, and the security of persons, unless such assistance will directly benefit the needy people in such country.[46]

Even tougher parallel provisions relate to military assistance. Section 502B(a)(1) of the Foreign Assistance Act makes human rights an integral part of all U.S. foreign policy. It provides that:

> (1) The United States shall, in accordance with its international obligations as set forth in the Charter of the United Nations and in keeping with the constitutional heritage and traditions of the United States, promote and encourage increased respect for human rights and fundamental freedoms throughout the world without distinction as to race, sex, language, or religion. Accordingly, a principal goal of the foreign policy of the United States shall be to promote the

increased observance of internationally recognized human rights by all countries.[47]

(2) Except under circumstances specified in this section, no security assistance may be provided to any country the government of which engages in a consistent pattern of gross violations of internationally recognized human rights. . . .[48]

In concrete terms, the President:

is directed to formulate and conduct military assistance programs. . . . in a manner which will promote and advance human rights. These programs are also designed to avoid identification of the United States with governments which deny to their people internationally recognized human rights and fundamental freedoms, in violation of international law or in contravention of the policy of the United States as expressed in Section 502B(a)(1) or otherwise.[49]

The law prohibits security assistance to a country and to the "police, domestic intelligence, or similar law enforcement forces of a country," as well as the export of crime control and detection instruments and equipment to a country "the government of which engages in a consistent pattern of gross violations of internationally recognized human rights," unless the President certifies that "extraordinary circumstances" warrant otherwise.[50]

By its actions in Cyprus, Turkey was and is in clear and incontrovertible violation of Section 116 of the Foreign Assistance Act. Turkey has engaged and continues to engage "in a consistent pattern of gross violations of internationally recognized human rights." Similarly, Turkey's actions in Cyprus make her ineligible under Section 502B(a)(1) of the Act which provides that "no security assistance may be provided to any country the government of which engages in a consistent pattern of gross violations of internationally recognized human rights." A list of Turkey's human rights violations in Cyprus includes:

1. the abduction, clandestine detention without charges and murder of five American citizens;[51]
2. the abduction and prolonged and clandestine detention without charges of 1495 Greek Cypriots (the period of detention is now over forty years);
3. the taking by force of over 35,000 thousand Greek Cypriot homes and property in the occupied north of Cyprus (most of these homes have been taken for a period of over forty years);
4. the prevention by armed force of the return of the Greek Cypriots to their homes and lands in safety in the occupied north;
5. the giving or selling of these Greek Cypriot homes and lands to the illegal Turkish settlers, occupation forces and Turkish Cypriots in the occupied north of Cyprus;[52]
6. the illegal use on a continuing basis by the illegal Turkish occupation forces, the Turkish settlers/colonists and Turkish Cypriots of Greek Cypriot homes and property in the occupied north of Cyprus;
7. the illegal selling of these Greek Cypriot homes and lands to British and other foreign persons and entities; and,
8. the illegal taking of property owned by United States citizens and the illegal use on a continuing basis of such property by the illegal Turkish occupation forces, the illegal Turkish settlers/colonists, and Turkish Cypriots.

Military grant aid to Turkey was finally halted in the early 1990s, and economic grant aid was halted in the mid-1990s after an all-night debate and vote at 5:00 a.m. in the House. As the purported goal of U.S. foreign policy is to promote human rights, Turkey's offenses against Greek Cypriots and continued occupation of Cyprus should not and must not be ignored. The United States should consider removing all economic and commercial benefits Turkey enjoys, including textile quotas and most favored nation treatment until Turkey removes all of its troops and settlers/colonists from Cyprus and is in full compliance with unanimous General Assembly Resolution 3212 of November 1, 1974 and other UN resolutions.

On the transnational level, the regional European Convention for the Protection of Human Rights and Fundamental Freedoms (European Convention on Human Rights (ECHR) is, by the terms of its preamble, an extension of the UN Universal Declaration of Human Rights of 1948. The UN Charter stipulates legal obligations on the part of its members to "promote. . . . universal respect for and observance of human rights. . . ."[53] The United Nations Universal Declaration of Human Rights of 1948 defines the term "human rights and fundamental freedoms."[54] Its provisions have been duplicated or amplified in subsequent international instruments, including the European Convention on Human Rights, which explicitly acknowledges the Universal Declaration as the matrix of principles of human rights. Consequently, when Turkey violates provisions of the European Convention, it also violates comparable provisions of the Universal Declaration of Human Rights and the United Nations mandate on human rights.

The government of Cyprus filed four applications to the European Commission on Human Rights. The first application to the Commission, No. 6780/74, was filed on September 17, 1974; the second application, No. 6950/75, was filed on March 21, 1975; the third, No. 8007/77 in 1977; and the fourth, No. 25781/94 on November 22, 1994.

The Commission issued its report on the charges made in the first two applications on July 10, 1976. The report was not officially published until January 20, 1979, after it had been considered by the Committee of Ministers of the Council of Europe. The report clearly established that Turkey committed war crimes and crimes against humanity. In the report, the Commission found Turkey guilty of violating the following articles of the European Convention on Human Rights:

(1) Article 2—by the killing of innocent civilians committed on a substantial scale;[55]
(2) Article 3—by the rape of women of all ages from 12 to 71;[56]
(3) Article 3—by inhuman treatment of prisoners and persons detained—a continuing violation;[57]
(4) Article 5—by deprivation of liberty with regard to detainees and missing persons—a continuing violation;[58]
(5) Article 8—by displacement of persons creating more than 170,000 Greek Cypriot refugees, and by refusing to allow the refugees to return to their homes—a continuing violation;[59]
(6) Article 1 of the First Protocol to the Convention—by deprivation of possessions, a continuing violation, looting and robbery on an extensive scale.[60]

On January 23, 1977, the London *Sunday Times* published excerpts of the report and stated: "It amounts to a massive indictment of the Ankara government for the murder, rape and looting by its army in Cyprus during and after the Turkish invasion of summer 1974."[61] There is no statute of limitations on war crimes and crimes against humanity. Turkey's civilian and military personnel involved in these crimes during the 1974 invasion should be brought before the International Criminal Court.

Turkish depredations were rampant during the invasion itself, and have continued in the years since. For example, Turkey's armed forces have ethnically cleansed 200,000 Greek Cypriots from the occupied north by forcing them from their homes and properties: 180,000 in the initial days of aggression in July and August 1974 and 20,000 in the ensuing years, creating 200,000 refugees in their own country. And apart from such ethnic cleansing, Turkey is also responsible for the "cultural

cleansing" of the occupied north of its Hellenic and Christian heritage and presence, as well as the important cultural presences of
its Armenian, Maronite, and Jewish minority communities.

The destruction, desecration, looting and pillaging by
Turkey's armed forces is set forth in the July 10, 1976 report
of the European Commission on Human Rights. It began with
the arrival of the Turkish armed forces on July 20, 1974 and
was extensive in the early years of the occupation as set forth
in the Commission's report. In the years since, such acts have
not stopped. Turkey's armed forces, the Turkish Cypriots, and
Turkish settlers and colonists from Anatolia have continued
over the forty years since Turkey's aggression and land grab to
desecrate the cultural heritage of Cyprus.[62]

Political scientist Michael Jansen has characterized Turkish
ethnic cleansing and "theft of the island's rich cultural heritage"
as occurring in three phases, beginning "as soon as Turkish
soldiers stormed ashore on July 20th, 1974":

> During the first [phase] . . . archeological sites, museums,
> churches, monasteries, castles, libraries and private collec-
> tions were robbed and vandalized, sometimes at random
> by rampaging soldiers, sometimes by professional art and
> antiquities thieves belonging to a well-organized network on
> the island. . . . Looters who culled artifacts from archaeolog-
> ical sites not only diminished their value by 80 percent by
> removing them from their historical and geographical con-
> text but also destroyed sites they plundered. . . . During the
> second phase, . . . Turkish Cypriot smugglers systematically
> targeted specific treasures. These were shipped to the lead-
> ing wholesaler of Cypriot loot, Aydin Dikmen in Munich. . . .
> During the third, ongoing phase . . . looting has continued
> from unexplored sites.

To Jansen, the cultural heritage of Cyprus is in danger because
of this plundering—as well as the "illegal excavations, dissolu-

tion by neglect and destruction by developers" in the Turkish-controlled north. The consequences are severe:

> Sixteen thousand icons, mosaics and frescoes and 60,000 ancient artifacts have been torn from their contexts, smuggled, hoarded by dealers, consigned for sale to auction houses, and sold to museums and private collectors. While looting generally accompanies warfare and unrest in countries with rich heritages, the case of Cyprus is particularly dramatic because it is confined to a small, well defined geographical area. . . . In the Turkish occupied north, both Christian and ancient sites have been mercilessly plundered and scholarly investigation has been disrupted. Meanwhile in the government-controlled south, sites have been largely preserved and scholars have been at work uncovering the distant past, pushing back the history of the island by 3,000 years. . . . In 1974, archaeologists spoke of Cyprus as having 9,000 years of history but scholarly exploration over the past three decades revealed that Cyprus has, at least, 12,000 years of history.[63]

A "Report for Congress" in April 2009 titled *"Cyprus—Destruction of Cultural Property in the Northern Part of Cyprus and Violations of International Law"*[64] reinforces Jansen's claims. The report, prepared by Theresa Papademetriou, Esq., Senior Foreign Law Specialist in the Law Library of Congress, refers to a number of sources that confirm the destruction, desecration and pillaging of cultural property. This includes churches, mainly Greek Orthodox but also Armenian churches, Maronite Catholic churches, and Jewish synagogues.[65] The list, in part, is as follows:

- 500 Greek Orthodox Churches and chapels have been pillaged, vandalized or demolished;
- The whereabouts of 15,000 paintings are unknown; and

- 77 churches have been turned into mosques, 28 are being used by the Turkish military forces as hospitals or camps and 13 are used as agricultural barns.[66]

In this report and in remarks at the 50th anniversary commemoration of the independence of Cyprus, Ms. Papademetriou presents a damning overview of the cultural damage and of the legal framework regarding cultural property, which includes religious and archeological property in Cyprus. It is a devastating report.

Turkey, the neighborhood bully

Turkey's brutalization of Cyprus is not an isolated case, but part of a pattern. The Turkish government has a history of human rights violations and is a destabilizing force in the region. These tendencies have led to some degree of cooling in the relationship between the United States and Turkey, surely much to the chagrin of Henry Kissinger, who wanted nothing more than to be in bed with the Anatolian power. But this cooling is not difficult to understand intuitively, given Turkey's treatment of its own people and cultures.

Turkey has a substantial Kurdish minority, which makes up twenty percent of its population. Residing primarily in eastern and southeastern Turkey, these fifteen million Kurds do not have full political, civil, or human rights. Eric Rouleau, former French ambassador to Turkey, details Turkey's horrendous treatment of its Kurdish minority. In its battle against Kurdish separatists, the Turkish military believes it has *carte blanche* to ignore international law: the army's Deputy Chief of Staff has said that the army refused to "be bound hand and foot by democracy and human rights." As a result, according to Rouleau, "individuals who advocate conciliation, including parliamentarians of Kurdish origin, have been imprisoned by the hundreds. . . . Torture has become widespread, and disappearances and assassinations of lawyers, journalists, politicians, and business executives suspected of sympathizing with the rebels have multiplied."[67] Yet the State Department lists the PKK, the main separatist Kurdish organization, as a terrorist group. While the PKK is not blameless in this internecine warfare, it is in reality a rebel/guerrilla organization fighting for the freedom of the Kurds, not a terrorist group. Responsible media, including the Associated Press and the *New York Times*, recognize this, using the terms "rebel" or "guerilla" to describe the PKK.

Turkey's attitude towards its religious minorities is even more indefensible. The country is currently listed as a major violator of religious freedom by the United States Commission on International Religious Freedom (USCIRF), a U.S. government agency that monitors religious freedom worldwide. In its 2012 annual report, the USCIRF recommended Turkey be designated as a "Country of Particular Concern" (CPC). Previously on the USCIRF Watch List, Turkey was placed on the most serious list of religious freedom violators, the Country of Particular Concern list. The new designation was recommended "due to the Turkish government's systematic and egregious limitations on the freedom of religion or belief that affects all religious communities in Turkey, and particularly threaten the country's Non-Muslim religious minorities." The Commission reversed the designation in 2013. It has been criticized for so doing.

Religious persecution directed against Eastern Orthodox Christians is just one example among many, albeit a highly visible and disturbing example, given that Turkey is the historical home of the Orthodox faith. Turkey does not recognize the Ecumenical Patriarch and his position worldwide as first among equals in Eastern Orthodox Christian religious groups. There are an estimated 300 million Eastern Orthodox Christians, yet Turkey restricts full religious freedom for the Ecumenical Patriarchate. It illegally closed the Halki Theological School in 1971. Turkey has illegally seized several thousand properties of the Ecumenical Patriarchate. The United States should call for the recognition by Turkey of the status of the Ecumenical Patriarchate and should call for the return of illegally seized church properties.

Turkey's anti-Christian stance has resulted in some of history's most horrific mass killings. In the early decades of the twentieth century, Turkey's predecessor, the Ottoman Empire, committed genocides against its Armenian, Assyrian and Greek Pontian and Greek Anatolian Christians. On July 13, 2007, the International Association of Genocide Scholars issued a resolution on those genocides and called the government of Turkey "to acknowledge the genocides . . . , to issue a formal apology, and to take prompt and meaningful steps toward restitution."[68]

In September 1922 the Turkish army led by Ataturk destroyed the predominantly Greek city of Smyrna on the western coast of Turkey. Scholar Dr. Marjorie Housepian Dobkin gives an in-depth account of the horrific events in her 1972 book *Smyrna 1922: The Destruction of a City* (Faber & Faber, London, 1972, previously published in 1971 by Harcourt Brace Jovanovich, New York, as *The Smyrna Affair*). The book was on the *New York Times* list of its "100 Notable Books" of 1971, and in 1972 was considered by the *Sunday Times* of London as the "Book of the Year."

Dr. Dobkin recounted that:

Within hours of Ataturk's victorious entry into the beautiful, thriving and predominantly Greek city of Smyrna (now Izmir), Turkish soldiers began the killing and raping of Greeks and Armenians, and the looting and pillaging of their homes and shops. Over 100,000 Greek and Armenian civilians were killed by the Turks.

After breaking down the doors and entering Armenian and Greek homes house by house (the Greek and Armenian quarters overlapped), Ataturk's soldiers killed and raped the inhabitants, and emptied the furnishings into waiting trucks. This was the finale of the Armenian Genocide of the

First World War when close to two million Armenian men, women and children had in 1915-1916 been dispatched to their deaths by the Young Turks from all points in Turkey— except Smyrna.

On September 6, 1955 Turkey organized a massive pogrom against the 100,000 Greek Orthodox Christians living in Istanbul (they were there under the terms of the exchange of populations of 1923). Following the pogrom the Greek Orthodox Christians started leaving Istanbul. Today there are only about 2,000 Christians left, reduced from a height of three to four million Christians at the beginning of the twentieth century. Turkey was formed on the bodies of over 2 million Christian victims of genocide and forced removal.

Turkey's authoritarian style does not end with the persecution of its own ethnic and religious minorities. It is well known that Turkey lacks full freedom of the press and media. There are over 100 journalists, the largest of any nation, sitting in jail even today on trumped-up charges. And the country's highest leadership often seems intent on adopting a hostile stance toward foreigners. Turkey's relationship with Israel is a prime example. Turkish Prime Minister Recep Tayyip Erdoğan has made many vicious comments against Israel and its leaders including President Shimon Peres. Although Turkey had longstanding cooperative military ties with Israel,[69] this relationship was ended in early 2011 after the controversial Gaza flotilla raid. Erdoğan has also defended Sudan's President Omar Hassan Ahmad Al-Bashir, indicted for war crimes and genocide by the International Criminal Court (ICC). Erdoğan said that Bashir is his friend and that "it is not possible for those who belong to the Muslim faith to carry out genocide."[70]

Thousands of Turks protested in May–July 2013 against Prime Minister Erdoğan's proposed conversion of Gezi Park, a small park in the Taksim area of Istanbul, into a shopping mall. Erdogan crushed the demonstrations with brute force.

Turkey's actions have been as controversial as its words. One example of international concern is its role in the drug trade. Turkey is not only the main transit route for illegal drugs from Afghanistan to Europe, but also produces opium which is illegally shipped to Europe. In fact, the State Department's 2013 International Narcotics Control Strategy Report (INCSR) states that: "Turkey remains a significant transit country for illicit drug trafficking. Heroin, opium, and cocaine are generally trafficked through Turkey to European markets, and methamphetamine and amphetamine-type stimulants (ATS) are trafficked to markets in the Middle East and elsewhere in Asia."

More relevant to the case of Cyprus is Turkey's relationship with its most immediate historical neighbor Greece. Turkey has made ludicrous claims to one-half of the Aegean Sea, which separates the two countries, and disputes Greece's sovereignty over the Dodecanese Islands and adjacent islets which were ceded to Greece in the 1947 Paris Peace Treaty. However, Turkey refuses to take its maritime boundary claim to the International Court of Justice at The Hague for a binding ruling. Turkey for decades has periodically violated the air space of Greek islands in the Aegean Sea. The United States, also of course a signatory to the 1947 Paris Peace Treaty and a NATO ally of Turkey, has said nothing to ameliorate such encroachments. Intervention by the U.S. might head off future crises, as Turkey has stated that if Greece extends her continental shelf from its existing six miles to twelve miles, which it has a legal right to do, it would be a *casus belli* (cause for war).

Further, there is Turkey's aggressive attitude toward Cyprus itself. Turkey has not recognized Cyprus's sovereign rights in the Eastern Mediterranean Sea, its continental shelf, and its Exclusive Economic Zone (EEZ) in the waters south and southeast of Cyprus, which all other nations, including the United States, do. The U.S. ambassador to Cyprus, John M. Koenig, reiterated the U.S. position in his confirmation hearing before the Senate Foreign Relations Committee on

July 18, 2012: "The Administration recognizes the Republic of Cyprus' right to develop its Exclusive Economic Zone." In sharp contrast, Turkey has threatened the use of force to stop Cyprus's exploration and development of the natural gas reserves in its EEZ, including attacks on Cyprus's agreements with Egypt, Israel, and Lebanon regarding the hydrocarbons in their respective EEZs. Former Minister of Foreign Affairs of Cyprus, Dr. Erato Kozakou-Marcoullis, made the following remarks in a speech at the London School of Economics on January 25, 2012:

> During the past six months we were dismayed to witness yet again the hostile and aggressive face of Turkey . . . The start of exploratory drilling in the Cypriot EEZ, something which had been planned several years in advance and which was not a secret, sparked an angry verbal assault on the part of Turkish leaders, at the highest levels. . . . Then, came the blatant threats of violence and provocations which involved Turkish warships and aircraft, air and naval exercises in the sea south of Cyprus and illegal seismic surveying and seabed mapping carried out by ships on behalf of Turkey inside our Exclusive Economic Zone, in blatant violation of Cypriot sovereign rights . . . [Turkey's] newfound confidence, based on real or imagined successes, its economic growth and, I am sorry to say, the unbridled support it receives in some countries, has given rise to a neighborhood bully. A Turkey whose Foreign Minister promoted a policy of "zero problems" with its neighbors, is now asserting a policy of "only problems."[71]

The recent attacks on Cyprus's right to explore its EEZ are an unpleasant reminder of Turkey's past repression of the rights of Cypriots and of Cyprus as a nation. Its relationships in recent years with its neighbors and, indeed, its own population, sadly mirror this same attitude.

Turkey's increasingly intransigent political and diplomatic stance has also affected its relationship with the United States. The government of Prime Minister Erdoğan came into power on March 14, 2003 and has steadily moved away from the United States and the Western European nations. Erdoğan, re-elected in 2007 and 2011, has succeeded in subordinating the military to civilian rule but Turkey remains a partial democracy according to Freedom House's 2012 annual report.

Robert L. Pollack, a senior editorial page writer at the *Wall Street Journal*, in an article on February 16, 2005, detailed the extreme anti-American and anti-Jew hatred in Turkey. Pollack wrote that a "combination of old leftism and new Islamism" of the Justice and Development Party (AKP) of Prime Minister Recep Tayyip Erdogan "explains the collapse in relations" between Turkey and the United States. He states:

> And what a collapse it has been. On a brief visit to Ankara earlier this month with Undersecretary of Defense Doug Feith, I found a poisonous atmosphere—one in which just about every politician and media outlet (secular and religious) preaches an extreme combination of America- and Jew-hatred that . . . *voluntarily* goes far further than anything found in most of the Arab world's state-controlled press. If I hesitate to call it Nazi-like, that's only because Goebbels would probably have rejected much of it as too crude.

Ted Galen Carpenter, former Vice President for defense and foreign policy studies at the Cato Institute, has detailed the growing split in U.S.-Turkey relations in several speeches. He has analyzed Turkey's refusal in early 2003 to allow the use of Turkey's soil to open a second front against Saddam Hussein's dictatorship (unless it received additional billions of dollars). He has noted as well Turkey's relations and policy positions with Iran contrary to U.S. views: Turkey's moves away from the West and to the Arab Muslim nations of the Middle East;

Turkey's split with Israel; and Turkey's closer relations with Russia.

In a speech on November 13, 2007 Carpenter cities the following four assertions of "conventional wisdom in American foreign policy circles regarding Turkey" and argues that they are "either partially false or totally false:"

> First, that Turkey has been a loyal ally of the United States since the earliest days of the Cold War and remains a loyal ally.

> Second, that Turkey is a force for stability in the Middle East and Central Asia in addition to its role within NATO and European affairs.

> Third, that Turkey is basically a Western secular country.

> Fourth, Turkey is a good candidate that should be admitted to the European Union in the near future.

Let's examine these four assertions in turn.

First, is Turkey a loyal ally of the United States? Carpenter stated: "Well if that was ever true it's not true any longer." He cited the U.S. mission in Iraq in 2003, during which "Ankara refused to allow U.S. troops to invade Iraq from positions in Turkey" and refused to allow the Incirlik Air Base to be used for bombing strikes against Iraq. According to Carpenter, "those two actions . . . made the U.S. military task more difficult than it had to be." Carpenter also refers to differences between the U.S. and Turkey regarding Iran and Russia.

Second, Carpenter flatly denies that Turkey is a force for stability in the region:

> I don't think that has ever been true. You have fairly obvious things like the invasion of Cyprus in 1974. . . . Turkey certainly was not a force for stability on that occasion and in the years since, as it has continued its illegal occupation. . . . We have the ongoing claims to Greek territory in the Aegean and the provocative overflights, by Turkish planes. We have the

economic blockade of Armenia and the continuing strategy of historical denial that the government and population of Turkey practices. . . .

Again, all of those actions suggest to me that Turkey is more an **aggressively revisionist power** [emphasis in original] than a stabilizing, status quo power. Turkey certainly has not been a stabilizing force regarding Iraq. We have, as we have seen very recently, periodic threats to launch new military operations in northern Iraq to go after the PKK rebels even if such actions would destabilize the one area of Iraq that has done reasonable [*sic*] well under the U.S. occupation. And it's not just threats to northern Iraq over the PKK. Let's remember that Ankara has issued repeated threats to mount a full-scale invasion of Iraqi Kurdistan if the northern regional government is given control of the oil-rich city of Kirkuk. Again, not exactly cooperative stabilizing behavior.

As we have seen, Turkey's invasion of Cyprus can in a sense be thought of as a dress rehearsal for its current belligerence — something that someone with a less myopic view of East-West relations than Henry Kissinger might have been expected to realize in the 1970s.

Third, regarding whether Turkey "is basically a Western secular country," Carpenter believes that "if anything the trend appears to be in the opposite direction." Carpenter cites Robert Pollack, an editorial writer from the *Wall Street Journal*, who described his interpretation of the Turkish scene: "I found a poisonous atmosphere — one in which just about every politician and media outlet (secular and religious) preaches an extreme combination of America — and Jew — hatred that voluntarily goes much further than anything found in most of the Arab world's state-controlled press." Carpenter continues:

Indeed the Islamist newspaper *Yeni Sabak,* the favorite paper of the Turkish Prime Minister Erdogan, routinely prints stories accusing the U.S. of the most outrageous war crimes in both Iraq and Afghanistan. Just one example of a story that is absolutely typical is the allegation that U.S. forces raped women and children and left their bodies in the streets to be eaten by dogs. Utterly preposterous, yet this is kind of routine fare in the newspaper that the Prime Minister reads religiously.

The secular newspapers in Turkey unfortunately have become nearly as extreme, which is a very disheartening trend.

Such religiously-tinged extremism was joined by nationalist sentiment in an unhealthy mix. Indeed, to Ted Carpenter this sort of nationalism puts the lie to the fourth assertion, regarding Turkey as "a good candidate" for the European Union, Carpenter writes:

Turkey shows signs of becoming an increasingly bizarre and intolerant cauldron of populist nationalism. It's difficult to reconcile that Turkey with a worthy candidate for admission to the European Union. And that doesn't even take into account Ankara's continuing unwillingness to end its illegal occupation of Cyprus. To be very polite about it, Turkey's bid to join the E.U. is decidedly premature.

Carpenter also cites Turkey's "growing cooperation with Iran" in opposition to U.S. views. In his view, Turkey is not a "constructive partner" of the United States: "Ankara seems to be causing some rather serious trouble. Most troubling is the trend in Turkish opinion, strongly anti-U.S. sentiment combined with elements of anti-Semitism and political extremism. That is a very troubling brew. With allies like Turkey, I'm not sure that America needs any adversaries."

In speeches on April 14, 2010 "A Chill in the Air: Relations with Washington's Turkish 'Ally' in the 21st Century" and on

April 26, 2010 "Loose Cannon: Washington's Turkish 'Ally' in the 21st Century" Carpenter reiterated in detail Turkey's views about U.S. policy in Iraq, and about Iran, its moves away from the West and the U.S. to the Arab Muslim nations, its split with Israel, and its closer relations with Russia. In its courting of Turkey, the United States does serious harm to its avowed adherence to democratic governance and international law. Even worse, it fails to challenge the continued Turkish occupation of Cyprus. The United States needs to change its position.

Not everyone in America's government is willing to go along with the abandonment of Cyprus. In an op-ed article in the *Washington Times* on June 15, 2012, the then Chairman of the House Foreign Affairs Committee, Ileana Ros-Lehtinen (R-FL) told Turkey to get out of Cyprus, a position she has espoused for many years. She wrote:

> It is time for Turkey to withdraw its military troops, end all support for illegal immigration to Cyprus and let the true inhabitants of the island determine their own future. Only then will the long-suffering Cypriot people finally enjoy the peace and security they have been trying so desperately to achieve for decades.

In a broad-ranging article Chairman Ros-Lehtinen sharply criticizes Turkey's invasion of Cyprus and occupation of the northern area of Cyprus—37.3 percent of Cyprus's land area. She details the plight of the 200,000 Greek Cypriot refugees driven from their homes by the Turkish invaders, and describes the religious and cultural destruction that followed:

> The desolation of Cypriot properties and cultural sites . . . is a reality in all the areas under Turkish military occupation. In fact, an estimated 520 Greek Orthodox churches and cha-

pels, and 17 monasteries in the occupied areas have been pillaged, vandalized or destroyed. Often these religious sites have been converted into stables, bars, nightclubs, casinos or hotels, leaving more than 15,000 religious artifacts unaccounted for. This widespread destruction of Cypriot historic, religious and cultural identity certainly does not seem like the behavior of a "protective guardian."

Chairman Ros-Lehtinen criticized Turkey's statements and actions aimed at limiting "Cyprus' sovereign rights to develop its energy resources" in the Eastern Mediterranean. She attacked Turkey's continuing promotion of "illegal immigration by Turks to the northern occupied areas of Cyprus with the goal of changing the demographic composition of the island. . . ." The Turkish Cypriots are outnumbered by the illegal settlers by over two to one.

On Thursday, September 22, 2011, Ros-Lehtinen issued the following pointed statement regarding threats from Turkish authorities against U.S. commercial ships off the southern coast of Cyprus.

It is clearly unjustified and indefensible for Turkey to interfere in the lawful agreement between the sovereign Government of Cyprus and the U.S. firm Noble Energy to explore the gas fields in Cypriot territorial waters.

Turkey's decision to escalate tensions by increasing its military presence in the Mediterranean poses a clear threat to U.S. citizens and interests in the region.

The exploration of these potentially lucrative gas fields could provide new sources of energy supplies, as well as an economic boost, to everyone on the island, Greek and Turkish-Cypriots alike.

The officials in Ankara should focus on supporting the Cyprus reunification talks, rather than further militarizing the conflict.

I urge the U.S. Administration to press the Turkish government to refrain from any course of action that could provoke an outbreak of violence in the Mediterranean. The Administration must also demand that the Turkish government respect the rights of U.S. companies to conduct their explorations without threats of military interference.

Ros-Lehtinen has an unusual personal connection to the Cyprus situation. In a speech in Miami on February 10, 2012, as part of the premier of a public television documentary on Cyprus — "Cyprus Still Divided: A U.S. Foreign Policy Failure" — she spoke of her own experience: "because I, too, am a refugee. . . . My family was forced to flee the tyranny of Castro's communist rule half a century ago, and I am still waiting for the day when I can return to what has become a devastated country." Her personal experience, she continued, prompted her to take action:

In January, I traveled to Turkey with Majority Leader Eric Cantor, where I raised the issue of Turkey's continued interference and occupation of Cyprus in meetings with the Turkish President, Prime Minister and Foreign Minister.

I can tell you that those meetings were quite heated as I and the other members pressed hard to make certain that those officials understood that the U.S. Congress was committed to bringing about a just resolution of the division of the island.

In fact, just yesterday I met again with the Turkish Foreign Minister and delivered the same strong message.

As you can imagine, he was not exactly thrilled to hear me again on this issue, especially when I used the word "occupation."

But I am determined to continue to press him and every Turkish official I meet with until they understand that the

U.S. will not abandon Cyprus and will continue to make it an issue in U.S.-Turkish relations until there is a just settlement.

Let me end by saying that I will continue to do all that I can to ensure that the U.S. government uses its enormous influence to support the reunification efforts, until the people of Cyprus can finally live in a country that is whole, free and at peace.

The goodwill and determined action of political leaders like Ros-Lehtinen is a step in the right direction for American policy toward Cyprus and Turkey. Indeed, her sentiments are not limited to her side of the political aisle. The late Senator Edward M. Kennedy at a dinner in honor of Cyprus's President George Vassiliou at the Kennedy Library on September 21, 1990, stated:

We are all familiar with the unconscionable invasion by Turkish troops in 1974 and the Turkish occupation of the northern part of Cyprus, which continues to this day. The Bush Administration must give higher priority to Cyprus in America's foreign policy. Aggression is aggression is aggression. President Bush has made it clear that Iraq's invasion and occupation of Kuwait is unacceptable. And it is time he made clear to Turkey that their invasion and occupation of Cyprus is just as unacceptable. . . . We know the speed with which productive change can come, and we hope that it will come to Cyprus soon. In less than two weeks, East will meet West when Germany unites. It is also time for North to meet South on Cyprus. The Wall has disappeared in Berlin, and the Green Line must disappear in Cyprus.[72]

Cyprus has broad support in the U.S. Congress on both sides of the aisle. A majority of the members in the House of Representatives and the Senate would support the removal of Turkish troops and colonists/settlers from Cyprus; and a free and independent Cyprus with a government based on majority rule, the rule of law and protection of minority rights. Senator Robert Menendez (D-NJ), Chairman of the Senate Foreign Relations Committee issued the following statement in October 2012 in response to an American Hellenic Institute questionnaire:

> For many years I have called on Turkey to end its illegal occupation of Cyprus. I also believe that Cypriots deserve a final resolution to the Cyprus questions that adequately addresses all issues, including the issues of property, territory and security and that the negotiations leading to that solution must be Cypriot-owned and led, with the momentum being determined by the process itself and not outside entities
>
> In June 2012, I introduced S. Con. Res. 47 in the U.S. Senate, which highlights Turkey's efforts to colonize northern Cyprus in violation of the Geneva Convention; urging president Obama to call on Turkey to end it illegal colonization and occupation of Cyprus and to cease illegal interference with Cyprus' efforts to develop energy resources in its Exclusive Economic Zone.
>
> In September 2011, I sent a letter to President Obama signed by 27 Senators underscoring the importance of a strong U.S.-Cyprus relationship. I reiterated that message in another letter to the President in June 2012, in which I asked the President to conduct a thorough re-evaluation of U.S. policy toward the region taking into account Turkey's belligerent stance in the eastern Mediterranean and the growing strategic importance of Cyprus.

The Chairman of the House Foreign Affairs Committee, Ed Royce (R-CA) holds similar views regarding Turkey and Cyprus. At a July 25, 2013 AHI breakfast meeting on Capitol Hill, Chairman Royce also lamented the destruction of Cyprus's cultural and religious heritage by Turkey. He stated: "It is as if the Turks are trying to erase history." He also said he would take a strong stance in support of Cyprus's right to develop its natural gas resources in its Exclusive Economic Zone.

What comes next for America's relations with Cyprus and Turkey? Voices like Ros-Lehtinen's and Kennedy's are an important counterbalance to official U.S. policy, which remains, under the Obama Administration, seemingly mired in a conciliatory attitude towards an increasingly aggressive Turkish state. Cyprus remains divided. Administration officials should be reminded, however, that Cyprus is a sovereign state, a fact that Turkey itself once admitted, since it was a signatory to the London–Zurich Agreements of 1959–60 which established the sovereign state of Cyprus and recognized that state. Following its aggression and illegal land grab, Turkey renounced its recognition, and remains the only country in the world that does not recognize the sovereign government of Cyprus.

In July 2005, Turkey signed the Ankara Protocol regarding the ten new member nations, including Cyprus, of the European Union: this protocol was intended to extend economic ties to the new members. But despite its signature, Turkey continues to refuse to recognize the government of Cyprus and refuses to allow Cypriot ships and planes to enter Turkish ports and airports. It is another example of Turkey's lawless and arrogant conduct. The United States should inform Turkey that the United States will hold no meetings or telephone discussions with Turkish officials until Turkey publicly recognizes the government of Cyprus and allows full access of Cypriot ships and planes to Turkish ports and airports and air space and sea lanes.

What of Cyprus itself? Ultimately, the two Cypriot communities must decide their relationship, bearing in mind the demographic makeup of the island. The Turkish Cypriots have also been victims of Turkey's actions in Cyprus. Ozker Ozgur, leader of the Turkish Cypriot opposition party, in a speech at his party's district congress in Nicosia on April 14, 1989, accused the

Denktash regime and the Ozal government in Turkey of cooperating in turning the north of Cyprus into a Turkish province. Ozgur stated that from 1974 to 1989, 30,000 Turkish Cypriots had emigrated, to Britain primarily; that if emigration continues at the same rate in five or ten years' time the Turkish Cypriots would become a minority in the north of Cyprus; that an early solution to the intercommunal problem would stop the process. He said:

> We are against the use of the workers and peasants from Turkey for the destruction of the identity of the Turkish Cypriots and in rendering the Turkish Cypriots ineffective as a communal entity. . . . We must tell the Turkish workers that the Denktash regime sees them as cheap labour and vote depots for their own selfish interests.[73]

In 2011 the Turkish Cypriots protested against Turkish rule. Erdoğan attacked them as ungrateful.

The apartheid policy applied by Turkey and the illegal Turkish Cypriot administration in Cyprus can no longer be tolerated. The opening of several border crossings, started in April 2003, has demonstrated that Greek and Turkish Cypriots can work and live together peacefully. There have been over 15 million crossings of Greek and Turkish Cypriots since April 2003 without serious incident. Six thousand Turkish Cypriots now work in the free area of Cyprus. These crossings by themselves put the lie to Kissinger's efforts to turn Turkey's aggression and occupation into an ethnic conflict.

Basically, Turkey has moved away from the West, the U.S. and Israel and focused its attention on the East and to Russia in the north. Gregory R. Copley details this situation in two articles—"Black Sea Watershed: How Turkey's New Axis with Russia Affect's U.S. Interests in the Eastern Mediterranean and South-Eastern Europe" (April 14, 2010), and "Did Turkey Declare

War on Israel . . . and the West?" (May/June 2010).[74] In the latter article Copley sets forth the following "four major aspects which have defined the Turkish situation in recent years:

1. **No to the West:** The elected civilian Government of the *Adalet ve Kalkinma Partisi* (Justice and Development Party: AKP), and the Turkish General Staff have never consciously believed that Turkey would, or should, become a member of the European Union (EU), assuming that Turkey would have to meet the EU's entry and functioning conditionalities;

2. **Yes, Reluctantly, to Russia:** Turkey's trade and strategic interests necessitated, increasingly during the past decade, that it had to accommodate Russian interests and dominance, despite mutual dislike between Russia and Turkey. This meant, absolutely and unequivocally, placing an alliance with Russia ahead of any alliance with the West, although talking for as long as possible in ways which would keep the West calm;

3. **The Polite Civil War:** The AKP Government and the Turkish General Staff (*Genelkurmay Baskanlari:* GB) are engaged in a bitter battle for dominance, and part of the process of the AKP has been to minimize the essentially military based alliance with Israel. Opposing Israel effectively strengthens the AKP's hand in opposing the GB; and

4. **The Quiet Support for Jihad:** The Turkish Government has increasingly, over the past two decades, taken an active rôle in facilitating and supporting *jihadist* groups based out of the former Ottoman Empire territories of Bosnia-Herzegovina and Kosovo (and elsewhere in Serbia, as well as Albania, the Former Yugoslav Republic of Macedonia, and the like). This has not only meant working with Iranian and Saudi elements in financing, and providing logistical support to, terrorist groups aimed at the West, but more importantly—from Ankara's viewpoint—facilitating the move-

ment and support of *jihadist* terrorists out of the Balkans (groups such as *Kvadrat,* which *Defense & Foreign Affairs* was first to identify) via safe havens in Turkish-occupied Northern Cyprus, to fight the Russians in Chechnya and elsewhere in the Caucasus. This could not have occurred without official Turkish Government involvement, and included the group which organized—again with Turkish Government participation—the "Gaza flotilla" which appeared in late May 2010.

Copley asserts that these four points:

> are driving the revival of the imagined glories of pan-Turkism and Islamic identity . . . [T]he realities are there: Turkey—but emphatically the AKP Government—has abandoned its pretensions of being part of the West; Russia is the driver of the region, even though Turkey hopes to be able to outgrow that forced relationship; and there is a quiet "civil war" underway between the AKP and the GB [Turkish General Staff].

Copley concludes by pointing out the Turkish Government's admission of its involvement "with the terrorist support organization, *Insani Yardim Vakfi* (IHH)." He writes:

> Now, finally, the Turkish Government has admitted that it supports and has worked closely with the terrorist support organization, *Insani Yardim Vakfi* (IHH), which sponsored the Gaza flotilla. IHH has a long history of involvement with the *jihadist* movement, including those linked to *al-Qaida*, in the Balkans. This means that Ankara has admitted, finally, that it has been supporting the international *jihadist* movement against the West, and Russia.
>
> Still, there is always one party at a divorce which observes: "So, you've hated me for years."

Hudson Institute

In a July 3, 2013 Hudson Institute article, Seth Cropsey, Senior Fellow and former Deputy Undersecretary of the Navy, charges that Turkish Prime Minister Reçep Tayyip Erdogan has moved Turkey away from the West and that the "U.S. and Turkey have become rival powers in the Middle East and Eastern Mediterranean." He writes:

> U.S. strategy in the region was for years based on common interests among America, Israel and Turkey. Islamist Recep Tayyip Erdogan's 2002 ascension as Turkish prime minister put strains into the strategy. It shattered when Turkish Islamists tried forcefully to break Israel's naval blockade of Gaza, aimed at preventing more weapons from reaching Islamist terrorists. Erdogan's policy deliberately ended good relations between Ankara and Jerusalem. This was not an isolated incident. It was the result of a profound change in the Turkish government's direction under an Islamist ruler who as of this writing has blamed "foreigners" for the growing protests that demonstrate Turkish citizens' dissatisfaction with an increasingly repressive regime. It was the strategy of a politician who has emerged from what was once a secular state to use the Gaza incident as part of a broad Islamist enterprise to reorient Turkey toward the East and return the nation to the vision of its past Ottoman imperial rulers. Turkey has now imprisoned more journalists than any country in the world; it has become a dialogue partner of the Shanghai Cooperation Council, a bloc dominated by Russia and China. Mr. Erdogan's Justice and Development Party, known as the AKP, has replaced secular media, courts and civil society with the party's fundamentalist loyalists. One in five generals of the Turkish army—once the guardians of the Turkish state—is now behind bars. As the AKP tightens its hold in Turkey [its adage is] "Islamism at home,

pan-Islamism in the world." The shift toward fundamentalism risks isolating Turkey even more, and promises growing
instability for the entire region.

* * * *

The region's drift toward fundamentalism creates
an incentive for America to move closer to Israel, Cyprus
and Greece. The U.S. has been interested in a stable
Mediterranean since the early 19th century wars against
the Barbary pirates who, as Ottoman puppets, preyed on
American and European shipping. Turkey's growing political aspirations and economic clout are recapitulating its old
dreams of regional influence that directly oppose NATO's
interest in a calm south and southeastern flank. The U.S.
and Turkey have become rival powers in the Middle East
and Eastern Mediterranean. President Obama does not recognize this: His visit to Turkey took place less than four
months after his first inauguration in 2009, and underlines
the esteem in which he holds Erdogan. This esteem is mis-
placed. Turkey's return to an imperial and fundamentalist
policy supported tacitly by the U.S. is changing the region's
strategic balance, as it creates dilemmas that will outlive the
current U.S. administration.

Doug Bandow, former special assistant to President Reagan
for policy development, and senior fellow at the Cato Institute
in Washington, D.C. specializing in foreign policy and civil
liberties, spoke on April 26, 2010 at the American Hellenic
Institute Foundation forum on "U.S. Policy Toward Greece,
Turkey and Cyprus: Development and Prospects in the Obama
Administration." He set forth his concerns as to the reliability
of Turkey as an ally of the United States. Focusing on "what is
happening to Turkey internally" and "the implications of that
in terms of its policies toward the United States, toward the rest
of the West and with Greece and Cyprus and more," he stated:

The question is: what is the ultimate objective of the AKP? Prime Minister Recep Tayyip Erdogan, in a kind of prior incarnation, seemed to be much more of an Islamist than he has made himself out to be since 2002. So is there a hidden agenda?

* * * *

There has been massive use of wire taps—judges have been wire tapped, journalists wire tapped. It doesn't appear that this is for criminal activity. It is much more for the political advantage of the AKP.

Labor union officials and journalists are talking about increasing pressure from the government, the concern that the government is going after media owners.

* * * *

Although the State Department pointed out the positive developments, it also pointed out the negative developments. There are reports of a number of human rights problems and abuses in the country, of security forces committing unlawful killings . . . A number of things in the State Department report should give one pause.

* * * *

Assistant Secretary of State Phillip Gordon, speaking for the administration . . . had a couple of critical paragraphs in there—very carefully worded . . . Nevertheless he did note concerns about media freedom, the rule of law, open court proceedings, and how important it was to protect both democracy and secularism. So obviously within the administration there is some recognition that the internal dynamic in Turkey should give one pause.

* * * *

There's also perhaps much more concern over the long term, about the rise of a kind of virulent anti-Western, anti-American attitude and also anti-Semitism. In 2007 the U.S. received a 9 percent favorable rating in Turkey; the global pollsters said that Turkey at that point was the most anti-American country they were surveying . . . In the media you see all kind of images, cartoons, both anti-American and also anti-Semitic. And while we haven't had a repeat of the synagogue bombing of a few years ago, there's also concern there.

* * * *

At some level the jury is still out on where Ankara is going with all of this. Nevertheless, the fact that there is this kind of uncertainty in terms of the direction of Turkey, along with the changes in foreign policy that Ted [Galen Carpenter] has talked about, has to raise the question of the reliability of Turkey as an ally. The notion that one can look ahead in 5, 10, 15, 20 years and just assume that this nation is going to be a base of our position in the Middle East is very dangerous.

* * * *

And on the domestic Turkish side if one looks at what seems to be a relatively steady though modest increase of the role of Islam in the country, the strengthening of authoritarian power for the AKP, I don't see that as being very positive. I worry in the long term about Turkey's power and what that power will be used for.

* * * *

And unless we see a better organization of pro-Western elements, I fear domestic politics in Turkey will develop in a negative way.

* * * *

You put this all together and I perceive a rather negative future. It's not guaranteed. I believe the United States should try to promote positive results in Turkey, but we should be prepared for a negative result. I am afraid our policy makers don't want to think about that, they don't want to confront that possibility.

* * * *

Unfortunately I don't think incantations about Turkey's strategic importance can get around geopolitical reality. If we look at both domestic developments as well as the foreign policy, the transformation that Ted has been talking about, we see a potentially very negative future. The United States should prepare for a world in which Turkey will be moving more distant, not closer to us. In that world Washington should take into account the Greek side which, as I indicated earlier, has a stable relationship with the United States. Washington can trust in its bilateral ties with Athens,' in contrast to America's relationship with Turkey, which we really don't know where it is going.

Corruption Investigation

A major corruption investigation involving the Erdogan government became public on December 17, 2013. The *New York Times* in articles on December 18 through December 31, 2013, when this manuscript went to the printer, has detailed the charges of corruption and the extent of the investigation. On Tuesday, December 17, 2013, "the police raided the offices of several businessmen with close ties to" Erdoğan. Three cabinet ministers resigned. Their sons are under investigation and have been detained. One of the three ministers called for Prime Minister Erdoğan's resignation as did street protestors. The headline in the *Times* article on December 20, 2013, stated: "Growing Corruption Inquiry Hits Close to Turkish Leader." The articles highlight the dispute and tensions between Erdoğan and Fethullan Gülen, an influential Turkish Sufi preacher "who lives on a sprawling compound in the Poconos" in Pennsylvania. In one article the *Times* discussed "what has traditionally been the strategy of Turkish politicians facing a crisis: Blame foreign powers, in this case the United States."

9

Kissinger's National Security Argument

For decades, American foreign policy has operated under a double standard with regard to Cyprus. In the name of strategic value, and contrary to many other cases around the world, the United States has not pressed for the rule of law on Cyprus—to the benefit of Turkey. American presidents, for example, pressed for the removal of Soviet troops from Afghanistan, Cuban troops from Angola and Vietnamese troops from Cambodia, but have been mute about Turkish occupation troops and colonists in Cyprus. The U.S. government called for the rule of law, free elections, majority rule, and protection of minority rights in the Philippines, Nicaragua, Panama, the Eastern European nations, and elsewhere, but accepts a constitution in which an 18 percent Turkish minority in Cyprus had veto power over all major government decisions. American unwillingness to take action on Cyprus has even extended to individual cases where American citizens have been in danger. While the United States made intense efforts to get our hostages in Lebanon released, the government remained silent regarding five Americans kidnapped in Cyprus in 1974 by Turkey, our NATO ally, and doing nothing to determine their fate until

Congress acted by passing legislation requiring the president to investigate. It was determined that they were illegally abducted by the Turkish military and turned over to the Turkish Cypriot militia, who murdered them in cold blood. The State Department did nothing to bring their killers to justice.

How did this unusual situation come about? As noted earlier, it was the British who counted Cyprus among the states in its sphere of influence, from imperial Victorian England all the way through the mid-twentieth century. But the answer is quite simple: it was Henry Kissinger who wove from whole cloth the narrative of Turkey's strategic importance to the defense of the West and the United States in the Cold War era, to excuse his tragic failure to obey the law. The additional tragedy of Cyprus is that the alleged strategic importance of Turkey is highly questionable.[1] The reality is that Turkey is of limited strategic value to U.S. security interests. Actually, Turkey is an unreliable ally who actively collaborated with the Soviet Union militarily during the Cold War.

The most direct argument in favor of Turkey's importance to American national security is related to the "twenty-six electronic stations" that, Kissinger said, were "monitoring Soviet missiles and space activities from Turkish territory." Proponents of the security argument stressed the importance of these listening posts in Turkey for verification of any potential treaty, in particular the SALT (Strategic Arms Limitation Talks) Treaty between the United States and the Soviet Union, negotiations for which had begun in 1969, not long before the series of crises entangling Greece, Turkey, and Cyprus. If Turkish listening posts were indeed crucial to such verification, it would seem at first glance a strong argument for Turkey's strategic centrality to U.S. security—*if* they were crucial. Sadly, we can add this to the ledger of Kissinger lies, for he omitted to mention that the Turkish sites were of marginal use and that there were better active sites elsewhere—including sites in Cyprus. As then Secretary of Defense Melvin Laird said: "We don't need Turkey to verify a SALT agreement. U.S. interests are not protected if we have to depend on a third country."[2]

Experts concurred with this view. For example, Dr. Herbert P. Scoville, former Director of Research for the CIA, stated in a letter to Congressman John F. Sieberling (D-OH) dated July 20, 1975, that:

> In sum, the Turkish bases have only marginal utility in veri-
> fying past or possible future SALT agreements. Other obser-
> vation sites and satellites would appear much more useful.
> SALT cannot be reasonably used as a justification for making
> a decision on our Turkish aid program.[3]
>
> Dr. Scoville also stated in that letter regarding U.S. lis-
> tening posts in Turkey that:
> [T]o say that they are essential for verifying past or future
> SALT agreements would appear to be such an exaggeration
> as to raise questions as to the sincerity of those making the
> statements.

Dr. Scoville's comment is a polite way of saying Kissinger lied. Furthermore, it is significant that his letter was sent in the midst of the internal American debate over the provision of arms to Turkey. As we know, events would show that Dr. Scoville's expert opinion was ignored. Turkey would get its American weapons, and would continue to be considered an important Western ally.

Looking back at the record, however, reveals that Turkey's actions before and after 1974 demonstrates that she was and is an unreliable ally. Turkey's military collaboration with the U.S.S.R. during the Cold War raises serious questions as to whether it would have assisted the United States or NATO in a conflict with the Soviet Union. As long ago as 1974, the noted strategic analyst Edward Luttwak in his book, *The Political Uses of Sea Power,* published in 1974, points out that "the Turks have chosen to conciliate the Russians. . . . at the expense of western rather than specifically Turkish interests." He writes:

> No longer presenting a direct threat to the integrity of Turkish national territory, and no longer demanding formal revision of the Straits navigation regime, the Soviet Union has nevertheless successfully exercised armed suasion over Turkey, even while maintaining a fairly benevolent stance, which includes significant aid flows. Faced with a sharp relative increase in Russian strategic and naval power, and eager to normalize relations with their formidable neighbor, the Turks have chosen to conciliate the Russians, and have been able to do so at little or no direct cost to themselves. It is only in respect to strategic transit that Turkey is of primary importance to the Soviet Union, and this is the area where the concessions have been made. Examples of such deflection, where the Russians are conciliated at the expense of western rather than specifically Turkish interests, include the overland traffic agreement (unimpeded Russian transit to Iraq and Syria by road), the generous Turkish interpretation of the Montreux Convention, which regulates ship movements in the Straits, and above all, the overflight permissions accorded to Russian civilian and military aircraft across Turkish air space. The alliance relationship in NATO and with the United States no doubt retains a measure of validity in Turkish eyes, but it is apparent that its supportive effect is not enough to counteract Russian suasion, especially since the coercion is latent and packaged in a benevolent, diplomatic stance.[4]

Examples of Turkish conciliation regarding Soviet "strategic transit" are not hard to find—nor are counter-examples of Turkish intransigence to Western requests. Perhaps the most egregious example occurred during the 1973 Mid-East War (predating the Turkish invasion of Cyprus by one year). Turkey refused the

U.S. military overflight rights to resupply Israel and granted the USSR overland military convoy rights to resupply Syria and Iraq, and military overflight permission to resupply Egypt.[5] A member of the Turkish Foreign Policy Institute in Ankara wrote in an article in the *Foreign Affairs* journal: "During the Arab-Israeli war of 1973, Moscow's overflights of Turkish airspace were tolerated. On the other hand, during the same Middle East conflict, Turkey refused to allow the United States refueling and reconnaissance facilities during the American airlift to Israel."[6]

During the 1977–1978 conflict in Ethiopia, Turkey granted the Soviets similar military overflight rights to supply the pro-Soviet Ethiopian communists under Col. Mengistu, who eventually prevailed.[7] But again, this flexibility did not extend to the U.S.: during the Iranian hostage crisis in 1979, Turkey refused to allow the United States to send sixty-nine marines and six helicopters to American military facilities at Incirlik in Turkey for possible use in evacuating Americans from Iran.[8] That same year, Turkey refused a U.S. request to allow U-2 intelligence flights (for Salt II verification) over Turkish airspace "unless Moscow agreed."[9] This position was voiced over a period of months by Turkish officials, the opposition party and the military Chief of Staff, Gen. Kenan Evren.[10] Finally, Turkey even opened the strategically vital Bosporus connecting the Black Sea to the Mediterranean to the Soviets (a coup that Russia and the Soviet state had been pursuing for centuries). Over NATO objections, Turkey allowed three Soviet aircraft carriers, the *Kiev* on July 18, 1976, the *Minsk* on Feb. 25, 1979 and the *Novorossiysk* on May 16, 1983, passage rights through the Bosporus and Dardanelles straits into the Mediterranean in violation of the Monteux Convention of 1936.[11] The Soviet ships posed a formidable threat to the U.S. Sixth Fleet in the Mediterranean.

Turkish intransigence extended to spheres beyond transit over its territory. In May, 1989, Turkey rejected an American request to inspect an advanced MIG-29 Soviet fighter plane, flown by a Soviet defector to Turkey.[12] The Turkish government also refused repeated American requests for the installation of antennas in Turkey for transmitters whose broadcasts would have been directed primarily to the Soviet Union and its eastern European satellites. The initiative by the U.S. Department of State sought to improve the reception of programs broadcast by Radio Free Europe, Radio Liberty, and the Voice of America. Turkey further damaged NATO by vetoing NATO's effort to put military bases on various Greek islands in the Aegean for defensive purposes against the Soviet navy. Finally, in February 2003 Turkey asked for 6 billion dollars more than the 26 billion dollars irresponsibly offered by Deputy Secretary of Defense Paul Wolfowitz to allow use of Turkey to open a second front against Saddam Hussein's dictatorship. The United States refused. A senior administration official was quoted in the *New York Times* as calling Turkey's actions "extortion in the name of alliance."[13]

Despite the evidence of its dubious status as an ally, U.S. diplomats continued to truckle to what they perceived as Turkey's importance. Thus, the United States itself was implicated in the dismemberment of Cyprus. While Kissinger bears the major responsibility for the events of 1974, a number of career foreign service officers and defense department officials share some responsibility for the tragedy of Cyprus. Ultimately, their failure to support the rule of law, the UN Charter, and the North Atlantic Treaty against Turkey's aggression has damaged American interests and made the United States an accessory and an accomplice to Turkey's war crimes and crimes against humanity in Cyprus.

The Executive Branch of our government has nevertheless tried to create the perception of being a disinterested broker or mediator between Greece, Cyprus and Turkey. The reality is otherwise. As Laurence Stern wrote: "One of the most important keys to an understanding of the Cyprus muddle is the realization that the United States, far from being a disinterested broker to the disputes of the past, was a deeply involved participant" on Turkey's side.[14] The American role as Turkey's accomplice is apparent since our aid to Turkey from 1974 to the mid-1990s subsidized the costs of Turkey's illegal occupation of Cyprus and underwrote Turkish subsidies to the illegal Turkish Cypriot administration.

Turkey now has about 43,000 illegal troops and 200,000 illegal colonists/settlers in Cyprus. Former undersecretary of state William Schneider Jr. stated in testimony on February 21, 1984, before the House Foreign Affairs Subcommittee on International Security and Scientific Affairs, that it costs Turkey $9,000 annually to maintain and equip one Turkish soldier.[15] Thus, the cost to Turkey in 1984 to maintain 35,000 illegal occupation troops in Cyprus was $315,000,000. Figuring the costs in 1990 per soldier at $12,000, the cost to Turkey in 1990 was $420,000,000 for its 35,000 troops; and in 2000 at $15,000, the cost is $525,000,000; and in 2010 at $18,000 each for 43,000 illegal troops is $774,000,000.

According to the International Institute for Strategic Studies (London), the Turkish Cypriot administration's total budget for 1988 was $138,000,000, of which Turkey provided $75,900,000. This consisted of $46,000,000 of direct aid and $29,900,000 in credits. U.S. military and economic aid to Turkey in 1989 amounted to $563,000,000. Since money is fungible, the United States, in effect, paid for the entire cost of Turkey's maintaining 35,000 illegal occupation troops in Cyprus in 1988 and for the 1988 subsidy Turkey paid to the illegal Turkish Cypriot administration. Specific figures are not available as to any annual payments to the illegal Turkish colonists/settlers.

The United States bears a responsibility to redress the situation in Cyprus. It is in the interests of the United States in support of the rule of law to do so.

10

Bush on Kuwait Compared to Kissinger on Cyprus

It is instructive to compare President George H. W. Bush's reaction to Iraq's aggression against Kuwait on August 2, 1990, and Kissinger's reaction to Turkey's aggression against Cyprus on July 20, 1974 and August 14–16, 1974. Iraq's invasion and occupation of Kuwait was immediately characterized by President Bush as "naked aggression" and a violation of the UN Charter.[1] The United Nations Security Council unanimously condemned Iraq's actions and demanded Iraq's immediate and unconditional withdrawal from Kuwait.[2] Additionally, the Security Council voted for mandatory economic sanctions,[3] authorized the use of force[4] to achieve compliance with the sanctions through the naval blockade initiated by the United States, and, on November 29, 1990, authorized the use of force against Iraq if Iraq did not comply with Security Council resolutions to leave Kuwait by January 15, 1991.[5] We will see that there is no fundamental legal difference between Iraq's aggression against Kuwait and Turkey's aggression against Cyprus.

The similarities between the invasion of Kuwait and Cyprus are immediately apparent, as is the consistency of the UN's response to both crises. Just as with the more recent Iraqi

169

aggression, Turkey, a large nation of 38,000,000 people at that time, used military force against a smaller country, Cyprus, with about 650,000 people. In both cases, naked aggression elicited a clear and forceful response from the United Nations. Even if one could argue that those responses lacked effective enforcement mechanisms, the will of the international community was, in both cases, undoubtedly clear. The difference lies in the response of the United States and other Western nations.

The reason for the Western allies' different responses to these invasions rests, at least in part, on a crucial economic difference: the reliance of the United States and other nations, particularly those in Europe, on oil from the Middle East.[6] Kuwait is one of the major oil producing countries in the world. Cyprus had no oil in 1974. Furthermore, there was fear that Iraq's dictator, Saddam Hussein, would move militarily against Saudi Arabia, the United Arab Emirates, Bahrain, Qatar and Oman, and gain control of a major percentage of the world's oil production and reserves. Other factual differences are that Turkey was and is a member of the North Atlantic Treaty Organization (NATO) and Iraq is not; Turkey does not have a land border with Cyprus, an island, while Iraq has a land border with Kuwait. Additionally, Iraq asserted a border dispute, violation of OPEC oil production quotas and irregular activity in drilling for oil. Turkey, citing the Treaty of Guarantee under the London–Zurich Agreements of 1959–1960, asserted she had the right to use armed force to invade Cyprus after the Greek junta–initiated coup against the Makarios government. Turkey had no such right, as I set forth in detail in chapter 8. However, in both cases the dictates of international law were unequivocal. Why did one invasion bring international intervention and the other only obfuscation?

In contrast to Kissinger's response to Turkey's invasion and occupation of 37.3 percent of Cyprus, President George H.W. Bush's actions following Iraq's invasion and occupation of Kuwait were decisively in support of the UN Charter and the rule of law. Some of Kissinger's actions were in direct violation of U.S. laws and most were contrary to the policy and spirit of U.S. foreign assistance laws, the UN Charter and the North Atlantic Treaty. On the other hand, President Bush immediately condemned Iraq's invasion as "naked aggression" and a violation of the UN Charter and international law. The White House issued the following statement within hours of Iraq's invasion of Kuwait:

> The United States strongly condemns the Iraqi military invasion of Kuwait and calls for the immediate and unconditional withdrawal of all Iraqi forces. We have conveyed this message to the Iraqi Ambassador in Washington and to the Iraqi Government through our Embassy in Baghdad. We deplore this blatant use of military aggression and violation of the U.N. Charter. Together with Kuwait we are calling for an emergency session of the U.N. Security Council.[7]

Strong words were accompanied by concerted action. Bush mounted a massive diplomatic effort to obtain multinational support for the rule of law from the world community, working through the United Nations and with Kuwaiti government officials who had fled to Saudi Arabia. As a result of his efforts, the United Nations Security Council met in emergency session on the morning of August 2, 1990. The Security Council unanimously passed, by a vote of fourteen to zero with Yemen not participating, Security Council Resolution 660 condemning Iraq's invasion and demanding Iraq's immediate and unconditional withdrawal from Kuwait.[8] The same day, Bush froze Iraqi and Kuwaiti assets under U.S. jurisdiction and stopped all commercial dealings with Iraq.[9] Britain, France, and Switzerland followed suit.[10]

The president's official censure was accompanied by statements in lockstep from diplomatic officials, both in the U.S. and worldwide. For example, on August 3, 1990, Secretary of

State James A. Baker III and Soviet Foreign Minister Eduard Shevardnadze issued a joint statement in Moscow condemning "the brutal and illegal invasion of Kuwait by Iraqi military forces" and urged a worldwide stoppage of arms deliveries to Iraq. They stated that "governments that engage in blatant aggression must know that the international community cannot and will not acquiesce in nor facilitate aggression." The Soviets stopped arms deliveries to Iraq and joined the call for withdrawal of Iraqi troops from Kuwait.[11] The joint statement reflected U.S.–Soviet post–Cold War comity—and of the intersection of human rights values with perceived economic interests. The Soviet action was particularly significant since Iraq was considered their ally and the Soviets had been Iraq's primary arms supplier.

Bush continued his diplomatic efforts through the United Nations and bilaterally. On August 6, 1990, the Security Council voted to impose mandatory economic sanctions on Iraq aimed at ending the occupation in Kuwait.[12] A sanctions committee was also established. On August 7, 1990, Bush obtained a formal request from the Saudi Arabian government to send American troops and equipment to Saudi Arabia for defensive purposes to prevent and deter any armed attack on Saudi Arabia by Iraq.[13] (Such a request is in accordance with article 51 of the UN Charter.) On August 9, 1990 the Security Council unanimously passed Resolution 662 stating that Iraq's annexation of Kuwait "has no legal validity, and is considered null and void."[14] On August 12, 1990, Bush ordered U.S. forces to halt all shipments of Iraqi oil exports and all imports except some food shipments. Bush had received a letter that morning from the Emir of Kuwait requesting that the United States, in accordance with article 51 of the Charter and the right of individual and collective self-defense, enforce the United Nations-mandated economic sanctions against Iraq and Kuwait.[15] On August 18, 1990, the Security Council unanimously passed Resolution 664 demanding that Iraq "permit and facilitate the immediate departure from Kuwait and Iraq" of all third country nationals.[16] On August 25, 1990 the Security Council passed Resolution 665, by a vote of thirteen to zero, authorizing the use of force to carry out the blockade of Iraq.[17] Cuba and Yemen abstained. The Security Council called for "measures commensurate to specific circumstances" to achieve compliance with economic sanctions against Iraq.

Bush met with Soviet President Mikhail Gorbachev in Helsinki on September 9, 1990. They issued a joint statement condemning Iraq's invasion of Kuwait and reaffirming their support for the United Nations Security Council Resolutions, declaring "that aggression cannot and will not pay." The joint statement included:

> We are united in the belief that Iraq's aggression must not be tolerated. No peaceful international order is possible if larger states can devour their smaller neighbors. Today, we once again call upon the Government of Iraq to withdraw unconditionally from Kuwait [and] to allow the restoration of Kuwait's legitimate government. . . . Nothing short of the complete implementation of the United Nations Security Council resolutions is acceptable. . . . We call upon the entire world community to adhere to the sanctions mandated by the United Nations, and we pledge to work, individually and in concert, to ensure full compliance with the sanctions. . . . As soon as the objectives mandated by the U.N. Security Council resolutions mentioned above have been achieved, and we have demonstrated that aggression does not pay, the Presidents direct their foreign ministers to work with countries in the region and outside it to develop regional security structures and measures to promote peace and stability.[18]

One can only speculate what the effect might have been of such a muscular public stance in the matter of Cyprus only a decade and a half earlier. The evolution of diplomatic relations with the

Soviet Union made such a joint statement possible, of course, but this was also not just mere words: it would be followed by action. There was no Kissinger behind the scenes to follow his own duplicitous path.

On September 13, 1990, the Security Council passed Resolution 666, by a vote of thirteen to zero supporting the humanitarian efforts to supply foodstuffs to Iraq and Kuwait.[19] Three days later, the Security Council condemned aggressive acts by Iraq against diplomatic personnel in Kuwait.[20] Next, the Security Council entrusted its Sanctions Committee to examine requests for assistance from countries with special economic problems and to make recommendations to handle such situations.[21]

On September 25, 1990, the Security Council, with thirteen of its fifteen members represented at the foreign minister level, passed Resolution 670 by a vote of fourteen to one.[22] Resolution 670 imposed an embargo on air traffic to Iraq and Kuwait, tightened the economic blockade against the Iraqi government, called for the detention of Iraqi merchant ships, and emphasized that measures would be considered against countries evading the sanctions. It was only the third time in the 45-year history of the United Nations that such a large number of foreign ministers represented the nations that comprise the Security Council. Secretary of State James A. Baker III took the seat for the United States. Soviet Foreign Minister Eduard Shevardnadze presided over the meeting.[23]

Shevardnadze also addressed the General Assembly and attacked Iraq with the strongest language the Soviet Union had used since the crisis began. He stated in part:

> An act of terrorism has been perpetrated against the emerging new world order. This is a major affront to mankind. Unless we find a way to respond to it and cope with the situation, our civilization will be thrown back by half a century.

Iraqi actions are having and will have the gravest consequences for the people of Iraq and for millions of men,
women and children in many countries of the world, for
their hopes and their future. War may break out in the gulf
region any day, any moment.

From this rostrum we would like to appeal once again
to the leaders of Iraq. We are doing it as their old friends
and as a country which has found the courage to condemn
its wrongdoings against certain states in the past. We call
upon them to hear reason, and to obey the demands of law
and also of plain common sense, to take a responsible and
humane attitude, above all vis-à-vis the Iraqi people, who
surely yearn for peace, tranquility and good relations with
their neighbors.

Some may find that Iraq is being judged by a different,
higher standard than that applied to other countries even
in the quite recent past. My answer is this. It is good that
we have reached this point; it is a good thing that we have
adopted a universal human yardstick of good and evil; that
we are calling aggression by its proper name and consider it
necessary to condemn and punish its perpetrator and to help
the victim of injustice.[24]

An aggressor country "being judged by a different, higher standard" after attacking a smaller neighbor? This statement and its
reference to the "quite recent past" must have been cold com-
fort to Cypriots wondering where such adherence to the rule of
law had been in their case.

On October 29, 1990, the Security Council set the groundwork for making Iraq legally liable for human rights violations
and financial damages caused by the invasion and occupation of Kuwait.[25] One month later, the Security Council unanimously passed Resolution 677 to take steps to safeguard the
demographic composition of Kuwait.[26] Finally, on November
29, 1990, following weeks of extensive diplomatic activity by

the United States, the Security Council at the foreign ministers level passed, by a vote of twelve to two with one abstention, Resolution 678 authorizing the use of force if Iraq did not comply with all Security Council resolutions by January 15, 1991.[27] China did not exercise its veto.

UN-sanctioned military action began the next day—January 16. That evening, President Bush noted the "historic moment":

> We have in this past year made great progress in ending the long era of conflict and cold war. We have before us the opportunity to forge for ourselves and for future generations a new world order, a world where the rule of law, not the law of the jungle, governs the conduct of nations.[28]

Similar rhetoric characterized Bush's State of the Union address two weeks later. It is worth quoting at length:

> What is at stake is more than one small country, it is a big idea: a new world order where diverse nations are drawn together in common cause to achieve the universal aspirations of mankind . . . peace and security, freedom and the rule of law. Such is a world worthy of our struggle and worthy of our children's future.
>
> The community of nations has resolutely gathered to condemn and repel lawless aggression. [Iraqi President] Saddam Hussein's unprovoked invasion, his ruthless, systematic rape of a peaceful neighbor, violated everything the community of nations holds dear. The world has said this aggression would not stand, and it will not stand.
>
> Together, we have resisted the trap of appeasement, cynicism and isolation that gives temptation to tyrants. The world has answered Saddam's invasion with twelve United Nations resolutions, starting with a demand for Iraq's immediate and unconditional withdrawal and backed up by forces

from 28 countries of six continents. With few exceptions, the world now stands as one.

Most Americans know instinctively why we are in the gulf. . . . They know we must make sure that control of the world's oil resources does not fall into [Hussein's] hands only to finance further aggression. They know that we need to build a new, enduring peace based not on arms races and confrontation but on shared principles and the rule of law . . .

The world can therefore seize this opportunity to fulfill the long-held promise of a new world order where brutality will go unrewarded and aggression will meet collective resistance . . .

The winds of change are with us now. The forces of freedom are together united. We move toward the next century more confident than ever that we have the will at home and abroad to do what must be done . . . the hard work of freedom.[29]

On February 27, 1991, President Bush announced to the nation that "Kuwait is liberated" and declared victory for the allied forces. He stated: "This is a victory for the United Nations, for all mankind, for the rule of law and for what is right."[30] At each step, Bush had stressed the illegality of Iraq's actions, the legal basis for U.S. actions, full support for and adherence to the Charter and Resolutions of the United Nations, and support for a multinational response to Iraq's aggression. In the span of a few months, President Bush, with the key support of Soviet President Mikhail Gorbachev, did more for the stature of the United Nations and the rule of law in international affairs than anyone since President Dwight D. Eisenhower condemned and reversed the invasion of Egypt by Britain, France and Israel in late October of 1956.

It is worth recalling Eisenhower's words during that crisis; they are pertinent today. In his October 31, 1956 television and

radio report to the nation on the Middle East crisis, Eisenhower
said:

> We believe these actions to have been taken in error, for we
> do not accept the use of force as a wise or proper instru-
> ment for the settlement of international disputes. . . . The
> present fact nonetheless seems clear. The action taken can
> scarcely be reconciled with the principles and purposes of
> the United Nations to which we have all subscribed. And
> beyond this we are forced to doubt that resort to force and
> war will for long serve the permanent interests of the attack-
> ing nations. . . . I assure you your Government will remain
> alert to every possibility of this situation and keep in close
> contact and coordination with the legislative branch of this
> Government.

Eisenhower went on to detail U.S. efforts to end hostilities in
Egypt through the United Nations, efforts that were stalled at first
by the Security Council veto of Britain and France. Eisenhower
remained "deeply convinced that the United Nations represents
the soundest hope for peace in the world." He also believed,
however, that its "processes . . . need further to be developed
and strengthened" if it was to "secure justice under international law." He ended with an exhortation that to a degree fore-
shadows George H.W. Bush's rhetoric during the Kuwait crisis:

> In all the recent troubles in the Middle East there have,
> indeed, been injustices suffered by all nations involved. But
> I do not believe that another instrument of injustice—war—
> is a remedy for these wrongs. *There can be no peace without
> law. And there can be no law if we were to invoke one code of
> international conduct for those who oppose us and another
> for our friends.* The peace we seek and need means much
> more than mere absence of war. It means the acceptance
> of law and the fostering of justice in all the world. To our

principles guiding us in this quest we must stand fast. In
so doing we can honor the hopes of all men for a world in
which peace will truly and justly reign.[31]

Henry Kissinger should have taken those words to heart:
"there can be no law" if our conduct shifts based on the perception of political friendliness. The United States should follow
the policy established by President Eisenhower: laws must be
applied to friend and foe alike; and the policy of Presidents
George H. W. Bush and Mikhail Gorbachev—"that aggression
cannot and will not pay." If, in 1974, the United States had
joined with the world community in condemning and taking
action to reverse Turkey's aggression in Cyprus, would Iraq's
dictator, Saddam Hussein, have invaded Kuwait in 1990? The
force of precedent should not be underestimated.

The European Union (EU) has already stated that consideration of Turkey's application for entry into the EU is
linked to progress on the Cyprus question and human rights
in Turkey itself. During the Kuwait crisis, EU officials explicitly linked Iraq's invasion and the international response to
the earlier crisis on Cyprus. In early 1991, the president of
the EU's (then European Community's) Council of Ministers,
Luxembourg Foreign Minister Jacques Poos, announced that
the European Community would soon mount an initiative to
promote an overall Cyprus settlement within the framework
of the United Nations resolutions. The European Parliament
unanimously passed a resolution (which included a reference
to Kuwait) endorsing Mr. Poos's statement and calling on the
Community's Council of Ministers and the foreign affairs ministers meeting in the European Political Cooperation group "to
intervene actively and to take all necessary steps to ensure that
the United Nations resolutions on the question of Cyprus are
complied with immediately."[32]

The European Parliament Resolution on Cyprus with reference to Kuwait, adopted March 14, 1991, reads in part:

A. Aware that the international community has taken, as its authority for action in the Gulf, the resolutions of the Security Council of the United Nations on the invasion of Kuwait;

B. Acknowledging the need for the consistent and impartial application of international law;

C. Whereas Turkey has occupied a part of the Republic of Cyprus since 1974;

D. Observing the extent to which the international community has collaborated to implement and to apply the United Nations Security Council's resolutions on Kuwait, and understanding that equivalent determination should be shown in order to implement all relevant United Nations resolutions on Cyprus by peaceful means:

(1) Calls on the Council and the Foreign Affairs Ministers meeting in EPC [European Political Cooperation] to intervene actively and to take all necessary steps to ensure that the United Nations resolutions on the question of Cyprus are complied with immediately;

(2) Endorses the statement made by the President of the Council, Mr. J. Poos, on 7 February 1991 that the Presidency regards it as part of its duties to resolve any crises that affect Community and allied countries, including the Cyprus crisis, and that it intends to take an initiative on the basis of the relevant United Nations resolutions under the auspices of Secretary-General Perez de Cuellar;

The United States, the other four permanent members of the Security Council—Russia, Britain, France and China—and the world community should follow the Kuwaiti precedent by applying international legal norms to Turkey and condemn that nation for its "naked aggression" against Cyprus. The aggression against Cyprus—made possible by Henry Kissinger's

POLITICAL CARTOONS

BY

PAT OLIPHANT

BEHOLD OUR ALLY, THE NOBLE TURK

'WHY, CERTAINLY YOU CAN BE OF ASSISTANCE—YOU CAN HELP ME BURY HIM!'

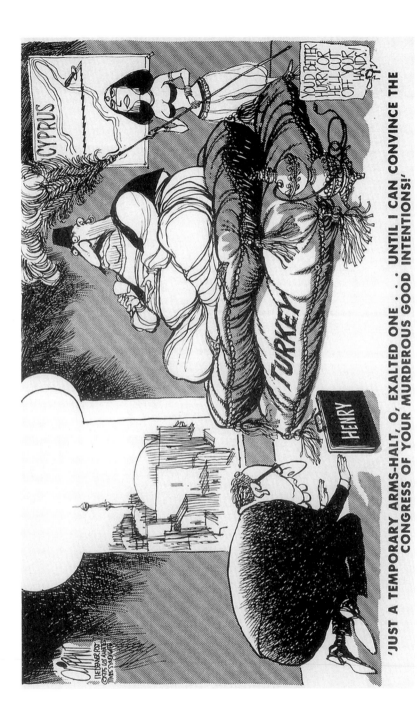

'JUST A TEMPORARY ARMS-HALT, O, EXALTED ONE . . . UNTIL I CAN CONVINCE THE CONGRESS OF YOUR MURDEROUS GOOD INTENTIONS!'

encouragement and mendacity—was in violation of a sovereign nation's territorial integrity. The long-standing illegal occupation by Turkish forces and the continuing illegal colonization by the aggressor country have exacerbated the problem. Moreover, viable government is not possible if, as the Turkish government and the Turkish Cypriot regime have advocated, the Turkish Cypriot minority has veto power over all major government decisions, including taxation, finance, security, and foreign affairs. However, it is also not a question of minority rights. Turkish Cypriots continue to enjoy full minority rights—the same individual rights as the Greek Cypriots. The Greek Cypriots have offered to have those rights guaranteed. And Cyprus's accession to the European Union in May 2004 gives added support to minority rights. The problem is simply one of Turkey's territorial aggrandizement, a Turkish land grab through brute force with Kissinger's encouragement. A solution is not difficult if the will to act is strong. The first step should be a policy decision by the Security Council to enforce its resolutions calling for an end to Turkey's illegal occupation and colonization of Cyprus.

On January 30, 1991, President George H. W. Bush met with the Greek foreign minister Antonios Samaras. A member of the Greek press corps asked Bush: "Does your resolve for implementation of all U.N. resolutions include the Cyprus issue as well?" Bush responded: "We've been looking at that for a long, long time. . . . [T]hat's a problem that I'd love to see solved, in keeping with these U.N. resolutions."[33]

The constitutional issues can be settled in accordance with the rule of law and the universally accepted democratic principle of majority rule with minority rights fully protected. Then-Vice President George H. W. Bush made the following policy statement on July 7, 1988: "We seek for Cyprus a constitutional democracy based on majority rule, the rule of law, and the protection of minority rights. . . . I want to see a democratic Cyprus free from the threat of war."[34] Once this is accepted, the road to a peaceful solution is clear.

11

"Kissinger the war criminal"

In his book review of *Nixon and Kissinger: Partners in Power* (2007), Professor Jussi M. Hanhimäki comments:

> "History," Henry Kissinger told Richard Nixon on the eve of the president's resignation in August 1974, "will treat you more kindly then your contemporaries have." He has been proven correct. When Nixon died in 1994, his achievements, particularly in foreign policy, dominated the historical assessments of the only U.S. president to have resigned.
>
> The opposite has been the case with Kissinger. Journalists fawned over him when he was in office. In 1973, he was awarded the Nobel Peace Prize for negotiating the imperfect end to the Vietnam War, even as Nixon was squirming in the purgatory of Watergate. But over time, "Kissinger the war criminal" came to replace the image of a globe-trotting super-diplomat.[1]

It seems unbelievable now that Henry Kissinger is a Nobel laureate—for peace. This supposed peacemaker won the award in 1973 only months before the Turkish invasion of Cyprus on July 20, 1974, which Kissinger encouraged and for which he was in large part responsible. Not only that, he encouraged the Greek junta–initiated coup of July 15, 1974 against the elected Makarios government of Cyprus, including the attempted assassination of President Makarios. He then encouraged the July 20, 1974 Turkish invasion of Cyprus and the second and massive phase of Turkey's aggression on August 14–16, 1974, without any pretext and three weeks after the legitimate government of Cyprus had been restored on July 23, 1974. In its initial aggression Turkey captured about four percent of Cyprus including the port town of Kyrenia on the north coast and a corridor to the Turkish Cypriot part of Nicosia. Cease-fire violations accounted for an additional three to four percent of Cypriot territory, and then Turkey grabbed an additional 30 percent in northern Cyprus in its August 14–16, 1974 aggression, for a total of 37.3 percent of Cyprus.

It is not just his complicity in the dismemberment of Cyprus that makes Kissinger's Nobel prize a sham. He was selected for supposedly bringing peace to a conflict that he had been largely responsible for extending. In fact, the major foreign policy disaster of the Nixon-Kissinger years was the needless extension of the Vietnam War from January 20, 1969, the beginning of Nixon's first term, to the signing of the Vietnam peace treaty in February 1973, four years later. In my view, Kissinger influenced Nixon more than anyone or anything else to extend the war instead of carrying out his 1968 presidential campaign pledge to end the war in Vietnam. As a result, up to 21,000 Americans in our armed forces in Vietnam lost their lives, needlessly in my judgment.

Consider Kissinger's Vietnam-era record. I was campaign manager for Nixon's 1968 presidential campaign in New York City, after working as a deputy manager for Governor Nelson Rockefeller's campaign for the Republican presidential nomination, which he lost. Rockefeller subsequently pledged his support to Nixon. I had known Nixon casually from the Eisenhower administration (I was special assistant to Undersecretary of the

Treasury Fred C. Scribner Jr. from mid-1958 to January 1961), and his campaign staff asked me to manage the New York City campaign. Nixon made several key speeches on issues in the 1968 campaign and I stressed two of them in our New York City campaign: his "I will end the war in Vietnam," and "The military balance must be tipped in Israel's favor." In office, however, it became apparent that Nixon's Vietnam campaign pledge would not be kept, and that Kissinger was the prime mover behind that reversal. The war would continue through the early 1970s, needlessly throwing away thousands of lives. Martin F. Nolan, who covered the Nixon White House for the *Boston Globe*, in a book review on May 6, 2007 of *Nixon and Kissinger: Partners in Power*, Harpers Collins, (2007), puts the blame on both Nixon and Kissinger:

> Their egocentric political scheming lengthened the war in Vietnam, so they already have monuments on the Mall in Washington. The Vietnam Memorial lists American combat deaths year by year. On the Nixon-Kissinger wall, the total exceeds 21,000, and for what?[2]

Regarding Kissinger and Vietnam, Anthony Lewis, the distinguish *New York Times* columnist, wrote the following in his January 13, 1977 column:

> History will remember him most of all for his policy in Indochina. In the teeth of evidence well known by 1969, this supposed realist pressed obsessively for indefinite maintenance of the status quo. To that end, in his time, 20,492 more Americans died in Vietnam and hundreds of thousands of Vietnamese. The war was expanded into Cambodia, destroying that peaceable land. And all for nothing.

Albert R. Hunt, *Wall Street Journal* columnist, in a May 26, 1994 column on *The Haldeman Diaries: Inside the Nixon White*

House, discusses a number of Halderman's comments on Henry Kissinger. Mr. Hunt writes:

> The recently released dairies of President Nixon's chief of staff, H.R. Haldeman . . . haven't gotten as much attention as they deserve. ABC-TV's 'Nightime' did an excellent two-part series, but otherwise they have been depicted as chiefly kiss-and-tell stories.
>
> They are much more. Historian Stephen Ambrose, author of a highly acclaimed three-part volume on Richard Nixon, says the diaries are so valuable that he could write another book just on them. . . . [W]ith extraordinary discipline, the chief of staff recorded the day's events.
>
> * * * *
>
> Mr. Ambrose . . . says that his research suggests that the diaries are amazingly reliable. Jo Haldeman, the author's widow, says her husband saw the diaries as 'a valuable research source for historians' that would 'help put the Nixon presidency in better perspective.'
>
> Both Ms. Haldeman and Prof. Ambrose agree that other than Richard Nixon the book's central figure is Henry Kissinger; it's not a flattering portrait. When Ms. Haldeman called Mr. Kissinger some weeks ago to tell him about the book, he expressed displeasure, suggesting it would be better if it never were published.
>
> Mr. Kissinger, who says he hasn't read the book, nevertheless suggests that many conversations 'may have been taken out of context.' Moreover, he questions Mr. Haldeman's expertise: 'Haldeman was not a foreign policy man.'
>
> Nice try, Henry, but no dice. Mr. Haldeman . . . shows an incredibly petty and insecure man. . . Walter Isaacson, who recently wrote a superb, if critical, biography of Mr. Kissinger, says that after reading the Haldeman diaries he fears he 'understated the paranoid atmosphere' that affected

the Nixon White House in general and Henry Kissinger in particular.

But Mr. Kissinger's greatest flaw was Vietnam. The president's foreign policy czar initially envisioned a get tough policy the first year that would drive Hanoi to the bargaining table. 'He [Mr. Kissinger] wants to push for some escalation, enough to get us a reasonable bargain for a settlement within six months,' Mr. Haldeman reports on July 7, 1969. This became a familiar, and movable, refrain.

'If we just had one more dry season, the opponents would break their backs,' Mr. Kissinger tells the president in San Clemente on Aug. 24, 1971, more than two years later. The ever-loyal chief of staff couldn't resist adding: 'This, of course, is the same line he's used for the last two years, over and over . . . it's amazing how it sounds like a broken record,' . . .

Today Mr. Kissinger still is one who perpetuates the myth that Vietnam was lost not because of a flawed policy, but due to a lack of political will at home.

* * * *

The next time Mr. Kissinger is pronouncing on some momentous event, take a look at the Haldeman diaries. They're a good reality check.

In a conversation with General Charles de Gaulle, Kissinger revealed his reasoning for extending the war—and revealed his grotesque lack of concern for the lives being spent. De Gaulle asked Kissinger: "Why don't you get out of Vietnam?" and Kissinger replied: "Because a sudden withdrawal might give us a credibility problem."[3] That was his concern vis-à-vis the quagmire of Vietnam: not spreading democracy, not upholding the rule of law, not even American casualties. It was credibility.

I have long contended as well that Kissinger was the godfather of "the plumbers unit" and Watergate. Martin Nolan has written:

> [E. Howard] Hunt [one of the Watergate burglars] has little to say about Kissinger, but Kissinger's overreaction to the 1971 publication of the Pentagon Papers actually led to the notion of White House burglars on 24-hour call, "the plumbers unit." The president's political advisers thought the publication of Vietnam documents was harmless, even beneficial, to Nixon because it documented Democratic mistakes in Vietnam. Laird called them "the McNamara papers" after Robert McNamara, defense secretary for Presidents Kennedy and Johnson.
>
> Kissinger prevailed, persuading Nixon that preserving secrecy was more important than law and order. So Hunt and G. Gordon Liddy deployed their burglar tools on Nixon's behalf, were caught and sent to prison. Unlike Nixon and Kissinger, they complained little. Hunt and Liddy retained, during and after that paranoid era, a sense of humor and a sense of honor.[4]

Just as with Turkey, Greece, and Cyprus, the end always justified the means to Kissinger. Burglary and intimidation would trump the rule of law as long as he considered secrecy of prime importance. Time after time — not only on Cyprus and at the Democratic National Headquarters in America, but also in Vietnam, Bangladesh, Chile, East Timor,[5] and elsewhere — Kissinger would follow this pattern. Even with his own staff, Kissinger was obsessed with secrecy and loyalty. As head of the National Security Council (NSC) Kissinger tapped the telephone conversations of his staff to determine their loyalty to him and whether they were leaking information to the media. When he took control (unofficially) of American foreign policy, he was perhaps in an unfamiliar situation: administrator. His position as the national security advisor to the president was a policy position managing a substantial staff. As an academic he had no management experience of any substance to prepare him to manage the National Security Council staff to say nothing of a major department of the government. Perhaps a small part of Kissinger's tendency toward backstage machinations was this very lack of management experience. But it certainly does not excuse his crimes.

Just as with Vietnam and Watergate, the means Kissinger employed during the Cyprus crisis were not only unlawful but in service of a goal that was harmful to U.S. interests. His actions and deliberate inactions, which encouraged Turkey's aggression against Cyprus on July 20, 1974 and the second and massive phase of the aggression on August 14-16, 1974, were the direct cause of Turkey's war crimes, crimes against humanity, ethnic cleansing, cultural cleansing and the planned emigration of illegal colonists from Anatolia to the occupied north of Cyprus. At a minimum Kissinger was and remains an accessory and accomplice to all these crimes.

Kissinger bears direct responsibility for the several hundred (331) Greek Cypriot deaths and 1,288 missing, the rape of women from 12 to 71 years old, the looting and pillaging of Greek Cypriots houses, properties and businesses (including American-owned homes and properties), the ethnic cleansing of 200,000 Greek Cypriots from the north of Cyprus and the cultural cleansing of the north of its Christian religious treasures and heritage, archeological treasures, and Jewish synagogues.

Kissinger should be indicted as a war criminal—as should have happened long ago—along with the Turkish military and political leadership and the Turkish military commanders in Cyprus for the war crimes set forth in the July 10, 1976 report of the European Commission on Human Rights on the first and second applications of the government of Cyprus verses Turkey.

Those war crimes consisted of the violations of the following articles of the European Convention on Human Rights:

1. Article 2—by the killing of innocent civilians committed on a substantial scale;
2. Article 3—by the rape of women of all ages from 12 to 71;
3. Article 3—by inhuman treatment of prisoners and persons detained—a continuing violation;
4. Article 5—by deprivation of liberty with regard to detainees and missing persons—a continuing violation;
5. Article 8—by displacement of persons creating more than 170,000 Greek Cypriot refugees, and by refusing to allow the refugees to return to their homes—a continuing violation;
6. Article 1 of the First Protocol to the Convention—by deprivation of possessions, looting and robbery on an extensive scale.

On January 23, 1977, the *London Sunday Times* published excerpts from that report, stating: "It amounts to a massive indictment of the Ankara government for the murder, rape and looting by its army in Cyprus during and after the Turkish invasion of summer 1974." Furthermore, as we saw earlier, Kissinger did nothing from the summer of 1974 to the end of the Ford Administration on January 20, 1977 to stop Turkey's violation of the Geneva Convention of 1949 by the "transfer. . . of its own civilian population into the territory it occupies" in Cyprus. These actions by Turkey can also be considered war crimes. The Geneva Convention of 1949, section III, article 49 prohibits colonization by an occupying power. Section III of the Geneva Convention deals with Occupied Territories. Article 49 states in its last paragraph: "The Occupying Power shall not deport or transfer parts of its own civilian population into the territory it occupies."

Consideration should be given to bringing Kissinger before the International Criminal Court. There is no statute of limitations for war crimes. The Turkish military and political leadership in 1974 and the Turkish military commanders in Cyprus in 1974 should also be brought before the International Criminal Court. But Kissinger has not been held accountable. Instead, his crimes have been brushed under the rug. The State Department has covered up Kissinger's lawlessness and wrongdoing ever since Kissinger left office on January 20, 1977. This whitewashing is one of the more troubling outcomes of the Cyprus crisis, and has tainted U.S. diplomacy for four decades. I assume its purpose was to placate Turkey. It is more important for the State Department to support the rule of law and democratic values, including democracy based on majority rule, the rule of law and protection of minority rights, rather than to appease Turkey. The State Department should tell the public of Kissinger's unlawful conduct regarding Cyprus in 1974. It should also denounce Kissinger's efforts in 1975 to remove the congressional rule of law arms embargo legislation on Turkey. Exposing Kissinger would enhance the credibility and prestige of the United States worldwide.

12

The Rule of Law in the National Interest

In the middle of the twentieth century, the United States led the way towards the institutionalization of international law, giving democratic voices around the world a chance to be heard. In the twenty-first century, it should be a truism that American credibility and prestige suffer when it itself turns away from the rule of law. Yet time and again we have had to re-learn this lesson. It was under Henry Kissinger's tenure that many of the worst episodes of the United States acting counter to international law in the service of a mistaken sense of national interest occurred. In fact, it is in the national interest of the United States to support the rule of law, and rectifying its wrong in Cyprus would be an important step in this direction.

Nor would it be an unfamiliar step. There is no fundamental legal difference between Iraq's aggression against Kuwait and Turkey's aggression against Cyprus that would prevent a comparable response against Turkey by the world community, short of a declaration of war. Turkey's aggression has been compounded over a forty year period, a fact which should weigh heavily against Turkey. Toleration of Turkey's occupation of 37.3 percent of Cyprus weakens the legal, moral, political, and diplomatic positions of the United States in the Middle East and throughout the world. The United States must insist that Turkey, as George Ball and Cyrus Vance said, "purge" itself of its aggression by removing its troops and colonists/settlers from Cyprus at once, without conditions.

The reaction of the world community to Iraq's aggression against Kuwait in 1990 gave hope at the time that Turkey's occupation of Cypriot territory would end through a peaceful and democratic solution in accordance with the UN Charter and resolutions on Cyprus. Unfortunately, it did not then and has not since. Nevertheless it could happen with sufficient effort. After all, the United States, with the full support of the Soviet Union, was able to mobilize the world community through the United Nations against Iraqi aggression against Kuwait in support of the rule of law. The United States has not taken any real steps since 1974 regarding Turkey to achieve a peaceful, just, and viable settlement of the Cyprus problem. Turkey's aggression against Cyprus and occupation of its northern third is now in its forty years. It is in the national interest of the United States to take concrete steps to pressure Turkey to get its troops and settlers out of Cyprus and to achieve a peaceful, just, and viable settlement. And it is not as if there is no element of what is generally thought of as economic self-interest in the matter of Cyprus, as there was with Kuwait's oil. In view of the natural gas discoveries in Cyprus's Exclusive Economic Zone (EEZ) and Cyprus's growing relationship with Israel, the United States would be well-served economically to bring the crisis to a close. But the opportunity to advance the cause of democratic self-rule should be incentive enough.

Cyprus is not a complex matter. The issue is aggression, the rule of law and the democratic principles of majority rule and the protection of minority rights. The United States sidesteps its responsibility by saying we will agree to anything acceptable to the parties. That has been used by recent administrations to placate and avoid pressuring Turkey, the aggressor. The United States needs to stand for a realistic policy, one we can support before the world community regarding Cyprus and in other current foreign policy issues, namely, the rule of law in international affairs, democracy based on majority rule, and the protection of minority rights[1] as set forth in the U.S. charters of freedom: the Declaration of Independence, the Constitution and the Bill of Rights.

The United States also should publicly state its support of the various United Nations substantive resolutions on Cyprus that call for recognition of the sovereignty, independence and territorial integrity of Cyprus. Specifically the United States should publicly reiterate its support for and implementation of unanimous General Assembly Resolution 3212 of November 1, 1974,[2] which called for the removal of all foreign military forces from Cyprus, and UN Security Council Resolution 365 of December 13, 1974, which endorsed General Assembly Resolution 3212. For its own part, the United States should exert diplomatic, political and economic pressure directly and through the United Nations on Turkey to get out of Cyprus. The United States should publicly call for the removal of Turkey's armed forces from Cyprus and the removal of the Anatolian settlers/colonist who are in Cyprus in violation of the Geneva Convention of 1949 .

In a July 7, 1988 speech in Boston, Vice President George H.W. Bush said, "We seek for Cyprus a constitutional democracy based on majority rule, the rule of law, and the protection of minority rights. . . . I want to see a democratic Cyprus free from the threat of war." That is a stance the United States should publicly adopt today, in word and deed.

There are three developments in recent years which should move the United States and the European Union to press Turkey to get out of Cyprus. The first is the discovery of significant natural gas resources in the Eastern Mediterranean in Cyprus's Exclusive Economic Zone (EEZ). The second development is Turkey's split with Israel and its current anti-Israel policy. Turkey has attacked Israel's Palestinian policy and initiated the flotilla against Israel, besides terminating its military arrangement with Israel. The third is the growing relationship of Israel with Greece and Cyprus.

For security and energy reasons, the United States should seek a "quadrilateral coalition or alliance" with Israel, Greece and Cyprus. As Seth Cropsey writes in his July 3, 2013 Hudson Institute article:

> A quadrilateral relationship—U.S., Greece, Israel and Cyprus—based on economic and security interests would help defend NATO's southeastern flank, offset the increasing presence of Russian, Chinese, Iranian naval forces in the region and deter the Turkish fleet as Turkey abandons the Kemalist enterprise in favor of Islamist fundamentalism. U.S. leadership of a high-level strategic dialogue that brings the four countries together annually to discuss regional developments would help bring common goals closer. Upgrading in size and scope the annual [U.S., Greece and Israel] special forces training, naval maritime interdiction exercises, intelligence sharing and joint counter-terrorism training would also improve security; so would effective action to ensure unhindered access to the strategic airbase of Paphos on Cyprus for U.S., Greek and Israeli air forces. All these measures will help secure the sea lines of communication and provide a powerful deterrent against hostile state and non-state actors.

There are Cypriot considerations other than geopolitical that commend the attention of the United States and other Western countries. The rule of law extends to human rights for all Cypriots. The State Department should follow the precedent of the European Court of Human Rights decision in the case of Loizidou v. Turkey and publicly call for compensation to Greek Cypriot owners of property and other owners—including

Americans—for the loss of use of their property in occupied Cyprus. The State Department should support legislation in Congress authorizing American owners of property in occupied Cyprus to sue Turkey in U.S. federal courts for the loss of use of their property.

The State Department should also publicly call for the immediate return of the vacant area of Famagusta/Varosha for the resettlement of refugees under UN supervision, as was promised by the Carter Administration and by Turkey and the Turkish Cypriots during the legislative battle in the summer of 1978 to lift the remaining rule of law arms embargo against Turkey. The return of Famagusta/Varosha was also in the U.S. twelve point plan for Cyprus released in November 1978.[3] The European Parliament, in a written declaration on February 14, 2012, signed by 390 members, called for the return of Famagusta/Varosha to its lawful owners.[4]

The United States should, either alone or in collaboration with Britain, a guarantor power, call for a UN war crimes tribunal on Turkey's actions in Cyprus, similar to the war crimes tribunal on Yugoslavia, or, failing that, bring Turkey before the International Criminal Court (ICC).

The United States should oppose any aid to Turkey from the IMF and other international organizations until Turkey gets its troops and settlers/colonists out of Cyprus. And the United States should support legislation in Congress suspending all current benefits to Turkey including textile quotas and most favored nation status until Turkey removes its troops and settlers/colonists from Cyprus.

Cyprus continues to be a key test today for the rule of law in international affairs. Is the rule of law to be applied uniformly, or is there to be a continuation of the double standard for and appeasement of Turkey's aggression? Enforcing the United Nations resolutions on Cyprus against Turkey would demonstrate that the era of this double standard for an ally on the rule of law is over. It would reinforce and confirm our efforts in 1990–1991 in the Persian Gulf for a new world order. To be credible the rule of law must be applied to our friends and opponents alike. As President Eisenhower stated in 1956:

> There can be no peace without law, and there can be no law if we were to invoke one code of international conduct for those who oppose us and another for our friends.

The historic action of the world community against Iraq's invasion and occupation of Kuwait is an extraordinary precedent.[5] President Eisenhower's historic actions in 1956 to stop and reverse the invasion of Egypt by Britain, France and Israel are also a significant precedent. These precedents hold great promise for liberating Cyprus. A unified world could force Turkey to relinquish her involvement in Cyprus and let the Cypriots come to a solution under their own terms. The value of such an outcome for the rule of law in international affairs, added to the Kuwait and Egypt precedents, would be highly significant. It is time to shed the last vestiges of the blunders, double-dealing, and mendacity of the Kissinger era in favor of open and honest dealings. It is time to end the Turkish occupation of Cyprus and reinvigorate the rule of law and democratic governance on that historic isle.

Appendix

Presidential campaign statements
1976–2008

Governor Ronald Reagan

Republican presidential candidate
May 14, 1976, Detroit, Michigan

The present tragic situation in Cyprus is another example of the failure of the Kissinger-Ford foreign policy. President Ford should have taken action to prevent the unlawful use of U.S.-supplied arms by Turkey in Cyprus. I believe in the right of self-determination for the people of Cyprus. My position is that the Turkish invasion troops and colonists should leave Cyprus and all refugees should return to their homes and land. If I am elected president I will uphold the rule of law at home and abroad and I will use my office to bring about that result.

Governor Jimmy Carter

Democratic presidential nominee
September 16, 1976, Washington, DC

The continuing tensions between Greece and Turkey damage the NATO alliance and endanger stability in the Eastern

Mediterranean. If these two allies of the United States are to play a vigorous role in the alliance, there must be a just and rapid settlements of the tragic situation on Cyprus.

The policy of the Ford Administration of tilting away from Greece and Cyprus has proved a disaster for NATO and for American security interests in the Eastern Mediterranean.

Despite repeated warnings, the Administration failed to prevent the 1974 coup against President Makarios engineered by the former military dictatorship in Athens. The Administration failed to prevent or even limit the Turkish invasion that followed. The Administration failed to uphold either principle or the rule of law in the conduct of our foreign policy. American law requires that arms supplied by the United States be used solely for defensive purposes.

Today, more than two years later, no progress toward a negotiated solution on Cyprus has been made.

The lack of progress is disappointing and dangerous. Peace must be based upon the United Nations General Assembly Resolution 3212 of November 1, 1974 endorsed by Cyprus, Greece and Turkey, calling among other things, for the removal of all foreign military forces from Cyprus. The widely reported increase in colonization of Cyprus by Turkish military and civilian forces should cease. Greek Cypriot refugees should be allowed to return to their homes. Both Greek and Turkish Cypriots should be assured of their rights, both during and after the withdrawal of all foreign troops from Cyprus.

The impasse on Cyprus must be broken. The United States must be prepared to work with others, including the United Nations, to insure the independence, territorial integrity and sovereignty of Cyprus.

In addition, the dispute over rights in the Aegean must be resolved peacefully, under international law. Provocations must be avoided.

Greece and Turkey are and must remain our allies within NATO and neighbors at peace with each other within the community of nations.

The United States must pursue a foreign policy based on principle and in accord with the rule of law.

If and when I am elected President I intend to enforce and carry out the provisions of the statement.

Governor Ronald Reagan

Republican presidential nominee
September 26, 1980, Washington, DC

Republican presidential nominee Governor Ronald Reagan issued a statement on September 26, 1980 in which he stated that Carter had "reneged on his pledges" regarding Cyprus. Excerpts dealing with Cyprus follow:

Statement by the Honorable Ronald Reagan
on Greece, Cyprus, Turkey

* * * *

In 1976, while campaigning for the presidency, candidate Jimmy Carter stated, "We would be negligent of the moral issues and courting longer-range disaster if we fail to couple the improvement in relations with Turkey with increased fair progress on the Cyprus issue." And in a news release dated September 16, 1976, he declared, "The impasse on Cyprus must be broken. The United States must be prepared to work with others, including the United Nations, to insure the independence, territorial integrity and sovereignty of Cyprus. . . If and when I am elected President, I intend to enforce and carry out the provisions of the statement."

Given those words, one might have assumed that something positive regarding a settlement would have emerged by now. As in so many other cases of Carter's campaign declarations and promises, he reneged on his pledges.

* * * *

The tragic situation in Cyprus has lasted six years. It must not continue. The foreign military forces on that island should be substantially reduced, and Cypriot refugees, be they Greek or Turkish, should be permitted to return to their homes and land.

I support the full implementation of unanimously approved United Nations Resolution 3212 of November 1974 which:

"Calls upon all States to respect the sovereignty, independence, territorial integrity and non-alignment of the Republic of Cyprus and to refrain from all acts and intervention directed against it; Urges the speedy withdrawal of all foreign armed forces and foreign military presence and personnel from the Republic of Cyprus, and the cessation of all foreign interference in its affairs."

Vice President George H. W. Bush

Republican presidential nominee
July 7, 1988, Boston, MA

We seek for Cyprus a constitutional democracy based on majority rule, the rule of law, and the protection of minority rights. . . I want to see a democratic Cyprus free from the threat of war.

As President, George H. W. Bush elevated the Cyprus issue to the White House level and thought that he had a deal among the parties. At a Paris conference to close the deal in late 1991, Turkey at the last minute reneged on the deal.

Governor Bill Clinton

Democratic presidential candidate
October 2, 1992

Statement by Governor Clinton on Issues of Special Concern to the Greek American Community.

* * * *

In this world of extraordinary change, it is tragic that a just solution to the Cyprus problem remains elusive. Since 1974 the northern part of Cyprus has been under Turkish military occupation. The United States has a moral obligation as well as a national security interest to see that this illegal occupation of Cyprus comes to an end.

The United States and the world community will not accept the permanent division of Cyprus. The search for a just and viable solution to the Cyprus problem must be vigorously pursued. Such a Cyprus settlement should be consistent with the fundamental principles of human rights and democratic norms and practices. Accordingly, a Cyprus settlement can be just and viable only if it provides for the withdrawal of Turkish occupation forces; satisfactorily accounts for all American and Greek Cypriots missing since 1974; provides for the rights of refugees; ensures the sovereign independence and territorial integrity of the state; and establishes a democratic constitution which respects and guarantees the rights of both communities.

I will give the Cyprus issue a high foreign policy priority in my administration and, working with the European Community and the United Nations, I will press hard for a lasting solution to the tragedy of Cyprus. Such a solution will serve not only the best interests of Cyprus, but also the best interests of our allies, Greece and Turkey, and above all the best interests of the United States. In this respect, I believe that the 7:10 ratio of military aid to Greece and Turkey advances the cause of peace and stability in the region.

President Bill Clinton

October 19, 1996
Washington, DC

During my administration, I have made the resolution of the Cyprus problem a high foreign policy priority, and have taken several steps to advance this goal. In January, 1995, I appointed Richard Beattie as a Special Presidential Emissary for Cyprus, the first such Emissary in 17 years. Last July, I sent Ambassador Madeleine Albright to the region with Mr. Beattie to begin discussions, which we hope will lead to direct talks between the two communities and to a comprehensive settlement that is long overdue. I have sustained our program of $15 million in annual bilateral assistance to Cyprus, which is intended to foster greater bicommunal interaction on the island. My administration played an active role in encouraging the European Union to schedule accession talks for Cyprus. Our Ambassador in Nicosia, Robert Dillon, is conducting an investigation into the whereabouts of five American citizens who disappeared in 1974. When there have been setbacks, such as the recent unjustified and unwarranted killings of Greek Cypriots in the UN buffer zone, we have spoken out forcefully, while seeking agreement on measures aimed at preventing the recurrence of these tragedies. These incidents and the continued division of the island are unacceptable and I will continue to press for a comprehensive and lasting settlement to this tragic dispute.

Vice President Al Gore

Democratic presidential nominee
October 26, 2000

I have followed the situation in Cyprus for many years. It is my hope that the present UN-sponsored talks will resolve the bitter differences that have long divided the island for the good of the people of Greece, the people of Turkey, and most importantly, for the people of Cyprus.

President Clinton recently told President Ahmet Necdet Sezer in a meeting about his concern that the current UN-sponsored talks would break down if the Turkish Cypriot side made its status a precondition to negotiations on other issues. Secretary of State Albright made this same point in a meeting a few days later with Turkish Foreign Minister Cem. I am pleased that after President Clinton's and Secretary Albright's meetings, the two sides for the first time actually engaged in negotiations on core issues, without preconditions.

If I am elected President, I will make Cyprus one of my foreign policy priorities. My administration will continue to fully support the relevant UN Security Council resolutions calling for the establishment of a bi-zonal, bi-communal federation uniting Cyprus.

Cyprus is looking to become a member of the European Union and is working hard to fulfill the conditions for EU membership. Indeed, I understand that Cyprus is now further along than any other country in meeting these conditions. This reflects the high priority Cyprus gives to joining with other European countries in their common quest for peace, stability, and prosperity in Europe.

Last December in Helsinki, the EU heads of state adopted a declaration stating that a settlement is not a precondition to Cyprus's accession but that all relevant factors would be taken into consideration. I interpret this language to mean that both sides on Cyprus are being urged by the EU to make every effort to resolve their difference in order to unite Cyprus. At the same time, the failure of a good-faith effort alone should not prevent Cyprus from entering the EU, although this matter is for the EU itself to determine. However, my administration will do all that it can to encourage the two parties on Cyprus to arrive at a comprehensive settlement that unites the island.

Senator John Kerry

Democratic presidential nominee
October 2004

The entry of the Republic of Cyprus into the European Union is a major step forward both for Cyprus and for the EU. With its strong democratic institutions, vigorous economy and hard-working, well-educated and productive people, Cyprus has earned its EU membership. Cyprus will help carry the EU's fundamental political and economic principles to the Eastern Mediterranean and will contribute to stability and growth in the Balkans.

Since the Turkish invasion of Cyprus three decades ago, the island has been divided. It is a long-standing objective of U.S. policy to see the island reunited under the terms of a just and peaceful settlement that has the support of all its people. We have not yet reached that objective, to which I am strongly committed. In a recent referendum, the people of Cyprus rejected the United Nations-sponsored plan, in a vote that reflected widespread concern about the plan's deficiencies. While this vote could be viewed as a setback, we must not treat it as a defeat. The U.S. must stand firmly behind the continuing effort to reach an equitable agreement on reunification which commands the broadest possible popular support among the Cypriot people.

Senator Joe Biden

Democratic presidential candidate
May 17, 2007, Washington, DC

Presidential hopefuls Senator Joe Biden (D-DE), the chairman of the Senate Foreign Relations Committee, Senator Hillary Clinton (D-NY), and Senator Barack Obama (D-IL) spoke to a group of

Greek American leaders on May 17, 2007, in Washington, D.C. Voice of America correspondent George Bistis recorded their comments:

Bistis recorded Biden's comments as follows: "The only truly unresolved and unremitting injustice that exists in that . . . area of the world is Cyprus." Bistis said that "Senator Biden outlined a general policy towards Turkey that he plans to implement should his bid for the U.S. Presidency be successful." He recorded Biden's policy toward Turkey as follows:

> The U.S. should demand, should make absolutely clear, that the basis of the relationship is impacted upon by how Cyprus is resolved, Turkey disengaging completely, how disputes between Greece and Turkey in the Aegean are settled in the future, how we deal with those false claims relating to access to oil that has now been found essentially in the continental shelf of Cyprus and how the Patriarch is treated.

Senator Hillary Clinton

Democratic presidential candidate
May 17, 2007, Washington, DC

Mr. George Bistis interviewed Senator Hillary Clinton (D-NY) and recorded her comments on Cyprus as follows:

> We need to make it very clear that this [Cyprus] is an issue that is important to the world, especially to Europe, because they do not want this continuing occupation and the difficulties that flow from it in the midst of Europe. So, you've got to have an American presence that is consistent and steadfast and we will do that when I am President.

Senator Barack Obama

Democratic presidential candidate
May 17, 2007, Washington, DC

Voice of America correspondent George Bistis recorded the following comments of Senator Barack Obama (D-IL) on Cyprus:

> America has been able to rely on Cyprus in the war on terror and we were able to rely on Cyprus during the Lebanon crisis. So we should work to find a solution to the situation in Cyprus that is acceptable to both the Greek and Turkish Cypriot communities, one that is based on the rule of law, not on force, one that is based on the U.N. resolutions passed on the Cyprus issue and on the very principles and standards of the EU, of which Cyprus is a member.

Governor Bill Richardson

Democratic presidential candidate
July 6, 2007, Albuquerque, NM

Governor Bill Richardson, Democratic presidential candidate wrote the following letter to constituents and supporters:

> As Ambassador to the United Nations, I came to understand that the continued illegal occupation of Cyprus by Turkey adversely affects stability in the region and violates basic human rights.
>
> Although the United States recognizes only the Republic of Cyprus as the only government on the island of Cyprus, as President, I would assure that no organ of the United States government would act in any way that may compromise the effect of that recognition. I would also support legislation pending in Congress that would enable U.S. citizens to seek reimbursement for their exclusion from and the continued use of their property by Turkey and persons acting under the protection of the Turkish occupation.

Senator Barack Obama

Democratic presidential nominee
October 2008

As president, I will show U.S. leadership in seeking to negotiate a political settlement on Cyprus. I believe strongly
that Cyprus remain a single, sovereign country . . . within
a bi-zonal, bi-communal federation . . . A negotiated political settlement on Cyprus would end the Turkish occupation
of northern Cyprus and repair the island's tragic division
while paving the way to prosperity and peace throughout
the entire region.

List of Abbreviations

AHEPA	American Hellenic Educational Progressive Association
AHI	American Hellenic Institute
AHIF	American Hellenic Institute Foundation
AKP	Justice and Development Party (of Turkey)
CIA	Central Intelligence Agency
EEZ	Exclusive Economic Zone
EU	European Union
ECHR	European Convention on Human Rights
FAA	Foreign Assistance Act
FBIS	Foreign Broadcast Information Service
FMSA	Foreign Military Sales Act
FOIA	Freedom of Information Act
GB	Genelkurmay Baskanlari (Turkish General Staff)
ICC	International Criminal Court
IHH	Insani Yardim Vakfi (Turkish terrorist support organization)
INCSR	International Narcotics Control Strategy Report
IMF	International Monetary Fund
NATO	North Atlantic Treaty Organization
NSC	National Security Council
SALT	Strategic Arms Limitation Talks
UN	United Nations
USCIRF	United States Commission on International Religious Freedom
WSAG	Washington Special Action Group
U.S.S.R.	Union of Soviet Socialist Republics

Notes

1. CYPRUS: STRATEGIC, ECONOMIC AND POLITICAL VALUE

1. U.S. Army, *Area Handbook For Cyprus* 73 (1971). The 1970 census had the population at 628,000. *Id.*
2. Excerpts of remarks to the American Jewish Committee Global Forum, May 3, 2012.
3. *Id.*
4. Seth Cropsey is a Senior Fellow at Hudson Institute who served as Deputy Undersecretary of the Navy during the Ronald Reagan and George H.W. Bush administrations.
5. See Brookings Institution website for Minister of Foreign Affairs Ioannis Kasoulides' remarks on May 9, 2013.

2. A BRIEF HISTORY AND BACKGROUND ON THE 1974 CRISIS

1. *Convention of Defensive Alliance between Great Britain and Turkey,* June 4, 1878, 68 *British and Foreign State Papers* 744 (1877–1878); 3 *Martens Nouveau Recueil* 274 (ser. 2nd) (commonly known as the *Cyprus Convention of 1878*).
2. *The Treaty of Lausanne*, July 23, 1923, 28 L.N.T.S. 12, 25 [hereinafter Treaty of Lausanne], states: "Turkey hereby recognizes the annexation of Cyprus proclaimed by the British Government on the 5th Nov., 1914." *Id.* at art. 20.
3. *See generally,* Sir George Hill, *A History Of Cyprus* (1952), (four-volume history of Cyprus); Doros Alastos, *Cyprus In History* (1955); *Footprints In Cyprus* (D. Hunt ed. 1982); Costas Kyrris, *History Of Cyprus* (1985); Stavros Pantelis, *The Making Of Modern Cyprus* (1990). *See also* for the post–World War II period, M. Attalides, *Cyprus* (1979); Glafcos Clerides, *Cyprus: My Deposition* (1989), a three volume history and analysis, and a fourth volume (1992).
4. Robert Stephens, *Cyprus: A Place Of Arms* 118 (1966) [hereinafter Stephens]. "Official recruiting posters called on the Greek Cypriots

to volunteer and save the Greek motherland." *Id.* A Cyprus regiment fought in North Africa, Italy, Greece and elsewhere. Six hundred and fifty Greek Cypriots are buried in 15 countries. *See 50th Anniversary Of The Formation Of The Cyprus Regiment* 19 (1989).

5. 531 Parl. Deb. H.C. (5th ser.) 50708 (1954).
6. 52 U.N. GAOR, U.N. Doc. No. A/2703 at 1 (1954).
7. *See* Treaty of Lausanne, *supra* note 2, at art. 16.
8. The Tripartite Conference on The Eastern Mediterranean and Cyprus, CMND, No. 9594 (1955). *N.Y. Times,* Sept. 8, 1955, at A1, col. 1.
9. *See* Charles Foley, *Legacy of Strife* 35 (1964); N. Crawshaw, *The Cyprus Revolt* 123–24 (1978) [hereinafter Crawshaw].
10. John Phillips, *What Is The Matter With Mary Jane? The Tragicomedy of Cyprus, Harper's Magazine* 43, at 48 (June 1956). *See also N.Y. Times,* Sept. 7, 1955, at A1, col. 5; *Id.,* Sept. 12, 1955, at A8, col. 3.
11. *See* Michael Foot, & Mervin Jones, *Guilty Men 1957: Suez and Cyprus* (1957); C.L. Cooper, *The Lion's Last Roar* (1978); R. Fullick and G. Powell, *Suez: The Double War* (1979); K. Love, *Suez: The Twice Fought War* (1970); H. Thomas, *The Suez Affair* (1967); G. Regan, *Great Military Disasters* (1987); D. Nichols, *Eisenhower 1956, The President's Year of Crisis—Suez and the Brink of War.* (2011).
12. 102 Cong. Rec. 8,771–73 (1956) (Memorandum of the Ethnarchy of Cyprus on the Deportation of His Beatitude, Archbishop Makarios of Cyprus).
13. *NATO and the Rift Over Cyprus, N.Y. Times,* Mar. 10, 1956, at A1, col. 8. By tradition, the head of the Greek Orthodox Church is considered the Ethnarch, *i.e.,* the political leader of the community, when the people are under foreign rule.
14. *N.Y. Times,* Oct. 30, 1956, at A1, col. 8.
15. 562 Parl. Deb., H.C. (5th ser.) 1267–68 (1956). M. L. Evriviades, *The Legal Dimension of the Cyprus Conflict,* 10 *Texas Int'l L.J.* 227, 234–35 (1975). Stephen Zydis, *Cyprus: Conflict and Conciliation, 1954–1958, passim* (1967) [hereinafter Zydis]. If granted the right of self-determination, the 80% Greek Cypriot majority would have voted for "*enosis,*" union with Greece, a long-held aspiration. The 18% Turkish Cypriot minority called for "*taksim*" or partition.
16. 12 U.N. GAOR (731st plen. mtg.) at 618, U.N. Doc. No. A/3794, at 2 (1957).
17. *See* U.N. Dep't of Pub. Info., 1957 U.N.Y.B. 72–76 (1958); T. Ehrlich, *Cyprus, the 'Warlike Isle: Origins and Elements of the Current Crisis,* 18 *Stan. L. Rev.* at 1027–31 (1966) [hereinafter Ehrlich]; Zydis, *supra* note 15.
18. *See Cyprus: The Bitter Legacy* (BBC television broadcast, 1984).
19. Ehrlich, *supra* note 17, at 1060–61. Stephens, *supra,* note 4, at 160. McCaskill, *Cyprus Twenty-five Years Later A Diplomat Looks*

Back, [hereinafter McCaskill], in 2 *The Rule of Law and Conditions
on Foreign Aid to Turkey* 22–25, (Conference Proceedings of the
American Hellenic Institute, Washington, D.C.) [hereinafter *The Rule
of Law*].

20. The constitution may be found in 3 *Constitutions Of Nations—Europe*
138–221 (A. Peasley, 3d ed. 1968). *See also* S. de Smith, *The New
Commonwealth and Its Constitution* (1964); P. Polyviou, *Cyprus,
The Tragedy and The Challenge* 16–33 (1975); Ehrlich, *supra* note
17 at 1031–40; S. Kyriakides, *Cyprus: Constitutionalism and Crisis
Government* (1968); McCaskill, *supra* note 19, at 26–29; Bureau of
Intelligence & Research, U.S. Dep't of State, Pub. No. 8047, *Analysis
of the Cyprus Agreements* (1959), reprinted in *J. Hellenic Diaspora*
9–31 (Winter 1984); Criton Tornaritis, *Cyprus and Its Constitutional
and Other Legal Problems* (2d Ed. 1980).

21. *See generally supra* note 20 and accompanying text.

22. The 13 proposed amendments were:

    1. The right of veto of the President and the Vice-President of the
        Republic should be abandoned. *See* art. 57.
    2. The Vice-President of the Republic should deputize for the
        President of the Republic in case of his temporary absence or
        incapacity to perform his duties. *See* art. 44(2).
    3. The Greek President of the House of Representatives and the
        Turkish Vice-President should be elected by the House as a
        whole. Presently, the Greek members vote for the President of
        the House of Representatives and the Turkish members vote for
        the Vice President. *See* art. 72.
    4. The Vice-President of the House of Representatives should dep-
        utize for the President of the House in case of his temporary
        absence or incapacity to perform his duties. *See* art. 72.
    5. The constitutional provisions regarding separate majorities for
        enactment of certain laws by the House of Representatives should
        be abolished. *See* art. 78.
    6. Unified Municipalities should be established. *See* art. 173(I).
    7. The administration of Justice should be unified. This revision
        would affect a number of articles.
    8. The division of the Security Forces into Police and Gendarmerie
        should be abolished. *See* art. 130.
    9. The numerical strength of the Security Forces and of the Defense
        Forces should be determined by law. *See* art. 130.
    10. The number of Greek and Turkish Cypriots in the Public Service
        and the Armed Forces of the Republic should be proportioned
        according to the ratio of Greek and Turkish Cypriots in the pop-
        ulation. *See* art. 123.

11. The number of the Members of the Public Service Commission should be reduced from ten to five. *See* art. 124.
12. All decisions of the Public Service Commission should require a simple majority. *See* art. 125.
13. The Greek Communal Chamber should be abolished. *See* art. 86.

See Ehrlich, *supra* note 17, at 1043–44. Makarios, *Proposals to Amend the Constitution,* International Relations (Athens), Apr. 24, 1964, at 8–25. *See* McCaskill, *supra* note 19, at 29; Stephens, *supra* note 4, at 179; Crawshaw, *supra* note 9, at 366; J. Reddaway, *Burdened with Cyprus—The British Connection* 138 (1986).

23. Perry Anderson "The Divisions of Cyprus," *London Review of Books Vol. 30 (April 24 2008)*: 7–16.
24. *Id.*

3. KISSINGER'S ENCOURAGEMENT OF COUP AGAINST MAKARIOS

1. *N.Y. Times,* November 26, 1973.
2. *N.Y. Times,* July 6, 1974, at A2, col. 4.
3. *N.Y. Times,* July 16, 1974,at A1, col. 8.
4. *N.Y. Times,* July 17, 1974, at A1, col. 8.
5. *N.Y. Times,* July 18, 1974, at A1, col. 6.
6. Thomas Boyatt, "The View of the U.S. State Department in 1974," remarks given October 5, 2010 at the conference on the "Fifty Year Anniversary of the Republic of Cyprus," Washington, D.C.
7. *Id.*
8. *Id.*
9. *Id.*
10. *Id.*
11. *Id.*
12. *Id.*
13. *Id.*
14. *Id.*
15. *Id.*
16. In September 1974 Ambassador Nathaniel Davis, Director General of the Foreign Service at that time called Boyatt to inform him that be was to be assigned to the Senior Seminar in Foreign Policy for an academic year (September through June). Boyatt was surprised since the Seminar was the State Department's most senior training course reserved for those who were likely to go to senior ranks.

Subsequently towards the end of 1975 Boyatt was assigned as Minister Counselor and Deputy Chief of Mission (CDM) to the American Embassy in Santiago, Chile. It was an assignment widely seen as preparing the incumbent for a future ambassadorship. Undersecretary for Management Lawrence Eagleburger was instrumental in making this happen. In 1978 Boyatt was named Ambassador to Upper Volta and in 1980 Ambassador to Columbia.

The American Foreign Service Association presented to Boyatt its highest award, the Lifetime Contributions to American Diplomacy, on June 19, 2008. In 1969 he received the State Department's Meritorious Award "for heroism in helping injured passengers to safety and negotiating passenger release with Syria" during the 1969 hijacking by Palestinian guerillas of a TWA plane on which he was a passenger. In 1970 he received the William R Rivkin Award "for intellectual courage, creativity, disciplined dissent, and taking bureaucratic and physical risks for peace on Cyprus." In 1979 Boyatt was given the Christian A. Herter Award "for extraordinary contributions to the practice of diplomacy." In 1999 he received the Foreign Service Cup for post-retirement contributions to the Service.

17. Christopher Hitchens, *The Trial of Henry Kissinger* at 86 (2001) [herein after Hitchens.].
18. *Id.*
19. *Id,* at 83.
20. *Id.* at 81.
21. Association for Diplomatic Studies and Training, Arlington Hall, Arlington, Virginia, Ambassador Robert McCloskey, May 8, 1989.
22. Hitchens, at 87–88.

4. KISSINGER'S ENCOURAGEMENT OF TURKEY'S AGGRESSION

1. *N.Y. Times,* July 21, 1974, at Al, col. 8.
2. *The Christian Science Monitor,* July 19, 1974, at 1, col. 2.
3. *N.Y. Times,* July 18, 1974, at A1, col. 8.
4. *Id.*
5. S.C. Res. 353, 29 U.N. SCOR (1781st mtg.) at 7, U.N. Doc. S/11350 (1974) [hereinafter S.C. Res. 353].
6. Conference on Cyprus, CMND. 679 (1959). *See also* Cyprus, CMND. 1993 (1960). The Treaty of Guarantee is in CMND. 1253 (1961). The Treaty of Establishment is in CMND. 1252 (1961). See chapter 4 and accompanying text.
7. See note 5 supra.
8. *N.Y. Times,* July 23, 1974, at Al, col. 8. *See id,* July 24, 1974, at Al, col. 8, July 25, 1974, at A12, col. 7, July 26, 1974, at A1, col. 2, July 27, 1974, at A1, col. 2, July 28, 1974, at A1, col. 1, July 29, 1974, at A1, col. 5, July 30, 1974, at A1, col. 3.

9. *Id*. Robert McDonald, *The Problem of Cyprus,* 18–19 [hereinafter McDonald]. *Adelphi Papers* 234 (1989).

10. *Wash. Post,* July 24, 1974, at A1, col. 4–5.

11. Anthony Lewis, "Turks to Remain," *N.Y. Times,* July 31, 1974, at A1, col. 1.

12. *Id.*, Aug. 1, 1974, at A1, col. 5.

13. *Id.*, Aug. 14, 1974, at A1, col. 8.

14. Laurence Stern, *The Wrong Horse* 132 (1977) [hereinafter Stern]. Stern was a foreign correspondent for the *Wash. Post. See generally* Christopher Hitchens, *Hostage to History: Cyprus from the Ottomans to Kissinger.* (3rd Edition, 1997).

15. *N.Y. Times,* Aug. 14, 1974, at A3, col. 5.

16. Kostas Venizelos & Michalis Ignatiou, *The Secret Archives of Henry Kissinger* 434–35 (2002).

17. S.C. Res. 357, 29 U.N. SCOR (1792nd mtg.) at 8, U.N. Doc. S/11446 Rev. 1 (1974). S.C. Res. 358, 29 U.N. SCOR (1793rd mtg.) at 8, U.N. Doc. S/11448 (1974).

18. S.C. Res. 360, 29 U.N. SCOR (1794th mtg.) at 9, U.N. Doc. S/11450 Rev. 2 (1974).

19. Stern at 132–133. *N.Y. Times*, Aug. 15, 16 & 17, 1974.

20. *Yeniduzen*, Feb. 14, 1990.

21. FOIA request. Collection searched: Kissinger Transcripts. Department of State FOIA Electronic Reading Room, 2004. http://foia.state.gov/ SearchColls/CollsSearch.asp.

22. Association for Diplomatic Studies and Training, Arlington Hall, Arlington, Virginia, Ambassador Robert McCloskey, May 8, 1989.

23. *See* page vii for copy of the map; see *The Secret Archives of Kissinger* at 236 (2002); see *Cyprus Weekly,* August 10, 2007.

24. C. Hitchens, *The Trial of Henry Kissinger* 86–87 (2001).

25. *Id*. at 87.

26. Foreign Relations of the United States, 1969-1976, Volume XXX, Number 129. Memorandum of Conversation, at pages 423–424, August 13, 1974, 9 a.m.

5. KISSINGER'S VIOLATIONS OF U.S. AND INTERNATIONAL LAWS

1. *See* Exec. Order No. 10973, as amended, 3 C.F.R. 90 (1974), *reprinted in* 22, U.S.C. §2381, note (Supp. II 1972); Exec. Order No. 11501, as amended, 3 C.F.R. 267 (1974), *reprinted in* 22 U.S.C. §2751, note (1970 and Supp. II 1972).

2. *Id*.

3. Stern at 143.

4. *See generally infra* Chapter 6.
5. Stern at 142.
6. *N.Y. Times,* Feb. 27, 1975, at A8, col. 1.
7. *See generally infra* Chapter 6, and accompanying text.
8. Turkey's National Security Council made the decisions on national security, defense and foreign affairs matters at that time. It was chaired by the military chief of staff and a majority of its members were military officers. Hitchens, *Uncorking the Genie: The Cyprus Question and Turkey's Military Rule,* 122 Merip Reports 26 (Mar./ Apr. 1984).
9. *N.Y. Times,* Sept. 14, 1974, at A28, col. 1. Emphasis added.
10. *Id.,* Oct. 13, 1974, at A16, col. 1.
11. *Suspension of Prohibitions Against Military Assistance to Turkey, 1975: Hearing on S. 846, H.R. 8454 and other bills and resolutions Before the House Committee on International Relations,* 94th Cong., 1st Sess. 51 (1975) [hereinafter *Suspension of Prohibitions*] (statement of Cyrus Vance).
12. *Cyprus—1974, Hearings Before the House Comm. on Foreign Affairs and its Subcomm. on Europe,* 93rd Cong., 2nd Sess. 40–41 (1974) (statement of former undersecretary of state George Ball).
13. Graham Hovey, "How to Lose an Ally," *N.Y. Times,* August 27, 1974.

6. KISSINGER'S ACCOUNT IN HIS MEMOIRS

1. Henry Kissinger, *Years of Renewal* 192–239 (1999) [hereinafter Kissinger].
2. John Lewis Gaddis, "The Old World Order," *N.Y. Times Book Review,* March 21, 1999.
3. Jussi M. Hanhimäki, *Flawed Architect—Henry Kissinger and American Foreign Policy* (Oxford: Oxford University Press, 2004), at 472.
4. *Wash. Post Book World,* March 21, 1999, at 5.
5. *Id.*
6. Kissinger at 192.
7. Crossing points April 23, 2003 (*see N.Y. Times April 24, 2003).*
8. Foreign Ministry official interview 2011.
9. Kissinger at 196.
10. *Id.*
11. Stern at 7.
12. Kissinger at 196.
13. *Id.* at 199.
14. Christopher Hitchens, *The Trial of Henry Kissinger* 79–80 (2001). Emphasis added.
15. Kissinger at 198.

16. *Id.*
17. Andrei Gromyko, *Memories* 235–36 (1989).
18. Kissinger at 199.
19. *Id.* at 200.
20. *Id.* at 205.
21. *Id.*
22. *Id.* at 206.
23. *Id.* at 192.
24. *Id.* at 216.
25. *Id.* at 224.
26. *Id.* at 229.
27. *See* page vii for a copy of the map.
28. Foreign Relations of the United States, 1969–1976, Vol. XXX, 129 Memorandum of Conversation, pages 423–424, at 424.
29. Kissinger at 225.
30. Stern at 149.
31. *N.Y. Times,* Aug. 14, 1974, at A3, col. 5.
32. Kissinger at 225.
33. *Id.* at 215.
34. *Id.* at 216.
35. *Id.* at 217.
36. *Id.* at 219.
37. *Id.* at 219.
38. *Id.* at 220.
39. *Id.* at 220.
40. *Id.* at 220–21.
41. *Id.* at 221.
42. *Id.* at 223.
43. *Id.*
44. *Id.* at 224.
45. *Id.* at 228–29.
46. *Id.* at 229.
47. James Callaghan, *Time and Chance* 331–357 (1987), [hereinafter Callaghan].
48. *Id.*
49. Kissinger at 209.
50. *Id.*
51. *Id.* at 210.
52. *Id.*
53. *Id.* at 210–11.
54. *Id.* at 211.
55. *Id.* at 211–12.
56. *Id.* at 212.

57. Callaghan at 341.
58. Kissinger at 228.
59. *Id.*
60. Callaghan at 351–354.
61. Kissinger at 213.
62. *Id.* at 212.
63. *Id.*
64. Kissinger at 201.
65. *Id.* at 192.
66. *Id.*
67. *Id.* at 232.
68. *Id.*
69. Sept. 5, 1974 Cong. Rec. *N.Y. Times,* Sept. 6, 1974.
70. Kissinger at 233.
71. *Id.*
72. *Id.*
73. *Id.*
74. *Id.* at 233–34.
75. *Id.* at 235–36.

7. THE ARMS EMBARGO BATTLE IN CONGRESS

1. Act of Dec. 30, 1974, Pub. L. No. 93-559, (1974) U.S. Code Cong. & Admin. News (90 stat.) 2072–73, 6742–43.
2. 120 Cong. Rec. 28,306 (1974); *Cyprus—1974, Hearings Before the House Comm. on Foreign Affairs and its Subcomm. on Europe,* 93rd Cong., 2nd Sess. 83 (1974) (statement of Rep. John Brademas) [hereinafter *Cyprus Hearings*].
3. Kissinger press conference, Aug. 19, 1974, *referred to* in Stern, *The Wrong Horse* 142 (1977).
4. *Cyprus Hearings, supra* note 2, at 57.
5. *Id.* at 49–50.
6. 120 Cong. Rec. 30,700 (1974).
7. 120 Con. Rec. 32,439–40 (1974); *N.Y. Times,* Sept. 25, 1974, at A1, col. 8.
8. Stern at 143–44.
9. *Id.*
10. *Cyprus Hearings, supra* note 2, at 59; *see also* Stern, *supra* note 3, at 145; *N.Y. Times,* Sept. 20, 1974, at A4, col. 2; *Wash. Post,* Sept. 20, 1974, at A1, col. 1.
11. Telephone interviews with former Senator Thomas F. Eagleton (D-Mo) (Oct. 3, 1990) and Brian Atwood, Sen. Eagleton's chief foreign policy legislative assistant (Sept. 19, 1990).

12. 120 Con. Rec. 32,948 (1974); *N.Y. Times,* Oct. 1, 1974, at A1, col. 4.
13. 120 Cong. Rec. 33,272 (1974); *N.Y. Times,* Oct. 2, 1974, at A1, col. 8.
14. Stern at 143. *See* Boyatt, *1974 In Retrospect and Its Importance Today,* in 2 The Rule of Law and Conditions on Foreign Aid to Turkey 7, (1989) (Conference Proceedings of the American Hellenic Institute, Washington, D.C.). *N.Y. Times,* Dec. 2, 1974, at A7, col 1
15. Opinion letter from Comptroller General to Senator Thomas F. Eagleton at 13, 16 (Oct. 7, 1974) [hereinafter Opinion Letter]. At pages 2 and 3 of the opinion letter the following provisions of the 1947 bilateral agreement are set forth:

Article I states:

> The Government of the United States will furnish the Government of Turkey such assistance as the President of the United States may authorize to be provided in accordance with the Act of Congress approved May 22, 1947, and any acts amendatory or supplementary thereto. The Government of Turkey will make effective use of any such assistance in accordance with the provisions of this agreement.

The second paragraph of Article II states in part:

> *The Government of Turkey will make use of the assistance furnished for the purposes for which it has been accorded.* (Emphasis in original.)

Article IV of the Agreement states:

> Determined and equally interested to assure the security of any article, service, or information received by the Government of Turkey pursuant to this agreement, the Governments of the United States and Turkey will respectively take after consultation, such measures as the other government may judge necessary for this purpose. *The Government of Turkey will not transfer, without the consent of the Government of the United States,* title to or possession of any such article or information nor *permit,* without such consent, *the use of any such article* or the use or disclosure of any such information by or to anyone not an officer employee, or agent of the Government of Turkey or *for any purpose other than that for which the article or information is furnished.* (Emphasis in original).

16. *Id.*
17. *Id.* at 13.
18. *Id.* at 15.
19. Stern at 149.

20. 120 Cong. Rec. 34,672 (1974). "[T]he legal case . . . was sufficiently compelling so that Kissinger never, in the course of the harshest conflict he experienced with Congress, chose to defend his policies on legal grounds." Stern at 149.

21. 120 Cong. Rec. 34,673 (1974). The statements took place during consideration of S.J. Res. 247, which authorized the President to suspend, in the case of Turkey, the application of the provisions of § 505(d) of the Foreign Assistance Act of 1961 and § 3(c) of the Foreign Military Sales Act.

22. 120 Cong. Rec. 34,677 (1974); *N.Y. Times,* Oct. 10, 1974, at A1, col. 3.

23. 120 Cong. Rec. 35,429 (1974); *N.Y. Times,* Oct. 12, 1974, at A1, col. 2.

24. *N.Y. Times,* Oct. 15, 1974, at A1, col. 1.

25. 120 Cong. Rec. 35,608–9 (1974); *N.Y. Times,* Oct. 16, 1974, at A1, col. 5.

26. 120 Cong. Rec. 35,733 (1974); *N.Y. Times,* Oct. 17, 1974, at A1, col. 3.

27. 120 Cong. Rec. 35,908 (1974); *N.Y. Times,* Oct. 17, 1974, at A1, col. 3.

28. *N.Y. Times,* Sept. 14, 1974, at A28, col. 1.

29. *Id.,* Sept. 26, 1974, at A28, col. 1.

30. *Id.,* Oct. 13, 1974, at A16, col. 1.

31. 120 Cong. Rec. 36,018-19 (1974); *N.Y. Times,* Oct. 18, 1974, at A1, col. 2.

32. Humanitarian aid continued annually at $25 million, then at $15 million and reduced amounts, and totals over $400 million. There was no appropriation for 2014.

33. 120 Cong. Rec. 36,023 (1974); *N.Y. Times,* Oct. 18, 1974, at A1, col. 2.

34. *N.Y. Times,* Oct. 19, 1974, at A5, col. l.

35. 120 Cong. Rec. 38,084 (1974); *N.Y. Times,* Dec. 5, 1974, at A8, col. 1.

36. 120 Cong. Rec. 39,142 (1974); *N.Y. Times,* Dec. 12, 1974, at A11, col. 1.

37. 120 Cong. Rec. 40,385 (1974); *N.Y. Times,* Dec. 18, 1974, at A1, col. 1.

38. *N.Y. Times,* Dec. 31, 1974, at A3, col. 7.

39. *Id.,* Feb. 27, 1975, at A8, col. 1.

40. Section 304(a) of the International Security Assistance and Arms Export Control Act of 1976 (90 Stat. 751) (1976) amended §505(d) to remove the "immediately ineligible for further assistance" language and thereby eliminated the mandatory nature of the penalty/sanction for misuse of our arms assistance and sales.

41. The name of the committee had been changed from the House Committee on Foreign Affairs. It was changed back to the House Committee on Foreign Affairs, effective February 5, 1979, by House Resolution 89, 96th Congress.

42. *Suspension of Prohibitions Against Military Assistance to Turkey, 1975: Hearing on S. 846, H.R. 8454 and other bills and resolutions Before the House Committee on International Relations,* 94th Cong., 1st Sess. 45 (1975) [hereinafter *Suspension of Prohibitions*] (statements of George Ball and Cyrus Vance). *See also N.Y. Times,* July 11, 1975, at A2, col. 3.

43. *Id.* at 46, 48 (emphasis added).

44. *See Suspension of Prohibitions, supra* note 42, at 45–72.

45. *Id.*

46. Pub. L. 94–104 (1975). On July 24, 1975, the House of Representatives defeated the Administration's proposal, S. 846, to lift the embargo on the sale of American arms to Turkey by a vote of 223 to 206. 121 Cong. Rec. 24480–526 (1975). The Senate had passed S. 846, by a vote of 41 to 40, in May, 1975. 121 Cong. Rec. 24,526 (1975); *N.Y. Times,* July 25, 1975, at A1, col. 1. The Administration had a new bill introduced in the Senate, S. 2230, which passed in late July by a vote of 47 to 46. Following the August recess, the House Committee on International Relations passed S. 2230 by a vote of 20 to 9 on September 17, 1975. On October 2, 1975, the House of Representative passed S. 2230 by a vote of 237 to 176 which partially lifted the embargo for arms contracted by Turkey prior to the imposition of the embargo and permitted the issuance of licenses in connection with commercial sales. It did not authorize any military grant assistance and delayed resumption of government-to-government credit sales until enactment of new foreign military sales legislation for fiscal year 1976. 121 Cong. Rec. 31457-60 (1975); *N.Y. Times,* Oct. 3, 1975, at A1, col. 8. President Ford signed S. 2230 on October 7, 1975. The embargo was fully lifted in August, 1978, following intense pressure from the Carter Administration. The Senate passed repeal legislation on July 25, 1978 by a vote of 57 to 42. 124 Cong Rec. 22510–57 (1978). On August 1, 1978, the House voted 208 to 205 to repeal the remaining rule-of-law embargo. As a presidential candidate, Carter had specifically endorsed U.N.G.A. Res. 3212, stating that: "Peace must be based on the United Nations General Assembly Resolution 3212 of 1 November 1974 endorsed by Cyprus, Greece and Turkey, calling among other things for the removal of all foreign military forces from Cyprus." Carter further said that the United States must work "to insure the independence, territorial integrity and sovereignty of Cyprus," that Greek Cypriot

refugees should be allowed "to return to their homes," that the "United States must pursue a policy based on principle and in accord with the rule of law" and that "[i]f I am elected president I intend to enforce and carry out the provisions of my statement." Statement and speech by James Carter in Washington, D.C. (Sept. 16, 1976).

Presidential candidate Ronald Reagan stated that President Carter had "reneged on his [campaign] pledges" regarding Cyprus. Candidate Reagan stated: "The tragic situation in Cyprus has lasted six years. It must not continue. The foreign military forces on that island should be substantially reduced, and Cypriot refugees, be they Greek or Turkish, should be permitted to return to their homes and land. I support the full implementation of unanimously approved United Nations Resolution 3212 of November 1974 which 'Calls upon all States to respect the sovereignty, independence, territorial integrity and non-alignment of the Republic of Cyprus and to refrain from all acts and interventions directed against it; Urges the speedy withdrawal of all foreign armed forces and foreign military presence and personnel from the Republic of Cyprus, and the cessation of all foreign interference in its affairs.'" Reagan-Bush Committee news release (Sept. 26, 1980). President Reagan did not follow through on his pledge.

47. *N.Y. Times*, July 30, 1973, at A27, col. 1

8. TURKEY THE ROGUE STATE

1. 22 U.S.C. § 2301 (1990).
2. 22 U.S.C. § 2751 (1990) (renamed The Arms Export Control Act).
3. 22 U.S.C. § 2301 (1990).
4. 22 U.S.C. § 2314(d) (1990) (emphasis added). Section 304(a) of the International Security Assistance and Arms Export Control Act of 1976 (90 Stat. 751) (1976) amended § 505(d) to remove the "immediately ineligible for further assistance" language and thereby eliminated the mandatory nature of the penalty/sanction for misuse of our arms assistance and sales. Subsection (d) presently reads as follows:

(1) Assistance and deliveries of assistance under this chapter to any country shall be terminated as hereinafter provided, if such country uses defense articles or defense services furnished under this Act, the Mutual Security Act of 1954, or any predecessor Foreign Assistance Act, in substantial violation (either in terms of quantities or in terms of the gravity of the consequences regardless of the quantities involved) of any agreement entered into pursuant to

any such Act (A) by using such articles or services for a purpose not authorized under section 502 or, if such agreement provides that such articles or services may only be used for purposes more limited than those authorized under section 502, for a purpose not authorized under such agreement; (B) by transferring such articles or services to, or permitting any use of such articles or services by, anyone not an officer, employee, or agent of the recipient country without the consent of the President; or (C) by failing to maintain the security of such articles or services.

(2) (A) Assistance and deliveries of assistance shall be terminated pursuant to paragraph (1) of this subsection if the President so determines and so states in writing to the Congress, or if the Congress so finds by joint resolution.

(B) The President shall report to the Congress promptly upon the receipt of information that a violation described in paragraph (1) of this subsection may have occurred.

(3) Assistance to a country shall remain terminated in accordance with paragraph (1) of this subsection until such time as-

(A) the President determines that the violation has ceased; and

(B) the country concerned has given assurances satisfactory to the President that such violation will not recur.

(4) The authority contained in section 614(a) of this Act may not be used to waive the provisions of this section with respect to further assistance under this chapter. Section 304(b) similarly amended § 3(c) of the Foreign Military Sales Act, 22 U.S.C. §§ 2451–3900, at 310 (1990).

5. 22 U.S.C. § 2302 (1990)(emphasis added).

6. 22 U.S.C. § 2314(a) (1990).

7. 22 U.S.C. § 2753(c) (1974).

8. *Id.*

9. Opinion letter from Comptroller General to Senator Thomas F. Eagleton at 3 (October 7, 1974) [hereinafter "Opinion Letter"].

10. *Id.*

11. The Treaty of Alliance, one of three treaties comprising the London–Zurich Agreements, authorized 950 Greek troops and 650 Turkish troops to be stationed on Cyprus. The Treaty of Alliance, reprinted in *Royal Institute of International Affairs, Cyprus: The Dispute and The Settlement* 72–120 (1959) [hereinafter Treaty of Alliance].

12. The exchange of notes is *reprinted in Hearings on United States Security Agreements and Commitments Abroad, Greece and Turkey, Before the Subcommittee on United States Security Agreements and Commitments Abroad of the Senate Committee on Foreign Relations,* 91st. Cong., 2nd Sess., pt. 7, 1780 (1970).

13. *See* Opinion Letter, *supra* note 9, at 4.
14. *Id.* at 6.
15. *Id.* at 12.
16. *Id.*
17. *Id.* at 13.
18. *Id.*
19. 120 Cong. Rec. 30,700 (1974).
20. Hunt, *Cyprus: A Study In International Relations* 10 (1980) (Sir David Hunt, the 1980 Montague Burton Lecture on International Relations in the University of Edinburgh) [hereinafter Hunt]. Hunt was Britain's High Commissioner in Cyprus from 1965 to 1966.
21. The Security Council resolutions refer to the removal of foreign military forces except those authorized by international treaty. The Treaty of Alliance, *supra* note 11, authorized 950 Greek personnel and 650 Turkish personnel only. Unanimous G.A. Res. 3212 (Nov. 1, 1974) refers to the removal of all foreign military forces. G.A. Res. 3212, 29 U.N. GAOR (2275th plenary mtg.) at 3, U.N. Doc. S/11557 (1974) [hereinafter G.A. Res. 3212]. Security Council Resolution 365, Dec. 13, 1974, endorsed G.A. Res. 3212.
22. S.C. Res. 186, 19 U.N. SCOR Supp. (1102d mtg.) at 102, U.N. Doc. 8/5575 (1964); *see also* 19 U.N. SCOR Supp. (Apr.-June 1964) at 105, U.N. Doc. S/5679 (1964). S.C. Res. 186 reads as follows:

THE SECURITY COUNCIL,

Noting that the present situation with regard to Cyprus is likely to threaten international peace and security and may further deteriorate unless additional measures are promptly taken to maintain peace and to seek out a durable solution,

Considering the positions taken by the parties in relation to the Treaties signed at Nicosia on 16 August 1960,

Having in mind the relevant provisions of the Charter of the United Nations and its Article 2, paragraph 4, which reads: "All Members shall refrain in their international relations from the threat or use of force against the territorial integrity or political independence of any State, or in any other manner inconsistent with the purposes of the United Nations,"

1. *Calls upon* all member states, in conformity with their obligations under the Charter of the United Nations, to refrain from any action or threat of action to worsen the situation in the sovereign Republic of Cyprus, or to endanger international peace;

2. *Asks* the Government of Cyprus, which has the responsibility for the maintenance and restoration of law and order, to take all additional measures necessary to stop violence and bloodshed in Cyprus;

3. *Calls* upon the communities in Cyprus and their leaders to act with the utmost restraint;

4. *Recommends* the creation, with the consent of the Government of Cyprus, of a United Nations Peace-Keeping Force in Cyprus. The composition and size of the force 1991] Cyprus and the Rule of Law 51 shall be established by the Secretary-General, in consultation with the Governments of Cyprus, Greece, Turkey and the United Kingdom. The commander of the force shall be appointed by the Secretary-General and report to him. The Secretary-General, who shall keep the Governments providing the force fully informed, shall report periodically to the Security Council on its operation;

5. *Recommends* that the function of the force should be, in the interest of preserving international peace and security, to use its best efforts to prevent a recurrence of fighting and, as necessary, to contribute to the maintenance and restoration of law and order and a return to normal conditions;

6. *Recommends* that the stationing of the force shall be for a period of three months, all costs pertaining to it being met, in a manner to be agreed upon by them, by the Governments providing the contingents and by the Government of Cyprus. The Secretary-General may also accept voluntary contributions for that purpose;

7. *Recommends further* that the Secretary-General designate, in agreement with the Government of Cyprus and the Governments of Greece, Turkey and the United Kingdom a mediator who shall use his best endeavours with the representatives of the communities and also with the aforesaid four Governments, for the purpose of promoting a peaceful solution and an agreed settlement of the problem confronting Cyprus, in accordance with the Charter of the United Nations, having in mind the well-being of the people of Cyprus as a whole and the preservation of international peace and security. The mediator shall report periodically to the Secretary-General on his efforts;

8. *Requests* the Secretary-General to provide, from funds of the United Nations, as appropriate, for the remuneration and expenses of the mediator and his staff. *Id.*

23. *See* S.C. Res. 193, 19 U.N. SCOR Supp. 1 (1143rd mtg.) at 152, U.N. Doc. S/5868 (1964) [hereinafter S.C. Res. 193].

24. S.C. Res. 353 reads as follows:

THE SECURITY COUNCIL,

Having considered the report of the Secretary-General at its 1979th meeting about the recent developments in Cyprus,

Having heard the statement made by the President of the Republic of Cyprus and the statements by the representatives of Cyprus, Turkey, Greece and other member countries,

Having considered at its present meeting further developments on the island,

Deeply deploring the outbreak of violence and continuing bloodshed,

Gravely concerned about the situation which led to a serious threat to international peace and security, and which created a most explosive situation in the whole Eastern Mediterranean area,

Equally concerned about the necessity to restore the constitutional structure of the Republic of Cyprus, established and guaranteed by international agreement,

Recalling Security Council resolution 186 of 4 March 1964 and subsequent resolutions of the Security Council on this matter,

Conscious of its primary responsibility for the maintenance of international peace and security in accordance with Article 24 of the Charter of the United Nations:

1. *Calls upon* all states to respect the sovereignty, independence and territorial integrity of Cyprus;

2. *Calls upon* all parties to the present fighting as a first step to cease all firing and requests all states to exercise the utmost restraint and to refrain from any action which might further aggravate the situation;

3. *Demands* an immediate end to foreign military intervention in the Republic of Cyprus that is in contravention of operative paragraph 1;

4. *Requests* the withdrawal without delay from the Republic of Cyprus of foreign military personnel present otherwise than under the authority of international agreements including those whose withdrawal was requested by the President of the Republic of Cyprus, Archbishop Makarios, in his letter of 2 July 1974;

5. *Calls on* Greece, Turkey and the United Kingdom of Great Britain and Northern Ireland to enter into negotiations without delay for the restoration of peace in the area and constitutional government in Cyprus and to keep the Secretary-General informed;

6. *Calls on* all parties to cooperate fully with UNFICYP to enable it to carry out its mandate;

7. *Decides* to keep the situation under constant review and asks the Secretary General to report as appropriate with a view of adopting further measures in order to ensure that peaceful conditions are restored as soon as possible. *Id.*

25. G.A. Res. 3212 reads as follows:

THE GENERAL ASSEMBLY,

Having considered the question of Cyprus,

Gravely concerned about the continuation of the Cyprus crisis, which constitutes a threat to international peace and security,

Mindful of the need to solve this crisis without delay by peaceful means, in accordance with the purposes and principles of the United Nations,

Having heard the statements in the debate and taking note of the Report of the Special Political Committee on the question of Cyprus:

1. *Calls upon* all states to respect the sovereignty, independence, territorial integrity and non-alignment of the Republic of Cyprus and to refrain from all acts and interventions directed against it;

2. *Urges* the speedy withdrawal of all foreign armed forces and foreign military presence and personnel from the Republic of Cyprus, and the cessation of all foreign interference in its affairs;

3. *Considers* that the constitutional system of the Republic of Cyprus concerns the Greek-Cypriot and Turkish-Cypriot communities;

4. *Commends* the contacts and negotiations taking place on an equal footing, with the good offices of the Secretary-General between the representatives of the two communities, and calls for their continuation with a view to reaching freely a mutually acceptable political settlement, based on their fundamental and legitimate rights;

5. *Considers* that all the refugees should return to their homes in safety and calls upon the parties concerned to undertake urgent measures to that end;

6. *Expresses* the hope that, if necessary, further efforts including negotiations can take place, within the framework of the United Nations, for the purpose of implementing the provisions of the present resolution, thus ensuring to the Republic of Cyprus its fundamental right to independence, sovereignty and territorial integrity;

7. *Requests* the Secretary-General to continue to provide United Nations humanitarian assistance to all parts of the population of Cyprus and calls upon all states to contribute to that effort;

8. *Calls* upon all parties to continue to cooperate fully with the United Nations Peace-Keeping Force in Cyprus, which may be strengthened if necessary;

9. *Requests* the Secretary-General to continue to lend his good offices to the parties concerned;

10. *Further requests* the Secretary-General to bring the present resolution to the attention of the Security Council. G.A. Res. 3212

was endorsed by the Security Council (S.C. Res. 365) on Dec. 13, 1974. *Id.*

26. *See* Van Wynen Thomas & A.J Thomas, *The Cyprus Crisis 1974–75: Political-Juridical Aspects,* 29 SW. L.J. 513, 543–46 (1975) [hereinafter Van Wynen Thomas & Thomas].

27. *See Suspension of Prohibitions Against Military Assistance to Turkey, 1975: Hearing on S.846, H.R. 8454 and other bills and resolutions Before the House Committee on International Relations,* 94th Cong. 1st Sess. 46 (1975) [hereinafter *Suspension of Prohibitions*] (statements of George Ball and Cyrus Vance). *See also N.Y. Times,* July 11, 1975, at A2, col. 3.

28. *FBIS,* Apr. 29, 1975, at Z1 and Z2.

29. *N.Y. Times,* Feb. 28, 1975, at A3, col. 6.

30. *N.Y. Times,* June 20, 1975, at A2, col. 4.

31. Conference on Cyprus, CMND. 679 (1959). *See also* Cyprus, CMND. 1993 (1960). The Treaty of Guarantee is in CMND. 1253 (1961). The Treaty of Establishment is in CMND. 1252 (1961).

32. *See id.*

33. Hunt, *Cyprus: A Study In International Relations* 8 (1980) (Sir David Hunt, the 1980 Montague Burton Lecture on International Relations in the University of Edinburgh) [hereinafter Hunt].

34. R. St. J. Macdonald, *International Law and the Conflict in Cyprus,* 19 *Canadian Y.B. of Int'l L.* 3–48 (1981). Macdonald and Hunt refer to article IV of the Treaty of Guarantee as article 4, using the Arabic. The Treaty uses article IV, the roman.

35. *Id.* at 16.

36. *Id.* at 29–30.

37. Hunt, *supra* note 33, at 11. *See also* Van Wynen Thomas & Thomas, *The Cyprus Crisis 1974–75: Political-Juridical Aspects,* 29 *SW.L.J.* 513 at 529–46 (1975) [hereinafter Van Wynen Thomas & Thomas]; and Ehrlich, *Cyprus, the 'Warlike Isle': Origins and Elements of the Current Crisis,* 18 *Stan. L. Rev.* at 1066–79 (1966) [hereinafter Ehrlich], regarding the August 1964 Turkish bombings of Cyprus.

38. Hunt, *supra* note 33, at 11.

39. *See generally Cyprus and the Rule of Law,* in 2 The Rule of Law and Conditions on Foreign Aid to Turkey at 1, (Conference Proceedings of the American Hellenic Institute, Washington, D.C. 1989).

40. *See* Van Wynen Thomas & Thomas, *supra* note 26, at 542.

41. *N.Y. Times,* Mar. 28, 1964, at A5, col. 4.

42. *Id.,* Aug. 9, 1964, at A1, col. 8.

43. *See* S.C. Res. 193, 19 U.N. SCOR Supp. 1 (1143rd mtg.) at 152, U.N. Doc. S/5868 (1964).

44. *Yeniduzen,* Feb. 14, 1990. *Guardian,* Oct. 13, 1975, at 1, col. 5.

45. Foreign Assistance Act of 1961, P.L. 87-195, 75 Stat. 424 (1961), as amended by International Development and Food Assistance Act of 1975, Pub. L. No. 94-161, § 310, 89 Stat. 860 (1975) (current version at 22 U.S.C. § 2151 (1988)) [hereinafter Foreign Assistance Act of 1961].

46. *Id*. The same content can also be found in § 112(a) of the Agricultural Trade Development and Assistance Act of 1954, as amended, Pub. L. 95-88, § 203, 91 stat. 545 (1977) (current version at 7 U.S.C. § 1712 (1988)), which likewise prohibits food aid to states that grossly violate human rights unless it can be shown that it would directly benefit the needy.

47. Foreign Assistance Act of 1974, Pub. L. No. 93-559, 88 Stat. 1795 (1974) *as amended* by the International Security Assistance and Arms Export Control Act of 1976, Pub. L. No. 94-329, § 301(a), 90 Stat. 748 (1976) (current version at 22 U.S.C. § 2304 (a)(2) (1988)) [hereinafter Foreign Assistance Act of 1974].

48. *See* Foreign Assistance Act of 1961, *supra* note 45, at § 502(B)(a)(2) (current version at 22 U.S.C. § 2304(a)(2) (1988)).

49. *Id*. at § 502(B)(a)(3) (current version at 22 U.S.C. § 2304(a)(3) (1988)).

50. *Id*. at § 502(B)(a)(2) (current version at 22 U.S.C. § 2304(a)(2) (1988)).

51. 127 Cong. Rec., 9,887 (1981); Det. Free Press, Feb. 15, 1981, at 3A, col. 1.

52. The Geneva Convention of 1949, § III, art. 49, 6 USTIA 3517, 3548 (1955) [hereinafter Geneva Convention]. The Geneva Convention prohibits colonization by the occupying power. *Id*.

53. U.N. Charter, art. 1, para. 55(c), 56.

54. G.A. Res. 217, U.N. GAOR (183rd plenary mtg.), at 71, U.N. Doc. A/810 (1948) [hereinafter Universal Declaration].

55. European Convention for the Protection of Human Rights and Fundamental Freedoms, Nov. 4, 1950, 213 U.N.T.S. 221 [hereinafter European Convention on Human Rights]. Article 2(1) states: "Everyone's right to life shall be protected by law. No one shall be deprived of his life intentionally . . . " *Id*.; *see also* Universal Declaration, art. 3, which states: "[e]veryone has the right to life, liberty and security of person."

56. *See* European Convention on Human Rights, *supra* note 55, at art. 3. Article 3 states, "[n]o one shall be subjected to torture or to inhuman or degrading treatment or punishment." This is the counterpart to article 5 of the Universal Declaration, *supra* note 54.

57. *Id*.

58. *Id*. at art. 5(1). Article 5(1) states, "[e]veryone has the right to liberty and security of person." *See also* Universal Declaration, *supra* note

54, at art. 3. Moreover, article 9 of the Universal Declaration reads: "No one shall be subjected to arbitrary arrest, detention or exile." *See* Universal Declaration, *supra* note 54.

59. *See* European Convention on Human Rights, *supra* note 55, at art. 8(1). Article 8(1) states that, "[e]veryone has the right to respect for his private and family life, his home and his correspondence." *Id.* Universal Declaration, *supra* note 54, at art. 12, reads: "No one shall be subjected to arbitrary interference with his privacy, family, home or correspondence. . . ." *See also* Universal Declaration, *supra* note 54, at art. 17(2) ("No one shall be arbitrarily deprived of his property"). *Id.* at art. 13(1) ("Everyone has the right to freedom of movement and residence within the borders of each State.")

60. *See* European Convention on Human Rights, *supra* note 55, at art. 1 to the First Protocol to the Convention. This section states: "Every natural or legal person is entitled to the peaceful enjoyment of his possessions. No one shall be deprived of his possessions except in the public interest and subject to the conditions provided for by law and by the general principles of international law." *Id.* One newspaper described the looting: "Confidential United Nations military documents...disclose that looting is being systematically carried out on a massive scale by the Turkish and Turkish Cypriot authorities in the north of the island." *The Sunday Times* (London), Dec. 13, 1976, at 1, col. h. The documents:

> state categorically that scores of Greek Cypriots are being forced to leave their houses . . . and that robbery is now wide-spread in parts of Turkish-held Cyprus. . . . [T]he documents . . . describe in detail how the Turkish authorities in Famagusta have for more than a year been organizing daily convoys of lorries to transport property from Greek Cypriot homes and shops. . . . The documents, which speak of Greek Cypriots being forced to sign applications to leave their homes in Turkish-held districts, also refer to attacks on Greek Cypriots. . . . [The documents] take the form of a summary of events in the United Nations' six military sectors and each is signed by an officer in the United Nations international police force.

Id. The U.N. confirmed the genuineness of the documents but had no comment on their contents. *Id.*

. On March 4, 1991, the European Human Rights Commission decided to consider Application Numbers 15299/89, 15300/89 and 15318/89 from three individual Greek Cypriots against Turkey for violations of human rights in the Turkish-occupied areas of Cyprus. Article 25 of the Convention authorizes applications from individuals. Turkey ratified the European Convention on Human Rights on January 28, 1987, with certain territorial restrictions aimed at excluding Turkey from cases of alleged violations in the occupied areas of Cyprus. The Commission ruled that Turkey's territorial restrictions were invalid and that Turkey was subject to the provisions of the Convention for actions occurring after January 28, 1987, the date of Turkey's ratification of the Convention. The first and second applicants, two Greek priests, complained about their detention on July 19, 1989, and alleged ill-treatment and violations of articles 1, 3, 5, 6, 7, 9, and 13 of the Convention. The third applicant, Titina Loizidou, alleged violations of articles 3 and 5 regarding her detention during the "Women Walk Home" march on March 19, 1989, and continuing violations of article 1 of Protocol No. 1 ("Every natural or legal person is entitled to the peaceful enjoyment of possessions. . . .") regarding Turkey's refusing her access to her property in the occupied district of Kyrenia, Cyprus, after January 28, 1987. She is the first Greek Cypriot to sue Turkey over property rights. The Commission will now consider the merits of the applications. The government of Cyprus described the Commission's decision as a significant landmark."

61. *The Sunday Times,* (London), Jan. 23, 1977, at 1, col. 1.
62. Complete studies of the cultural cleansing of Cyprus include: Michael Jansen. *War and Cultural Heritage: Cyprus after the 1974 Invasion* (2005); Charalambos Chotzakoglou, *Religious Monuments in Turkish-Occupied Cyprus: Evidence and Acts of Continuing Destruction* (2008); Cyprus Press and Information Office, Nicosia, *Flagellum Dei: The Destruction of the Cultural Heritage in the Turkish Occupied Part of Cyprus,* 2nd ed. (1989).
63. Michael E. Jansen, speech at National Press Club, Washington, D.C., May 15, 2006.
64. Law Library of Congress, Directorate of Legal Research, LL File No. 2008-01356.
65. For a description of the destruction of cultural property, *see* Charalambos Chotzakoglou, *Religious Monuments in Turkish-Occupied Cyprus: Evidence and Acts of Continuous Destruction* 28-29 (2008); Flagellum Dei: *The Destruction of the Cultural Heritage in the Turkish Occupied Part of Cyprus* (Nicosia, Cyprus: Press and Information Office, 2d ed. 1989); Michael Jansen, *War and Cultural Heritage: Cyprus After the* 1974 *Invasion* (2005).
66. *See* note 64 at page 8.
67. Eric Rouleau, "Turkey's Dream of Democracy," *Foreign Affairs,* November/December 2000: 100–114, 111.

68. The July 13, 2007 Resolution of the International Association of Genocide Scholars on Genocides Committed by the Ottoman Empire states as follows:

> WHEREAS the denial of genocide is widely recognized as the final stage of genocide, enshrining impunity for the perpetrators of genocide, and demonstrably paving the way for future genocides;

> WHEREAS the Ottoman genocide against minority populations during and following the First World War is usually depicted as a genocide against Armenians alone, with little recognition of the qualitatively similar genocides against other Christian minorities of the Ottoman Empire;

> BE IT RESOLVED that it is the conviction of the International Association of Genocide Scholars that the Ottoman campaign against Christian minorities of the Empire between 1914 and 1923 constituted a genocide against Armenians, Assyrians, and Pontian and Anatolian Greeks.

> BE IT FURTHER RESOLVED that the Association calls upon the government of Turkey to acknowledge the genocides against these populations, to issue a formal apology, and to take prompt and meaningful steps toward restitution.

69. That arrangement was initiated by the United States in 1996 and, in my view, was not in the best interests of the United States.

70. "Turkey PM: Israel War Crimes Worse than Sudan," *Haaretz,* Nov. 8 2009.

71. Speech, "The Geostrategic Importance of Cyprus: Long Term Trends and Prospects." Erato Kozakou-Marcoullis, London School of Economics. Jan 25, 2012.

72. Speech given by Sen. Edward M. Kennedy at the Kennedy Library (Sept. 21 1990).

73. *Yeniduzen,* Apr. 17, 1989. It should be noted that Turkey said it invaded Cyprus to protect the security and interests of the Turkish Cypriots. In a united Cyprus the Turkish Cypriots, in addition to minority rights (including educational and cultural autonomy), would have an improved economic condition which would be enhanced even more by the entry of Cyprus into the European Union in 2004.

74. These articles appeared in *U.S. Relations with Turkey and Its Impact on Greece and Cyprus.* Gregory R. Copley is President of the Washington-based International Strategic Studies Association (ISSA), the global organization for strategic policy professionals, and chair of its Balkan & Eastern Mediterranean Policy Council.

9. KISSINGER'S NATIONAL SECURITY ARGUMENT

1. *See* Devallon Bolles, "Turkey as an Ally—Myth and Reality," in 2 *The Rule of Law and Conditions on Foreign Aid to Turkey,* 56, (Conference proceeding of the American Hellenic Institute, Washington, D.C. 1990).
2. *Baltimore Sun,* August 20, 1975, at A4, col. 1.
3. Letter, July 20, 1975 from Dr. Herbert Scoville to Rep. John Sieberling, 121 Cong. Rec. 24019-20 (1975).
4. Edward Luttwak, *The Political Uses of Sea Power* 60–61 (1974).
5. *Id.*
6. Ali L. Karaosmanoglu, *Turkey's Security and the Middle East,* 52 *Foreign Affairs* 157, 163 (Fall 1983).
7. Cord Meyer, *Facing Reality—From World Federalism to the CIA* 276–80 (1980).
8. *N.Y. Times,* Feb. 13, 1979, at A8, col. 3.
9. *N.Y. Times,* May 15, 1979, at A1, col. 3.
10. *Id.*
11. *See* generally *Wash. Post,* July 19, 1976, at A16, col. 1; *N.Y. Times,* Feb. 26, 1979, at A13, col. 1; *N.Y. Times* May 17, 1983.
12. *N.Y. Times,* May 28, 1989, at A12, col. 1.
13. *N.Y. Times,* Feb. 20, 2003, at A1, col. 6.
14. Stern, *The Wrong Horse* 7 (1977).
15. House Foreign Affairs Subcommittee on International Security and Scientific Affairs, February 21, 1984; International Institute for Strategic Studies (London) report.

10. BUSH ON KUWAIT COMPARED TO KISSINGER ON CYPRUS

1. *N.Y. Times,* Aug. 3, 1990, at A1, col. 6; White House Press Release, Aug. 1, 1990, 31 WEEKLY COMP. PRES. DOC. 1182, 1184 (Aug. 6, 1990).
2. S.C. Res. 660, 45 U.N. SCOR (2932d mtg.) U.N. Doc. S/21425 (1990) [hereinafter S.C. Res. 660]; *N.Y. Times,* Aug. 3, 1990, at A10, col.1.
3. S.C. Res. 661, 45 U.N. SCOR (2933d mtg.) U.N. Doc. S/21441 (1990) [hereinafter S.C. Res. 661]; *N.Y. Times,* Aug. 7, 1990, at A1, col. 6.
4. S.C. Res. 665, 45 U.N. SCOR (2938th mtg.) U.N. Doc. S/21640 (1990) [hereinafter S.C. Res. 665]; *N.Y. Times,* Aug. 26, 1990, at A1, col. 6.
5. S.C. Res. 678, 45 U.N. SCOR (2963d mtg.) U.N. Doc. S/21969 (1990) [hereinafter S.C. Res. 678]; *N.Y. Times,* Nov. 30, 1990, at A1, col. 6. As of Nov. 29, 1990, the Security Council had passed 12 resolutions regarding Iraq's invasion and occupation of Kuwait.
6. *See N.Y. Times,* Aug. 13, 1990, at A10, col. 1; Greenfield, *Another Kind of "Hostage," Wash. Post,* Aug 13, 1990, at A11, col. 1; Javetski,

Borrus & Harbrecht, *Oil War: The World v. Iraq, Business Week,* Aug 20, 1990, at 22–25; Buderi & Glasgall, *If Saddam Can be Stopped, Oil's Wild Ride May End, Business Week,* Aug. 20, 1990, at 26–27; Samuelson, *Why We Should Stay in the Gulf, Newsweek,* Aug. 20, 1990, at 41.

7. *See* White House Press Release, *supra* note 1.

8. *See* S.C. Res. 660, *supra* note 2. Yemen's representative explained his abstention by stating that he had not received instructions from his government.

9. Exec. Order Nos. 12722 and 12723, 55 Fed. Reg. 31803, 31805 (1990). International Emergency Economic Powers Act, 50 U.S.C. §§ 1701–1706 (1951 & Supp. 1990), the National Emergencies Act, 50 U.S.C. §§ 1601–1651 (1951), and 3 U.S.C. § 301 (1955 & Supp. 1990). *N.Y. Times,* Aug. 3, 1990, at 9, col. 1.

10. *Wash. Post,* Aug. 3, 1990, at A25, col. 6.

11. *N.Y. Times,* Aug. 4, 1990, at A6, col. 1.

12. *See* S.C. Res. 661, *supra* note 3.

13. *N.Y. Times,* Aug. 8, 1990, at A1, col. 6.

14. S.C. Res. 662, 45 U.N. SCOR (2934th mtg.) U.N. Doc. S/21471 (1990).

15. *N.Y. Times,* Aug. 13, 1990, at A1, col. 6.

16. S.C. Res. 664, 45 U.N. SCOR (2937th mtg.) U.N. Doc. S/21562 (1990).

17. *See* S.C. Res. 665, *supra* note 4.

18. *N.Y. Times,* Sept. 10, 1990, at A7, col.1.

19. S.C. Res. 666, 45 U.N. SCOR (2939th mtg.) U.N. Doc. S/21747 (1990).

20. S.C. Res. 667, 45 U.N. SCOR (2940th mtg.) U.N. Doc. S/21774 (1990).

21. S.C. Res. 669, 45 U.N. SCOR (2942d mtg.) U.N. Doc. S/21811 (1990).

22. S.C. Res. 670, 45 U.N. SCOR (2943d mtg.) U.N. Doc. S/21816 (1990) (Cuba opposed); *N.Y. Times,* Sept. 26, 1990, at A1, col. 6.

23. *Wash. Post,* Sept. 26, 1990, at A1, col. 4.

24. *N.Y. Times,* Sept. 26, 1990, at A10, col.1.

25. S.C. Res. 674, 45 U.N. SCOR (2950th mtg.) U.N. Doc. S/21911 (1990). The vote was 13 to 0 with Cuba and Yemen abstaining. *N.Y. Times,* Oct. 30, 1990, at A1, col. 6.

26. S.C. Res. 677, 45 U.N. SCOR (2962d mtg.) U.N. Doc. S/21966 (1990).

27. S.C. Res. 678, *supra* Note 5. Cuba and Yemen opposed and China abstained.

28. *N.Y Times,* Jan. 17, 1991, at A14, col. 1.

29. *N.Y. Times,* Jan. 30, 1991, at A12, col. 1.

30. *N.Y. Times,* Feb. 28, 1991, at A12, col. 1.

31. *N.Y. Times,* Nov. 1, 1956, at A14, col. 5 (emphasis added).

32. *See* Declaration on Cyprus by the European Council at their meeting in Dublin (June 27, 1990); announcement at the Council of Ministers meeting, Brussels (Feb. 7, 1991). *See also* Note, *Cyprus and the U.N.: A Case for Non-Military Collective Measures,* 54 Ind. L.J. 125 (1978–1979).

33. White House Press Release, Jan. 30, 1991, remarks by the President to the Greek press corps.
34. Speech of Vice President George H.W. Bush, Republican presidential nominee, at the 29th Biennial Clergy-Laity Congress, Greek Orthodox Archdiocese, Boston, July 7, 1988.

11. "KISSINGER THE WAR CRIMINAL"

1. From the book review by Jussi M. Hanhimaki of *Nixon and Kissinger: Partners in Power*, Robert Dallek, HarperCollins, 2007, in Columbia University Magazine 58–60, summer, 2007. Jussi M. Hanhimaki is professor of international history and politics at the Graduate Institute of International Studies (Geneva, Switzerland) and the author of *The Flawed Architect: Henry Kissinger and American Foreign Policy*, Oxford University Press (2004).
2. Martin F. Nolan book review in the *Boston Globe* May 6, 2007 of Nixon and Kissinger: Partners in Power, Robert Dallek (2007) and American Spy: My Secret History in the CIA, Watergate and Beyond, E. Howard Hunt with Greg Aunapu (2007).
3. *Id.*
4. *Id.*
5. See for example Christopher Hitchens, *The Trial of Henry Kissinger* (Verso, 2001). Hitchens' short volume is an invaluable resource as a broad overview of Kissinger's diplomatic crimes.

12. THE RULE OF LAW IN THE NATIONAL INTEREST

1. See Chapter 7.
2. See Chapter 8, Note 25.
3. See *N.Y. Times* June–Aug. 1978 and Nov. 12–13, 1978.
4. European Parliament Written Declaration No. 0042/2011 on the returned on the sealed-off section of Famagusta to its lawful inhabitants—See minutes of Feb 14, 2012 item 2, signed by 390 members. *Famagusta Gazette* Feb. 15, 2012. The Written Declaration states:

Declaration of the European Parliament of 14 February 2012
on the return of the sealed-off section of Famagusta to
its lawful inhabitants

The European Parliament,

– recalling its 1993 resolution on Cyprus,
– recalling its 2009 resolution on Turkey's progress report,
– having regard to Rule 123 of its Rules of Procedure,

A. whereas the city of Famagusta in the Republic of Cyprus was captured by the invading Turkish forces in August 1974,
B. whereas a section of Famagusta was then sealed off and remains uninhabited, under the direct control of the Turkish military,
C. whereas the return of the Famagusta sealed-off section to its lawful inhabitants would facilitate efforts toward a comprehensive settlement of the Cyprus problem,
D. noting the 1979 High Level Agreement and UNSC Resolutions 550(1984) and 789(1992),
E. noting the 2008 Report of the Committee on Petitions on Petition 733/2004,

1. Calls on the Government of Turkey to act according to the aforementioned UNSC Resolutions and Report Recommendations and return the Famagusta sealed-off section to its lawful inhabitants, who must resettle under conditions of security and peace;
2. Urges the EU institutions to coordinate their efforts with Parliament to promote Turkey's cooperation;
3. Instructs its President to forward this declaration, with the names of the signatories (*), to the Commission, the Council, the governments of the Member States, the UN Secretary General and the Government of Turkey.

   (*) The list of signatories is published in Annex 1 to the Minutes of 14 February 2012 (P7_PV(2012)02-14(ANN1)).

5. *See* D. Moynihan, *On The Law Of Nations* (1990); Rosenblatt, *Book Review, N.Y. Times,* Aug. 26, 1990, at 1, col. 1; Strasser; *Iraq Clash Tests New Alliances—International law could emerge victorious,* Nat'l L.J., Sept. 3, 1990, at col. 1; Frank & Patel, *UN Police Action in Lieu of War: 'The Old Order Changeth,'* 85 Am. J. Int'l L. 63 (1991); Glennor, *The Constitution and Chapter VII of the United Nations Charter, Id.* at 74; Caron, *Iraq and the Force of Law: Why Give a Shield of Immunity, Id.* at 89; *See* L. Henkin, S. Hoffman, J. Kirkpatrick, A. Gerson, W. D. Rogers & D. Scheffer, *Right v. Might: International Law and the Use of Force* (1989); D'Amato, *Book Review*, 85 Am. J. Int'l L., at 201.

BIBLIOGRAPHY

BOOKS

Alastos, Doros. *Cyprus in History: A survey of 5000 years*. London: Zeno Publishers, 1955.

Asmussen, Jan. *Cyprus at War—Diplomacy and Conflict During the 1974 Crisis*. London: New York: I.B. Tauris, 2008.

Attalides, Michael. *Cyprus: Nationalism and International Politics*. New York: St. Martin's Press, 1982.

Bass, Gary J. *The Blood Telegram—Nixon, Kissinger and a Forgotten Genocide*. New York: Alfred A. Knopf, 2013.

Birand, M. A. *30 Hot Days*. London: K Rustem & Brother, 1985.

Callaghan, James. *Time and Chance*. London: William Collins and Son., 1987.

Chotzakoglou, Charalambos. *Religious Monuments in Turkish-Occupied Cyprus: Evidence and Acts of Continuing Destruction*. Nicosia: World Forum for Religions and Cultures of the Holy Kykkos Monastery & Charalambos Chotzakoglou, 2008.

Clerides, Glafcos. *Cyprus: My Deposition*. Nicosia: Alithia Publishing, Volumes I-IV, 1988–1992.

Cooper, C. L. *The Lion's Last Roar*. New York: Harper and Row, 1978.

Coufoudakis, Van. *Cyprus: A Contemporary Problem in Historical Perspective*. University of Minnesota Mediterranean and East European Monographs, nr 15. 2006.

—— *International Aggression and Violations of Human Rights. The Case of Turkey in Cyprus*. Minneapolis, Minn.: University of Minnesota Mediterranean and East European Monographs, nr 17. 2008.

Crawshaw, Nancy. *The Cyprus Revolt*. London: George Allen & Unwin, 1978.

Crisis on Cyprus, Report for Senate Judiciary Subcommittee Regarding Refugees. Washington, D.C.: American Hellenic Institute, 1975.

Cyprus Press and Information Office. *Flagellum Dei: The Destruction of the Cultural Heritage in the Turkish Occupied Part of Cyprus*. Nicosia: PIO 2nd ed., 1989.

Dallek, Robert. *Nixon and Kissinger: Partners in Power*. New York: Harper Perennial, 2007.

de Smith, S. A. *The New Commonwealth and Its Constitutions*, London: Stevens, 1964.

Dobkin, Marjorie Housepian. *Smyrna 1922: The Destruction of a City*. London: Faber & Faber, 1972.

Foley, Charles. *Legacy of Strife: Cyprus from Rebellion to Civil War*. Middlesex, GB: Penguin, 1964.

Foot, Michael & Jones, Mervin, *Guilty Men-Suez and Cyprus*. New York: Rinehart & Co., 1957.

Foreign Relations of the United States, 1969–1976. *Volume XXX Greece; Cyprus; Turkey, 1973–1976*. Editor Laurie Van Hook, US Government Printing Office, Washington, DC, 2007.

Fullick, R. and Powell, G. *Suez: The Double War*. London: Hamish Hamilton, 1979.

Gunther, John. *Inside Europe*. New York: Harper & Brothers, 1938.

Graubard, Stephen. *Kissinger: Portrait of a Mind*. New York: Norton, 1973.

Gromyko, Andrei. *Memories*. London: Hutchinson, 1989.

Haldeman, H.R. *The Haldeman Diaries: Inside the Nixon White House*. New York: G. P. Putnam's Sons, 1994.

Hanhimäki, Jussi M. *The Flawed Architect: Henry Kissinger and American Foreign Policy*. New York: Oxford University Press, 2004.

Henkin, L., Hoffman, L., Kirkpatrick, J., Gerson, A., Rogers, W. D. & Scheffer, D. *Right v. Might: International Law and the Use of Force.* New York: Council on Foreign Relations Press, 1989.

Hersh, Seymour M. *The Price of Power: Kissinger in the Nixon Whitehouse.* New York: Summit Books, 1983.

Hill, Sir George. *A History of Cyprus.* Four Volumes. Cambridge: Cambridge University Press, 1940–1952.

Hitchens, Christopher. *Hostage to History: Cyprus from the Ottomans to Kissinger.* Third Edition, London, New York: Verso, 1997.

—— *The Trial of Kissinger.* London, New York: Verso, 2001.

Holland, Robert. *Britain and the Revolt in Cyprus, 1954–1959.* Oxford: Oxford University Press, 1998.

Human Rights Watch. *Denying Human Rights and Ethnic Identity: The Greeks of Turkey.* New York: Helsinki Watch, A Division of Human Rights Watch, 1992.

Hunt, David (ed.). *Footprints in Cyprus: An Illustrated History.* London: Trigraph, 1982.

Hunt, E. Howard & Aunapu, Greg. *American Spy: My Secret History in the CIA. Watergate and Beyond.* Hoboken, NJ: John Wiley & Sons, 2007.

Ioannides, Christos P. *Realpolitik in the Eastern Mediterranean— From Kissinger and the Cyprus Crisis to Carter and the Lifting of the Turkish Arms Embargo.* New York: Pella, 2001.

Isaacson, Walter. *Kissinger: A Biography.* New York: Simon & Schuster, 1992. Paperback edition 2005 with added introduction.

Jansen, Michael. *War and Cultural Heritage: Cyprus after the 1974 Invasion.* Minnesota Mediterranean and Eastern European Monographs XIV. Minneapolis: University of Minnesota, 2005.

Kalb, Marvin, and Bernard Kalb. *Kissinger.* Boston: Little, Brown, 1974.

Kissinger, Henry. *A World Restored: Metternich, Castlereagh and the Problems of Peace, 1812–1822.* Boston: Houghton Mifflin Company, Sentry Edition, 1979.

—— *For the Record: Selected Statements, 1977–1980.* Boston: Little, Brown 1981.

—— *White House Years.* Boston: Little, Brown, 1979.

—— *Years of Upheaval.* Boston: Little, Brown, 1982.

—— *Years of Renewal.* Boston: Little, Brown, 1999.

Kyriakides, Stanley. *Cyprus: Constitutionalism and Crisis Government.* Philadelphia: University of Pennsylvania Press, 1968.

Law Library of Congress. *Cyprus: Destruction of Cultural Property in the Northern Part of Cyprus and Violations of International Law,* Report for Congress, April 2009, LL File No. 2008-01356 (Washington, D.C.: Directorate of Legal Research for Foreign, Comparative, and International Law), 7–9. Available at: *http://www.csce.gov/index.cfm? Fuseaction=Files.Download&FileStore_id=1384*

Love, K. *Suez: The Twice Fought War.* London: Longman Group, 1970.

Luttwak, Edward. *The Political Uses of Sea Power.* Baltimore: Johns Hopkins University Press, 1974.

Meyer, Cord. *Facing Reality—From World Federalism to the CIA.* New York: Harper & Row, 1980.

Morris, Roger. *Uncertain Greatness: Henry Kissinger and American Foreign Policy.* New York: Harper & Row, 1977.

Nichols, David. *Eisenhower 1956: The President's Year of Crisis—Suez and the Brink of War.* New York: Simon & Schuster, 2011.

Pantelis, Stravros. *The Making of Modern Cyprus: From Obscurity to Statehood.* London: Interworld Publications, 1990.

Peaslee, Amos Jenkins. & Xydis, Dorothy Peaslee. *Constitutions of Nations—Europe* Volume III (Third Edition). The Hague: Martinus Nijhoff, 1968.

Polyviou, Polivios G. *Cyprus, Conflict and Negotiation, 1960–1980.* London: Duckworth, 1980.

—— *Cyprus. The Tragedy and The Challenge.* Washington, D.C.: American Hellenic Institute: 1975.

Pyrros, James G. *The Cyprus File: A Diary of the Cyprus Crisis in the Summer of 1974.* Washington, D.C.: Pella Publishing, 2010.

Reeves, Richard. *President Nixon: Alone in the White House.* New York: Simon & Schuster, 2001.

Regan, Geoffrey. *Great Military Disasters. A History of Incompetence on the Battlefield.* New York: M. Evans, 1987.

Rossides, Eugene T., ed. *Cyprus 35 Years Later What is Needed for a Solution?* Washington, D.C.: American Hellenic Institute Foundation, 2010.

—— *Greece's Pivotal Role in World War II and Its Importance to the U.S. Today.* Washington, D.C.: American Hellenic Institute Foundation, 2001.

—— *The Rule of Law and Conditions on Foreign Aid to Turkey.* Washington, D.C.: American Hellenic Institute, 1989.

—— *The Truman Doctrine of Aid to Greece: A Fifty-Year Retrospective.* New York and Washington, D.C.: The Academy of Political Science and the American Hellenic Institute Foundation, 1998.

—— *The United States and Cyprus—Double Standards and the Rule of Law.* Washington, D.C.: The American Hellenic Institute Foundation, 2002; co-editor Van Coufoudakis.

—— *U.S. Relations with Turkey and Its Impact on Greece and Cyprus.* Washington, D.C.: American Hellenic Institute Foundation, 2011.

—— *United States Foreign Policy Regarding Greece, Turkey and Cyprus—The Rule of Law and American Interests.* Washington, D.C.: American Hellenic Institute, 1988.

Royal Institute of International Affairs. *Cyprus: The Dispute and the Settlement.* London: Chatham House, 1959.

Schulzinger, Robert D. *A Time for War: The United States and Vietnam, 1941–1975*. New York: Oxford University Press, 1997.

Speer, Albert. *Inside The Third Reich*. New York: Simon & Schuster, 1970.

Stephens, Robert. *Cyprus: A Place of Arms*. London: Pall Mall Press, 1966.

Stern, Laurence. *The Wrong Horse—The Politics of Intervention and the Failure of American Diplomacy*. New York: Times Books—Quadrangle, 1977.

Law Library of Congress. *Cyprus: Destruction of Cultural Property in the Northern Part of Cyprus and Violations of International Law,* Report for Congress, April 2009, LL File No. 2008-01356 (Washington, D.C.: Directorate of Legal Research for Foreign, Comparative, and International Law), 7–9. Available at: *http://www.csce.gov/index.cfm? Fuseaction=Files.Download&FileStore_id=1384*

Theophanous, Andreas. *The Cyprus Question and the EU: The Challenge and the Promise*. Nicosia: Intercollege Press, 2004.

Thomas, Hugh. *The Suez Affair*. London: Weidenfeld & Nicolson, 1967.

Tornaritis, Criton G. *Cyprus and Its Constitutional and Other Legal Problems*. 2d Ed. Nicosia: [s.n.], 1980.

U.S. Army. *Area Handbook for Cyprus*. Washington, D.C.: U.S. Government Printing Office, 1971.

Venizelos, Kostas & Ignatiou, Michalis. *The Secret Archives of Kissinger (in Greek)*. Athens: Livani Publishing Organization, 2002.

Vryonis Jr., Speros. *The Mechanism of Catastrophe: The Turkish Pogrom Of September 6–7, 1955*. New York: Greekworks. Com Inc. 2005.

Weber, Frank G. *The Evasive Neutral: Germany, Britain, and the Quest for a Turkish Alliance in the Second World War*. Columbia: University of Missouri Press, 1979.

Weiner, Tim. *Legacy of Ashes: The History of the CIA*. New York: Doubleday, 2007.

Zydis, Stephen G. *Cyprus: Conflict and Conciliation, 1954–1958*. Columbus: Ohio State University Press, 1967.

ARTICLES

Anderson, Perry. "The Divisions of Cyprus." *London Review of Books*, Vol. 30, No. 8, April 24, 2008: 7–16.

Cropsey, Seth. "Will U.S. Choose the Right Side in the Eastern Mediterranean?" *Hudson Institute*, July 3, 2013. *http://www.hudson.org/index.cfm?fuseaction=publication_details&id=9659*

Evriviades, M. L. "The Legal Dimension of the Cyprus Conflict," 10 *Texas International Law Journal*, 227 (1975): 237–238.

Ros-Lehtinen, Ileana. "Time for Turkey to leave Cyprus in peace: Long-standing occupation amounts to annexation," *Washington Times*, June 15, 2012. *http://www.washingtontimes.com/news/2012/jun/15/time-for-turkey-to-leave-cyprus-in-peace/*

Macdonald, R.St.J. "International Law and the Conflict on Cyprus," 19 *The Canadian Yearbook of International Law* 29 (1981): 3-49.

McDonald, Robert. "The Problem of Cyprus," 18–19 *Adelphi Papers* 234 (1989).

Phillips, John. "What Is The Matter With Mary Jane? The Tragicomedy of Cyprus," *Harper's Magazine* 43, (June 1956): 43–52.

Rossides, Eugene T. "Cyprus and the Rule of Law," *Syracuse Journal of International Law* 17 (Spring 1991): 22–90.

Rouleau, Eric. "Turkey's Dream of Democracy," *Foreign Affairs*, November/December 2000: 100–114.

Thomas, A. Van Wynen & Thomas, A.J. "The Cyprus Crisis 1974–75: Political-Juridical Aspects," 29 *Southwestern Law Journal*, (1975): 513–541.

Television Broadcasts

BBC Television Broadcast, *Cyprus: The Bitter Legacy, 1984*.
American Hellenic Institute Foundation, *Cyprus Still Divided: A U.S. Foreign Policy Failure,* 2010. The documentary aired on Detroit Public TV on September 13, 2010, and Maryland Public TV on October 17, 2011

Speeches

Kasoulides, Ioannis, "Geopolitics in the Eastern Mediterranean: A Cypriot Perspective," Brookings Institution: Washington, D.C., May 9, 2013.
Kozakou-Marcoullis, Erato, "The Geostrategic Importance of Cyprus: Long Term Trends and Prospects" London School of Economics: London, January 25, 2012.
Ros-Lehtinen, Ileana "Cyprus Still Divided: A U.S. Foreign Policy Failure," Miami, FL, February 10, 2012.

Index